THE LIGHTNING WAR

the lightning WAR

W. BYFORD-JONES

THE BOBBS-MERRILL COMPANY, INC.
Indianapolis • New York

The Bobbs-Merrill Company, Inc.
A Subsidiary of Howard W. Sams & Co., Inc.
Publishers / Indianapolis • Kansas City • New York

Library of Congress Catalogue Card Number 68-15806
First American edition

First published by Robert Hale Ltd., London, 1967.

CONTENTS

ILLUSTRATIONS

Maps

And God spake unto Israel in the visions of the night, and said, Jacob, Jacob. And he said Here am I. And he said, I am God, the God of thy father: fear not to go down into Egypt; for I will there make of thee a great nation: I will go down with thee into Egypt. . . .

Book of Genesis, Ch. 46, v. 2-4

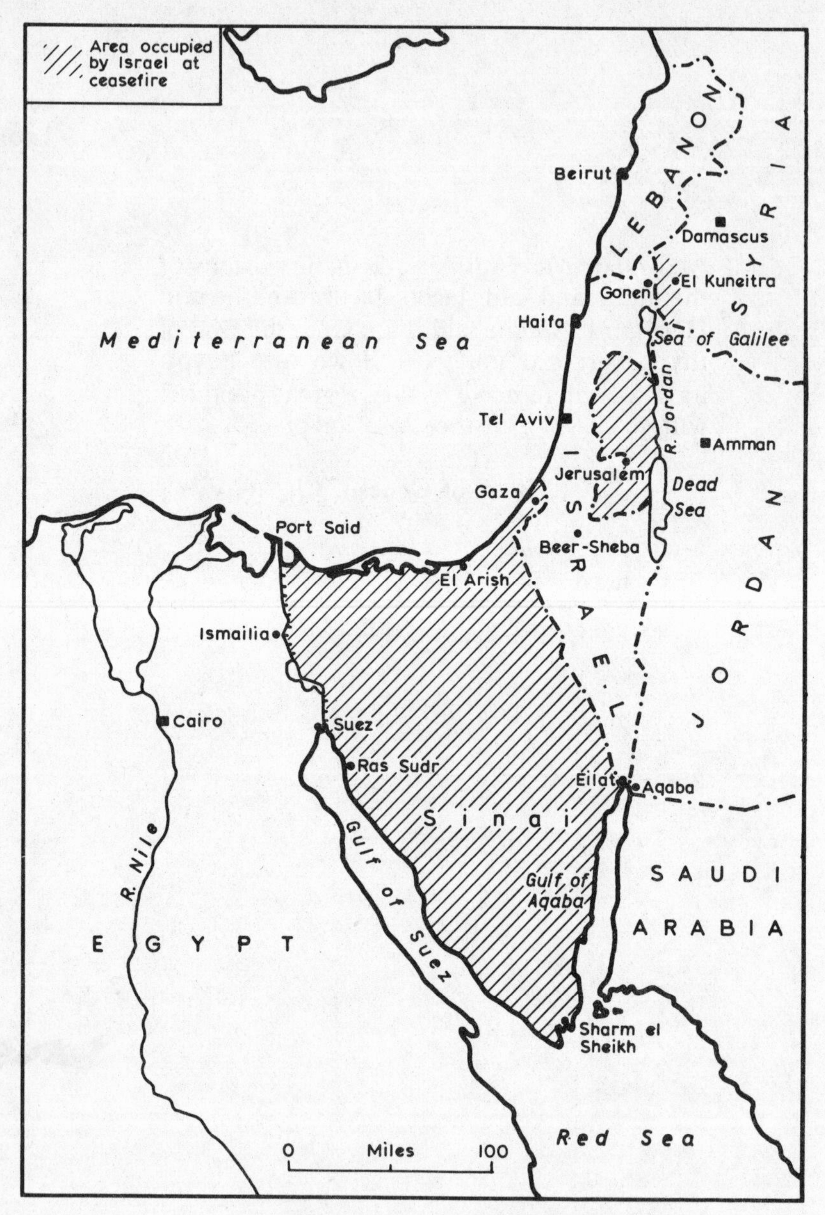

I Israel and her Arab Neighbors

1

RETURN TO ISRAEL

Looking out of my bedroom window the day I arrived in Israel I realized with a start that I was in a country completely encircled by hostile troops, heavy artillery, jet bombers and fast tanks. I would be trapped if an attack came in the night. Once the war began there would be no movement out of the country until it was over. Looking left, I could see the Mediterranean. Looking right, I could see the Jordanian border. Troops stood on the alert. I was not only near four of the most dangerous borders in the world. I was in a country only twelve miles wide on the average at this part of the coastal plain that runs from north of Haifa to south of Tel Aviv. In the gathering twilight I realized that if the specter of war screamed along this flat strip of land in the hours of darkness there would be absolute panic. Three-quarters of the entire population of Israel would be sleeping in just this small area. It would be so much the worse because we would all be cast into dungeon-like black-out immediately the first bomb fell or the first gun went off. Only now did I realize the full significance of the bulging suitcases tied with string, the parcels, water bottles and flashlights which I had seen at the bottom of the stairs as I came up to bed.

I remembered also bits of paper stuck on the walls. Scrawled on them were Hebrew words which must have been "Air Raid Shelter" together with red arrows pointing the way to them. I left the window and went out of my room on to the landing. My host, whom I had known as long as Israel had existed, and who had brought me from Lod Airport to spend the night with him, met me. The hotel he ran was nearly full and he was anxious to know if the little room he had given me was satisfactory.

"It has a splendid view," I said. "Two countries at a glance. If the Jordanians come I shall have a grandstand view."

"We've lived with it so long," he said as he led me to his first-floor office and study for coffee. "All the time I've been here until now I've felt fairly secure. Remember my last place? You stayed there. That was in Jerusalem. I used to lie in bed at night and watch sentries of the Arab Legion lighting each other's cigarettes. I'm sure those sentries and I knew each other well."

When we reached his office my friend showed me a map of Israel on the wall.

"Your country looks so small," I said for want of something to say.

"See," he said, sipping his coffee. "The country is all border. Except in the Negev no inhabited place is more than twenty miles from an Arab frontier. You and I know what that means in these days of long-range fire. You just can't live out of range of Arab fire no matter where you go. We've gotten used to it. It's a bit unnerving at times like these with all the reports of Arab troops all round our borders, especially when, as in my case, you have all your capital sunk in a little hotel that just makes ends meet. Of course, they'll attack in the night if they come at all. If they could make a breakthrough—but they never will—they'd be here in minutes by plane and twenty minutes in mechanized vehicles."

From time to time as we talked there came a knock on the door and one of the guests looked in to wish my friend good night. There was never a reference to the crisis, not to speak of any mention of the fear of invasion. No one seemed to talk about this subject unless a foreigner mentioned it. The practice then was to make light of any danger. "Shalom," each visitor said to my friend. The word means *peace*. It may have been my imagination but people seemed to utter the word now in a way different from what I remembered in the past. It was now intoned like "Amen" at the end of the Lord's Prayer. "Shalom," my friend replied. One old lady varied the salutation. *"Shalom—shalom aleichem,"* she said and my friend used the same three words in reply. They meant "Peace be with you." Later, after I had left the proprietor's sanctum I heard the words echoing all over the house like some dismal refrain.

"That's Mrs.—" said my friend after the old lady had left. "I think she is a little concerned this time. She's lived through the two previous wars. They had a farm once but it was attacked by saboteurs. She's a bit older now. What she worries about is her husband. He walks with difficulty. 'What shall I do with him if they come?' she said to me the other day. 'I've tried to order a car so that I can get him away, but it's impossible. Most of them are requisitioned in the event of war breaking out.' "

After I had gone to bed, earlier than usual because I had a good deal to do early in Tel Aviv, I began to think of Israel's plight. The country was not only encircled by overwhelmingly bigger forces who would regard any hostilities as a holy war, but it had to stand up to continual peril without any certain help from any quarter. Before leaving London I had heard the indecisive pronouncements by President Johnson about the Egyptian blockade of the Gulf of Aqaba at the Straits of Tiran, and been sure that no help would be forthcoming from that quarter. I had also read the hostile speeches against Israel by Russian leaders. Prime Minister Wilson had not cut a very impressive figure in his efforts to give the lead to legal action. Britain's impotence to act made nonsense of the East of Suez policy. The British were in Aden, Cyprus, the Persian Gulf, even in Bahrein, but could not do anything even to prevent the Arabs stopping the flow of oil. Someone has said that British troops had to move aside a little in Bahrein so that the Arabs there could the easier cut off her oil. Britain's failure to do anything before the war or after it had begun to protect "her vital interests"—always the parrot cry to justify the maintenance of costly forces east of the Suez—made her a laughing stock throughout the world. This will not prevent Prime Minister Wilson from making the same kind of statements to justify the maintenance of military bases.

If America intervened with the Sixth Fleet, now the subject of all kinds of optimistic speculations in Israel, the country would be in even greater peril. There could then be a great power conflict as well as a regional war. Israel would be faced with the double danger of attack from the sea by Russia and attack from her hinterland by the Arabs. Just before I fell off to sleep I decided that Israel was unique. Not only did all her neighbors refuse to recognize that she existed, except when they wanted to insult her or make war, but the foreign powers in the West, even those who were handmaidens at her birth, refused to make treaties with her. Israel's security was not guaranteed by any pact or treaty. She was the recipient of arms from the West it is true, but they came surreptitiously. Even the lifeblood of modern industry, of which her neighbors possessed massive resources, was denied to her by the blockading of Eilat. While the alarming plan of encirclement continued, Israel's maritime approaches with the Eastern half of the world were strangled at Tiran. Even the United Nations, Israel's reluctant foster father and her one hope for survival, seemed to have acted against her interests in removing the ten-year-old Peace army. The three big forces in the world, America, the Soviet Union and the United Nations, seemed impotent to act. It was as if the Israelis didn't matter any more. It amazed me that a crowd of them could be together in one room so near to the border of one of their Arab enemies, as had been the case that evening, and yet not even mention the peril about which they must all be thinking. Two of the guests had small babies. Maybe I thought I had received an exaggerated view of the crisis in Britain, and the danger of war was not so great as I had thought.

I was awakened by arrangement early next morning. The first thing I did after I had gotten out of bed was to go to the window, open the black-out curtains and look left towards the Mediterranean, then right to the Jordanian border. The sun shone warmly and the world at that early hour seemed to be at peace. But the threat remained and the longer it remained the worse it would be. Time was certainly on the side of the Arabs. When I left the hotel that morning little did I dream that in only about sixty-eight hours Israel and the Arabs would be at war. In eighty hours that hotel would have lost one of its gables in Jordanian shell fire.

2

DIPLOMATIC TANGLE

Russia's behavior in the Middle East for some months before the crisis began had the effect of increasing the tension which led to war. She encouraged Syria, which had included for the first time in its history two communists in its cabinet, in its provocative attitude to Israel. Syria openly supported the activities of Arab commandos who laid land mines in Israel to blow up trains and trucks. Russia was aware of this. Dr. Zayiyen, the Syrian Premier, said publicly seven months before the Middle East War (on October 11th) that Syria would continue to aid and provide bases for Arab guerillas making raids on Israel. A week later the Syrian Chief of Staff said: "The battle to liberate Palestine has begun." Israel asked the UN on October 13th to take up its earlier complaint of Syrian aggression. On October 17th Israel appealed to the World Powers and to the UN to stop Syria's aggression. Israel said she was prepared immediately to sign a non-aggression pact with Syria. Syria scorned the offer. Sabotage continued. The Security Council discussed a resolution dealing with Israel's complaint for three weeks. Then Russia imposed its veto. The discussion ended inconclusively. Unable to obtain redress through the UN, Israel viciously attacked Jordan, through whose territory Syrian-aided saboteurs were wont to come. Israel was condemned universally for this, though no one had condemned Syria for its acts. On January 2nd, about five months before the war, Syria claimed that it had destroyed three Israeli outposts on the border of the Sea of Galilee. U Thant appealed to both countries to keep the peace. Russia and the United States did the same. Syria obeyed Russia which had just advanced her 90 million dollars aid to build a railroad from the Euphrates Valley to the Mediterranean. On January 25th, the Syrian and Israeli delegates to the Mixed Armistice Commission met for the first time in six years and decided to keep the peace.

Mainly because of Russian intervention, Egypt had become involved in what Syria did to Israel and what Israel was likely to do to Syria. On May 10th 1966, just over a year before the war, Alexei Kosygin, the Soviet Premier, visited Cairo for ten days. It so happened (and the Russian knew this from his Syrian friends) that relations between Egypt and Syria were at a particularly low ebb. For some reason Kosygin wanted to see them improved. He urged Colonel Nasser to return to Egypt's relations with Syria before Syria defected from the original partnership in the UAR. So indebted was Nasser to Russia that he did Kosygin's bidding. Egyptian President Sidky Soliman visited Syria almost at once, the first Egyptian President to do so for six years. A Syrian military pact of defense was signed between the two countries on November 4th, seven months before the war began. At the beginning of April, two months before hostilities, Gromyko, the Russian Foreign Minister, followed his master to Cairo. No reason was given for the visit, the purpose of which remains a question for conjecture.

The quiet had not long continued on the Israeli-Syrian border. Incidents caused by Arabs were, however, not serious, except in a few cases. In one of these, on April 7th, less than two months before the war, after a further incident over the cultivation of land in the demilitarized zone above Galilee, there was an air battle between Syria and Israel, in which Israel shot down seven of Syria's Russian-made Migs. The Arab world had then expected Egypt to come to the assistance of Syria with which it had the defense pact. Colonel Nasser was not in a position to make any move.

Syria continued to aggravate Israel by further infiltrations. Israeli leaders became angry and threatened Syria but in terms not nearly as belligerent as those used by the Arabs against Israel. Israel sent a small number of additional troops to the northern border though these by no means threatened aggression.

Early in May, about a month before the war began, Russia sent by way of a trusted member of an Egyptian Parliamentary delegation that was visiting Moscow at the invitation of Gromyko, an extract from an Intelligence report which stated that there was a calculated intention by Israel to attack Syria with the support of the American Central Intelligence Agency. A similar extract had been sent to Syria, Egypt's ally.

Colonel Nasser got in touch with Moscow and asked for clarification. He had not received similar information from his own Intelligence.

Moscow apparently got in touch with their Ambassador to Israel and asked him to go to the Israeli government and challenge them with the report of troop concentrations. Levi Eshkol, Israeli Prime Minister, was asked for an interview by the Soviet Ambassador, who withdrew when diplomatic relations were broken off. When Eshkol and the Ambassador met in the Prime Minister's Office, the Ambassador told him that Moscow had heard there were heavy concentrations of Israeli troops in the north, in the region of Syria. What had the Prime Minister to say about it? Eshkol said that the allegation was without truth but the Russian was not convinced.

Eshkol looked at his schedule and saw that he was free of engagements. He then told the Ambassador that he would have his car sent round and he would take the Ambassador into any part of the north of Israel where he could see for himself how many troops there were near Syria. If they went right away there would be no chance for the troops to be moved before they got there.

The Ambassador declined and left.

The story that had been told to Egypt and Syria was, therefore, untrue.

On May 9th, U Thant, from his own resources, and he had many UN observers in the area, ascertained there were no Israeli troop concentrations. He passed this information on to Syria and Egypt.

Syria had twice refused to cooperate with suggestions by the United Nations authorities, and accepted by Israel, for a simultaneous and reciprocal inspection of the Israeli-Syrian border.

In mentioning troop concentrations, Russia ignored Syria's provocations against Israel. Syria had bombarded Manara from the Lebanese border. An accumulation of such incidents had caused Israel to lose her temper but there were no concentrations of troops.

Although, eventually, the major conflict appeared to be between Egypt and Israel, the Israeli-Egyptian border had been the quietest of the Israeli borders with the Arabs since 1957. There had been absolute peace for eight years. The trouble had been mainly on the Israeli-Syrian line. Syria was openly training and arming Palestinian refugees, some of whom lived just inside the Israeli-Jordanian border, and then sending them back to operate as terrorists across the Jordanian line against the Jews. This deflected attention from the Syrians and placed the responsibility on Jordan. Hardened fighters had been recruited in two gangs, El Asefa and El Fatah, which became notorious. There had been seventy-four outrages in which seventy-one Israelis had died since Syria had organized the Palestine refugees.

In face of the so-called threat from the Israeli "concentrations" along the Syrian border, Colonel Nasser had to do something both to show his loyalty to Syria and to demonstrate his hatred of Israel. So he asked the Indian commander of UNEF in Sinai to move his troops into the Gaza Strip. Israel made hostile comments on this, whereupon Colonel Nasser demanded that all United Nations forces should be withdrawn from both Sinai and Sharm el Sheikh. Colonel Nasser was egged on by Syria at every step. He responded because he had to exceed Syria as protector of the displaced Palestinians.

A leading British correspondent, Patrick Seale, in Cairo on June 4th stated: "To an observer in Cairo, it seems irrefutable that Nasser is seeking to deter Israel. President Nasser's gaze is focused on internal Israeli politics rather than on the international reactions to the crisis." He did not think that the great powers would allow real war to break out between Egypt and Israel. He was hoping to provoke such a dangerous situation from a position of considerable Egyptian strength that the great powers would have to sponsor a settlement helpful to the Palestinian refugees and not to Israel.

If evidence is needed that Israel did not want war, one had only to remember her attitude early in 1967 to Syria, which of all Arab nations had been her most hostile neighbor. Israeli and Syrian delegates to the Mixed Armistice Commission had met for the first time in seven years. Moreover, they had pledged themselves to "refrain from all kinds of hostile or aggressive actions as provided for in the United Nations Charter and the general armistice agreement." Israel's economy was not in the best shape. She needed a long period of peace in which to build up her trade, increase her output. It was stated in March that ten percent of her entire labor force was unemployed, or would be so when the citrus season was over. It was because of this need for reconstruction and this deep-seated desire for peace that Israelis in all walks of life were shocked by the action of U Thant, Secretary General of the United Nations, when he complied with the request of President Nasser on May 18th to withdraw UNEF from the line laid down between the Israelis and the Egyptians. Israelis felt the withdrawal of UNEF was certain to be the cause of border incidents which would bring about another war. When Nasser replaced UNEF troops at Sharm el Sheikh, thus blockading Eilat of strategic materials, everyone was convinced that war was inevitable. It was only a matter of time. The only hope Israel had was that the United States and Britain would act. Only if they made a military demonstration that the Gulf of Aqaba was an international waterway and was going to be treated as such, would war be prevented. How little real influence Britain had in America was made clear when President Johnson ignored Prime Minister Wilson's appeal. The President decided not to stand by America's 1956 pledge to keep the Straits of Tiran open. The United Nations, although it was the foster father of Israel, had never been popular in the country. United Nations parentage was reluctant, as if the child had been discovered to be the illegitimate offspring of some sordid match.

Abba Eban, the voluble Israeli Foreign Minister, went further than normal diplomatic protocol allows when he criticized the United Nations. Just before I reached Israel he had made a slashing attack on the Secretary General because of his decision about the UNEF. "The United Nations, let me use the most massive understatement of this century, does not emerge from the events of the past few weeks with brilliance or credit," he said. "In fact, we find ourselves here with a situation which in very large measure arises from error of United Nations judgment. I recall again what the two main symptoms are. The build up of forces in the Sinai and the announcement of the intention to close the Straits of Tiran. Now each of those problems was one for which the United Nations took a specific responsibility in 1957. The object of the United Nations' presence was to ensure that there would be legality and non-belligerency in the Gulf and that there would be a less explosive situation regarding the balance of forces in the Sinai. The abandonment by the United Nations of both of these functions within a matter of a few hours, without any corresponding or parallel attempt to think about the consequences of the change, which were inevitable, or to work out alternative measures for securing the same results, this failure is massive and even of historic dimensions. When there occurs a disturbed situation, it is natural for people to ask themselves in a self-critical spirit why they should have been so surprised. There are many factors here which could have been and were taken into account, but I don't think it is reasonable to think that anybody should have believed, or need have expected, that a request for such a fundamental change in the structure of the area would be met with such an uncritical response, without the broad and deliberate international consultation that should have taken place. Of all the things which were unexpected, and that nobody of rational mind could have expected, I would say this was the thing least to be anticipated. Of course, at any time the Egyptian Government could have requested and secured the withdrawal of those forces, but to think that it could secure their withdrawal overnight, without any parallel attempt to solve the problems which the presence of the forces secured, this was such an irrational thing that everybody in the world could be forgiven for not having taken it into account. In fact, it had been solemnly agreed that the opposite would happen, that when a demand would come for this change there would immediately be a broad and deep international consultation before the change was effected, in order to see how under new conditions the same objectives would have been fulfilled."

People in all walks of life in Israel were saying with added anguish that the Secretary General's action had brought Israel to the brink of war. They declared that it might be the principal cause of a world war unless the United States and Britain did something soon to alleviate the situation in the Sinai and at Sharm el Sheikh. One respected member of the Knesset told me that Arabs living in Israel swore to him that Colonel Nasser was only bluffing. His request about UNEF to U Thant, they declared, was an effort to prolong a military situation which had developed too quickly. Nasser wanted the United States and Britain and France to intercede and do something to avoid the war he himself had made look inevitable. He wanted them to initiate a move to settle the Palestine-Arab problem in a way which was "fair to the refugees." I was told that Colonel Nasser had come to an agreement with Dag Hammarskjold, former Secretary General, which made it impossible for there to be any precipitate action in this matter. It would make necessary, in fact, a long period of diplomatic negotiations out of which, as the diplomat he fancied himself to be, Nasser hoped he would be able to win important concessions for himself, for the Arabs and for the Palestinian refugees. He had no doubt at all that the agreement was on the official files of U Thant and that the Secretary General would be bound by it. Colonel Nasser knew he had gone far too near the brink, mainly as a result of his competition with Syria to be the most anti-Israel Arab leader. He felt that his request to U Thant to move UNEF would provide a period in which the Israelis and the Arabs could cool off while negotiations took place.

It seemed to me that U Thant had been weak and unimaginative over Nasser's request. If he had known anything about Arab mentality he would have suspected that Nasser's move was merely an act of bravado; that it was calculated to stir up diplomatic activity to prevent war and win him points. If he took Nasser's request at face value, he should have been so alarmed at the possible consequences as the head of a peace organization that he should have used all his abilities to delay the fulfilment of Nasser's request. As any diplomat knows, there are a series of regulation delaying tactics employed regularly to allow a situation to cool off. What was more mysterious was that U Thant actually knew before he left New York for Cairo of the existence of a memorandum drawn up by Dag Hammarskjold to meet just such a situation. Whatever reservations he may have had about this (and he certainly had some), he could have used this knowledge to introduce an element of delay. So far as is known he did not mention the memorandum to Nasser. U Thant later gave the main reasons for his decision to comply promptly with Nasser's request for the withdrawal of the UNEF. As might be expected, he said that his decision was based on both legal and practical considerations. The legal considerations were that since UNEF was introduced on to the territory of Egypt on the basis of the consent of the Government of Egypt, and by an agreement between Secretary-General Dag Hammarskjold and President Nasser that consent was withdrawn—and the United Arab Republic's right to do this could not be questioned—the basis of UNEF's presence ceased to exist. The United Nations said that as a purely practical matter, apart from legal considerations, all the United Nations peace-keeping forces depend not only on the consent, but on the active cooperation of the host Government. The functions of a peace-keeping force could not be exercised without that consent and cooperation. The Security Council, of course, had authority under Chapter VII of the Charter to take enforcement measures. In the case of UNEF, its buffer function, which had been made possible for over ten years only by the cooperation of the United Arab Republic, had already lapsed before the request for withdrawal was received, by virtue of the decision of the United Arab Republic to move in its troops. Furthermore, the position and security of the personnel of the force would certainly have been gravely endangered if the Secretary General had sought to maintain the force against the express wish of the Government of the United Arab Republic.

It was generally felt in political circles in Israel that there was not adequate consultation within the United Nations or with the members before the decision was taken. The Secretary General was, however, firmly of the opinion that the decision for the withdrawal of the force, on request of the host Government, rested with the Secretary General after consultation with the Advisory Committee of UNEF. Secretary General Hammarskjold took the following position in reply to a question about the withdrawal of the Force from Sharm el Sheikh on February 26th 1957: "An indicated procedure would be for the Secretary General to inform the Advisory Committee on the United Nations Emergency Force, which would determine whether the matter should be brought to the attention of the Assembly." The Secretary General did consult the Advisory Committee before replying to the letter of May 18th 1967. This consultation took place within a few hours after receipt of the UAR request. The Advisory Committee was informed of the decision which the Secretary General had in mind to convey in his reply to the Foreign Minister of the UAR: "The Committee did not move, as it was its right to do."

Eban's remarks on this subject (on June 19th) were highly critical, said U Thant. "I personally welcome criticism when it is just, based on fact and does not obscure or ignore essential facts. The concern behind this intervention is that the picture which Mr. Eban gave yesterday can be very damaging to the United Nations with regard to its peace-keeping function, past and present. I seek only to restore in that picture the balance which the facts warrant. I was rather surprised at the breadth and vigor of the Foreign Minister's dissatisfaction with the withdrawal decision since we had discussed that issue and I had given a rather full explanation of just why the decision I took had to be taken in the way it was. I heard no such reaction as Mr. Eban projected to the General Assembly yesterday. Nothing like it! I wish now to say that I do not accept as having validity Mr. Eban's strictures on this matter. My position on the decision to withdraw UNEF and the reasons for it have been set forth clearly in reports which I have submitted to the General Assembly and the Security Council."

A wrench was thrown into the works when the memorandum between Nasser and Dag Hammarskjold, which had earlier been referred to as "secret," was made public on June 19th. It was described as a private agreement between the then Secretary General and Colonel Nasser that the United Nations would not withdraw the UNEF from Egyptian territory and that Cairo would not order that withdrawal *until both had agreed* that the troops had completed their task. Hammarskjold had held that all interpretations of the Agreement must be governed by his memorandum, which contradicted the views and policies of U Thant. U Thant had held that Nasser had a complete right to demand the withdrawal of UNEF. No negotiation or United Nations deliberation could delay that withdrawal.

Hammarskjold's memorandum said that he foresaw a dispute over withdrawal, and forced Nasser to agree to a procedure that would at the least have delayed the removal of the troops. The memorandum was written on August 5th 1957, nine months after the establishment of the peace force. Hammarskjold told friends that he was dissatisfied with public and legal discussions of the arrangements and felt obliged to deposit in United Nations files some of the history of his negotiations with Cairo. At the same time he gave a copy of his report to a former United States Deputy Representative at the United Nations, then a consultant to Mr. Hammarskjold and now a partner in a New York law firm. In May 1961 when the controversy foreseen in the memorandum developed, Mr. Gross gave a copy of it to Stephen M. Schwebel, executive vice-president and director of the American Society of International Law, for printing in the society's bimonthly documentary publication, *International Legal Materials.*

The Hammarskjold memorandum states that the matter of how and when the United Nations forces could be asked to leave Egyptian soil was virtually the only issue discussed by Hammarskjold and Nasser in a seven-hour meeting in Cairo on November 17th 1956. Public agreements bearing on this question were ambiguous, the document concedes. But it also says that Mr. Hammarskjold obtained Nasser's agreement to a circuitous formula limiting the Egyptian leader's use of the right to expel the troops. It contends that Nasser "showed that he very fully understood that, by limiting their freedom of action in the way proposed, they would take a very serious step."

Egypt had the sovereign right to expel the force from her soil at any time, Hammarskjold said. But he insisted that his formula obliged Egypt—if she wished to act in good faith under her agreement with him—not to exercise that sovereign right until she had persuaded the United Nations that the "task" of the peace-keeping forces was completed. It pledged Egypt, when exercising her rights on any matter concerning the presence and functioning of the forces, to be guided "in good faith" by her original acceptance of the assembly resolution that established the force and defined its task. And it committed the United Nations in directing the force, to be guided "in good faith" by the definition of the task and to keep the force in place until the task was completed.

U Thant was worried about publication of the fact that this policy was exactly the opposite to that in the memorandum attributed to his predecessor, especially when war developed as a result of his decision. He said there was little new on the memorandum; "It makes no revelations which would warrant the special significance being attributed to it in some quarters. In any case, such a paper could not alter the basis for the presence of UNEF on the soil of the UAR, as set out in official documents." Then U Thant made certain specific comments: "It is not an official document, it is not in the official files of the Secretary General's office, and its existence has never been reported in any way to any organ of the United Nations, including the UNEF Advisory Committee. It was thus of a purely private character."

3

A PHONY WAR?

Just in case Israel could not wait another day, I decided to go to Biet Sokolov, in Tel Aviv, where the Israeli Government had made provisional planning to install military censors, a military spokesman and its own civil officials in the event of war. I showed my credentials and became accredited, as I had done before the Sinai campaign of 1956. It seemed to me as if history had turned a full cycle. The only thing different was that Colonel Nasser was seeking the aid of the United Nations and its Secretary General before the war broke out instead of after it had finished. Was this not Suez all over again, but before a shot had been fired in anger?

I was convinced from the start that so far as Colonel Nasser was concerned this was a phony war which he was going to exploit politically and diplomatically. In the week ending May 20th he had achieved his greatest ambition. This was, as he had explained to me, "to be a better diplomat than a soldier." At the time he uttered the words to me I thought he had his tongue in his cheek. He was inordinately proud of his rank as a lieutenant-colonel in the infantry. So much so, he had kept his commission and lived privately in standard lieutenant-colonel's married quarters in Moustapha Kamal barracks at Manshiyat el Bakry, where he entertained me. Though he had known only military defeat (and he spoke candidly of his soldiering) he was a good fighter. He was called by his brother officers—to whom I talked at the barracks gate—the "Tiger of Falugja" because of the part he played in the Egyptian invasion of Israel. Looking back now, I know he spoke from the bottom of his heart when he told of his ambition. Because of his diplomacy, developed along lines laid down by one of his favorite writers, Nicolo Machiavelli, Colonel Nasser was proud of his score card in the week ending May 20th.

As a necessary preliminary he had first drawn the limelight of the world by staging a melodramatic military move in the Sinai. With the arrogance of the great Saladin he had dispersed the United Nations' one and only successful peace army, which had been maintained by ten nations for ten years, to separate Arabs from Jews at a cost of 16 million dollars a year. He had caused U Thant, United Nations Secretary General, to postpone unceremoniously his visit to Britain. He had caused George Brown, British Foreign Secretary, to put off at half an hour's notice his talks with Mr. Kosygin in Moscow. When U Thant decided to fly to Cairo to try to end the crisis, Nasser laid it down that the visit should be to Egypt only, not both sides. The grand total of this impressive sum of Nasserite gains was the re-establishment of the Egyptian leader as the supreme leader of the Arab world—at the very moment when the leadership was being challenged by the new Muslim Alliance being set up by the three kings, Faisal of Saudi Arabia, the Shah of Persia, and (more cautiously) Hussein of Jordan.

This fervid Arab nationalist, born in Alexandria fifty years back to a 15-year-old girl, had one aim: to restore the since decadent Arab race to its former glory by uniting them and driving out of the Middle East all imperialists. He was as clever as he was charming, far too clever I thought to start a war with the Israelis for whose superb fighting powers he had a healthy respect—though one could begin by accident! When I covered the Sinai war I saw one Israeli show himself to be the equal of twenty Arabs. In the 1948 conflict there were thirty Arab soldiers to one Israeli. In the first battle Colonel Nasser, driven back with his men into a slit trench near the sea at Falugja, blamed defeat on unpreparedness, poor equipment, arms and ammunition. The revolution which dethroned Farouk was born in that slit trench. And so was the obsession to accumulate weapons to impress his foes as well as his friends and help him on his way.

First up to the Sinai war, and again since, Colonel Nasser had built up his army and squandered money in search of the latest, most lethal arms. What happened at Sinai? Egypt had been invaded and was beaten on all fronts, as I saw myself, in the Sinai, the Gaza Strip, the Gulf of Aqaba. A fantastic number of tanks and guns worth millions were captured by the Israelis. Then came Colonel Nasser's one saving talent—his Machiavellian diplomacy. With the ready cooperation of the United Nations he turned defeat into victory. It was a decisive victory, diplomatically and economically. Some 6,000 men from seventeen countries under General Burns went to the Middle East. The British and the French had to go, tails between their legs. Even the Israelis had to go back home growling, leaving behind all their army had won, excepting only Sharm el Sheikh. Colonel Nasser's score card then read: forced withdrawal of French, British and Israeli troops; rejection of Britain's offer to help in the salvage operations in the Suez Canal; successful insistence by Colonel Nasser that the Suez Canal be run as he wanted to run it; Colonel Nasser's conditions of settlement of Suez accepted. Not one of the six principles for settlement accepted by the Security Council in 1956 was among them.

Soon Britain and France, the only two nations to stand out for long, were paying tolls to Colonel Nasser. Egypt, which had received in the past only 40 million dollars a year, now looked forward to 1970 when she would collect 240 million a year.

Once I talked to Nasser at his home until the clock of the nearby Cairo University struck 2 a.m. He talked sincerely of his hatred of violence. "Egypt does not want war," he asserted, and I quoted him in the book* I wrote afterwards. "We have a big program of internal development to cope with the rapidly growing population, with the needs of industrial development and agricultural expansion. All are necessary to raise the standard of living, for it is poverty that provides fertile ground for growing seeds of Communism." He had the same problems now, in spite of great development since then, including the Aswan High Dam project. Poverty was still rife. The problem of the soaring population was still a nightmare. The last census, completed in early 1967, showed

* *Adventure with Two Passports,* Robert Hale Ltd., 1957.

that between 1960 and 1966 the population had increased from 26,000,000 to 30,000,000, the highest ever recorded. He had warned his people early in 1967 that "unless the birth rate was checked, or there was greater output, the standard of living could not be raised." He confessed that the agricultural and industrial projects envisaged, or under way, could not keep pace with the rate of population increase. Egypt had only two hopeful developments, he said. The Suez Canal authority had reported in March 1967 that the expected income from the Canal, if nothing disturbed the passage of ships, would be over 240 million dollars by 1970. It would thus be the greatest source of income next to cotton. Proposals were in hand for expanding the Canal to take vessels with a loading capacity of 200,000 tons. He said he was also developing the oil industry. He wanted more effort put into that. He claimed that if progress continued as in March 1967, oil production was expected to rise by 1970 to 30,000,000 tons annually. It was now only 7,000,000 annually. Colonel Nasser also admitted publicly in the week ending March 22nd 1967, some two months before the war was to begin, that Egypt was in dire need of wheat. He said that Egypt was unwilling to buy wheat from the United States because the State Department had taken too long considering whether to sell her 140 million dollars' worth of grain. He said that Egypt would do without American wheat. He was making plans for setting aside 150 million dollars in hard currency to buy their annual supply elsewhere. Did that sound like a man who was preparing to wage a war? Or did it look as if Nasser's support of Syria was a phony threat of war, typically Arabic, aimed at winning diplomatic concessions?

Lionel Pytan, who was a key figure in all the manifold arrangements at Beit Sokolov, was an old friend. I had known him before the Sinai campaign in 1956 when I had been writing a book on Israel. During the Sinai campaign I had seen a great deal of him and grown to admire him as a tireless worker. He arranged for me to have a military briefing from an Israeli colonel on my arrival on June 3rd. Israel knows more about Egypt than Egypt knows about Israel. They can tell you what General Mohammed Fawzy, Chief of Staff of the

Egyptian Ground Forces, said about this and that on any date you care to mention; what Voice of Cairo announced about the Egyptian Foreign Minister on the morning of May 18th; what Field Marshal Amer on May 19th told the political correspondent of *El Ahram* in his office; what the Egyptian Commander of the Sinai forces, General Murtaji, said in an Order of the Day next morning. And so on. Israel must dog the footsteps, monitor the voice, of everyone of any value in Arab countries.

The first stage of an Egyptian plan of attack, I was told, was the significant reinforcement of their troops in the Sinai under the pretext of giving assistance to Syria. The second stage was the order to withdraw the UNEF. The third stage, begun on May 20th, was the taking over by Egyptian forces of United Nations positions at Sharm el Sheikh. In the fourth stage, Colonel Nasser increased the strength of the army stationed in eastern Sinai to 100,000 men and 900 tanks and deployed them in an offensive position opposite Israel. Colonel Nasser, I was told, then believed that he was able if he wanted (and he certainly did not) to enter into the fifth stage and take the initiative of attacking Israel. In a speech to the National Council of Egypt in Cairo in the evening of May 20th, I was told, he actually gave expression to his intent: "If we have succeeded in turning back the situation to what it was before 1956, then there is no doubt that God will help us and move us to turn it back to what it was before 1948."

A military pact was signed between Egypt and Jordan on May 30th and between Egypt and Iraq on June 4th. "Now the Arab armies surround Israel in the full meaning of the word," boasted Saut el Arab radio.

When I suggested that Nasser had gone to the brink in a desperate attempt to activate United Nations peace machinery to deal once and for all with the Palestine refugee question my companion smiled doubtfully. "There is not," he said with emphasis, "the shadow of a doubt that the trend of events from May 14th on was the result of a previously prepared plan by Nasser. It was not phony. It was not the fruit of his being dragged along by chance developments. Nasser thought himself ready for a decisive clash with Israel.

Moreover, he was interested in it. This was shown by his willingness to pull significant Egyptian forces out of Yemen. He believed that in the wake of a victory over Israel he would be able to obtain anything he wished in the inter-Arab sphere." I was assured that there was clear evidence of the Egyptian intent to carry out an attack on Israel in the Order of the Day of General Murtaji, commander of the Egyptian ground forces, on June 3rd 1967. This read: "The eyes of the whole world are on you, in your most splendid war against Israeli imperialist aggression. This is in expectation of seeing the results of your sacred war to conquer the rights of the Arab nation. . . . You will reconquer the plundered soil of Palestine, with the grace of God, and the ability of justice with the power of weapons and the unity of our faith."

4

MOSHE DAYAN

One of the politicians I met on June 3rd at Beit Sokolov in Tel Aviv was Major-General Moshe Dayan, whom I knew well as the victor of the 1956 campaign. In response to popular demand he had just been appointed Minister of Defense. When I congratulated him he made a great show of modesty. I formed the impression that he would far rather have rejoined the Israeli army as a commander on the Southern Front. In fact he had, I learned, actually offered to make himself available. Dayan was 52—he had celebrated his birthday at the height of the crisis—but that day he looked younger. He was worshipped by the young people. I noticed a crowd of them had followed him to the door. Dayan was a true Sabra. He was born at Dagania "A", in the Jordan Valley. His parents, whom I also met later, were among the original founders of Nahalal, the first workers' cooperative settlement. Dayan went to school at the village and later worked as a farmer there. He was still a boy when he became a member of the Haganah. He distinguished himself organizing Jewish defense units.

After the outbreak of the Arab troubles in 1936, Moshe Dayan served under Captain (later Major-General) Wingate in the Night Squads. In 1939, while acting as a Haganah instructor, he was arrested by the British Mandatory authorities. He was tried and sentenced to five years in prison, but pardoned after two years. At once he resumed active service in the Haganah (Palmach). He commanded a special reconnaissance unit of the Australian Forces during the invasion of Syria (then held by the Vichy French). On several occasions he penetrated enemy lines and seized vital bridges. He was seriously wounded in this action, losing an eye. Later Dayan was employed in connection with the mission of Jewish parachutists sent to Europe. In Israel's War of Independence, then a Lieutenant-Colonel, he commanded Israeli forces on the Syrian front. Late in 1948 he was appointed Commander of the Jerusalem area, where he conducted operations against the Jordanian army. He took part in the Rhodes Armistice talks with Jordan as Senior Israeli Delegate and later served as O.C. Southern Command, bordering on Egypt. After a course of military studies in England, Dayan was appointed O.C. Northern Command. He became Chief of General Staff with the rank of Major-General in 1953 and held the appointment until 1958, when he was granted leave for study purposes.

Moshe Dayan laughed when I asked him if he thought it was true that Israel had almost completely lost military initiative. "If you think because we have not started military action we stand no chance if there is an Egyptian attack I am sure you're wrong," was his reply. He repeated this answer later. This remark was the opening gambit in what seemed like an innocent exchange between a newly appointed minister and a group of foreign correspondents. We all felt obliged to him for sparing the time to answer our questions. As it turned out, we were doing him, and Israel, a great service. There was in progress an astute operation in military intelligence. What was happening in a dimension other than the superficial questioning was a brilliant verbal diversionary move which contributed to saving Israel from extinction and saving many of her sons from death. It sounds so far-fetched that it is not easy to explain.

To begin with, Dayan had approached this apparent public relations exercise with extreme caution. He had firmly declined to make a statement. He did not want to initiate or develop any line of information. He merely wanted to reply to questions. His replies were truthful but they were capable at times of more than one meaning. They were not intended exclusively for the world's newspaper readers who would devour his every word avidly at breakfast next morning. They were angled for Colonel Nasser and the Egyptian General Staff, and, for that matter, the rest of the Arab leaders. He knew that when he was appointed Minister of Defense all the Arab newspapers had cried out that now the Israelis were bent on war, and very soon.

Remembering Dayan as the brilliant victor of the Sinai in 1956, the Arabs called him "The Butcher of Israel." Dayan was astute enough to know that ever since his appointment the Arabs had waited impatiently for him to speak, as speak he must, to the nation who had put him where he was, or to the world. They suspected that he would utter bloodcurdling threats as to what he would do to the Arabs. But Nasser, who waited for the first press notices of the first speech, had ready a group of professional news analysts who would go over what Dayan said word by word to try to discover any clue in it which would tell the Arabs of his short-term intentions. Colonel Nasser was personally satisfied that Dayan would not dare move against such superior forces, fight on four fronts, in the air and on the ground, when he knew the Arabs had superior Russian-made equipment. But he wanted to verify, if he could, his conclusion. There were Arabs who feared that Israel would attack. One of these was King Faisal, but he had no respect for the Saudi Arabian's sense of strategy. Saad Jumma, Prime Minister of Jordan, had been in touch with Colonel Nasser, and other Arab leaders, to tell him what King Hussein had earlier told a group of Jordanian high officials assembled at the Basman Palace. Hussein had said that the Israelis would strike first, and at the Arab air fields, and that they would attack in the period June 5th-6th. It sounded like an inspired prophecy. Colonel Nasser had replied, warning Jordan against taking any aggressive action which might provoke war. That was on June 4th. General Dayan, who had learned the art of military diversionary moves as a pupil of Orde Wingate, wished to divert the attention of the Arab leaders from the belief that, under his leadership, war was going to be launched immediately. He was telling them in other words that he was going to play in a golf tournament during the weekend and that Rabin was going sailing. He wanted the Arab leaders to relax, enjoy their weekend.

It is my information that at some time after Dayan's appointment it had been decided by the cabinet that, in the circumstances in which Israel found itself, the country could no longer assume, as they had in the past, that aggressions on their borders were local affairs, aimed only at provocation. In such tension, with the country surrounded by enemies, they must assume that any enemy attack was part of a plan. They could not wait to see what it turned out to be unless they wanted to make a present of initiative to the Arabs. But, of course, he was careful not to say this. So he spoke with caution. He knew public men heed this, that a newsworthy statement made on a Saturday achieves maximum publicity. It may appear in the late editions of the evening newspapers, in the Sunday newspapers and be commented on in the newspapers on Monday. General Dayan's replies to our questions that afternoon, in the light of what happened some thirty-eight hours later, are worth careful attention.

Q. In some circles friendly to Israel it is clear that you are very confident. Do you think it is possible that you are underestimating the fighting potential of your enemy?

A. It may be that we are underestimating our enemy, I do not know.

Q. Do you believe Israel lost any major military element by agreeing to this long drawn-out diplomatic action to try to solve this crisis?

A. I have just joined the Government. As a matter of fact I have not yet formally joined it because I have not yet been sworn in. I accept the situation as it is. I know it is always easy to say last week we were in a better position. This is not the point. The point, I should think just now, is that it is more or less a situation of being too late and too early—too late to react regarding our chance in the military field—on the blockading of the Straits of Tiran—and too early to draw conclusions as to the diplomatic way of handling the matter.

Q. Could you give us an evaluation of the balance of power?

A. They have plenty of tanks and troops—too many—and we have much less than they have. But much depends on where the battle will be. For instance, with the same number of troops, if we have to go to Baghdad or Cairo, it would be very difficult. I hope it will be very difficult for them with their superior numbers to attack Tel Aviv because they will have to make their way from their bases to Israel. On the other hand, of course, the number of their forces is bigger than ours, but still I hope we can make it. But very much depends on where the battle will be.

Q. Some of your Government colleagues—Minister Allon—last night stated that unless the Egyptian troops were pulled back from the borders, the Straits opened and the sabotage across the border stopped, war is inevitable. Do you think it is possible to accomplish these three points diplomatically, or is war inevitable?

A. Do you want me to comment on what Allon said?

Q. As your party has been opposed to the present Government policy, does your participation mean that the Government has changed its policy, or have you changed yours?

A. I think they have changed their minds about accepting me in the Government. I do not think all of them wanted me very much there before, so I think they have changed their minds in this respect. As for policy, I do not know what the policy was before and I would not say there has been any change in the policy. Only on Sunday will there be the first meeting of the Government in which I shall take part. They wanted me to participate two nights ago, but it was more about the way I would be admitted to the Government and not about policy. Next Sunday—and I will not be a Minister till then—will be the first meeting. It is now too early for me to say anything about policy.

Q. In your book, the second paragraph, you said it is very doubtful Israel would have attacked in Sinai without the collusion of Britain and France. The risks appear to be greater this time, and they are not in collusion with you. Isn't there a greater chance you should attack on that basis?

A. I hope you read my book thoroughly because in the first part I noted that Mr. Ben Gurion had presented the proposal to the Government and to me as Chief of Staff of Israel ten months earlier, that the Israel Army at that time could free the Straits of Tiran without any other forces. No other forces were considered at that time. It was true I said in my book that under the circumstances of October 1956 our Government at that time would not have considered that operation without France and England, but eleven months earlier Israel would have done it alone. But now it is eleven years later.

Q. As Minister of Defense or as a civilian—we know you as a soldier—do you intend to visit the fronts now?

A. I am sorry you did not include also my being Minister of Agriculture for five years. But just now, I am afraid I will have to spend some time in my office. But I have already made up for that because for the last two weeks I have been going around to the troops, as a civilian, to see what it was like, and I am obliged to our Chief of Staff and to Mr. Eshkol for allowing me to see what it was like. Now I can take my time and devote myself to the office for the next few days.

Q. Are you going to proceed through diplomatic channels alone, or are you going to war?

A. I think this is our Government policy, as stated by Mr. Eban time and again, and I feel you should take this up with him. I understand that our Government is trying to get help, and more than help, to get the international forces and countries to secure the free passage to Eilat, and I know this is the present policy and I fully agree with it.

Q. Have you any promise for an international force to help you in this?

A. I do not know, I have not yet met with the Government. I think it is very difficult to define what is a promise. I am sure our Government obtained a positive reaction, otherwise they would not have relied on and would not have looked for action to insure the free passage to Eilat. But how practical and how binding such promises or actions are I cannot say. I should say our Foreign Minister, Mr. Eban, is in a position to go into details about it.

Q. Has the Government asked for guarantees on the other two conditions your Government has given for bringing about peace in the Middle East; that is, drawing back of the Egyptian troops from the borders and the ending of sabotage on your borders?

A. I do not know whether we got such promises or not, but let me say that I, personally, do not expect and do not want anyone else to fight for us. Whatever can be done in the diplomatic way I would welcome and encourage, but if somehow it comes to real fighting I would not like American or British boys to get killed here, and I do not think we need them.

Q. Do you think if it comes to fighting at this stage—or if you postpone action—you can win now?

A. In a month I do not know, but now I think yes. I was joking about "a month" because I do not anticipate any major changes in a month, two months, or six months, but I think we can win. I am really surprised that you ask the question.

Q. How long can Israel afford to keep its troops mobilized?

A. Some countries go into world wars which last for years.

Q. You appear to be very happy and peppy looking. How do you think President Nasser felt at the moment he heard you were appointed Minister of Defense?

A. I would like to meet someone who saw him at that moment, and would like to find out.

Q. In 1956, after Israel stormed the Straits of Tiran, you withdrew on the assurance of free passage through the Straits. If it should prove necessary for Israel to take the Straits again, would you surrender them this time?

A. I can say that it was my view at that time and later, that I thought that if the Egyptians were ready to promise free passage and navigation to Eilat, we should have handed them back to the Egyptians just on that promise and have gone back. I thought at that time that for them it was such a victory to get the Straits back and to have the Israeli troops go back to Israel that they would perhaps have agreed to it. If we could get such a promise I, for one—and this is my very own personal view—would be very satisfied that they mean they would stop hostilities and we withdraw and go back and they take it back but on the condition that we enjoy free navigation there.

Q. Is there any possibility of the Israeli Government asking Jews in overseas communities to come to Israel to fight alongside your own troops, or are you going to keep it on the present basis where they do only civilian jobs?

A. Just now we have more volunteers in Israel than we

think are necessary. My office is full of people who want to join the troops; we have more than we really feel we need now.

Q. Are you going to tolerate the situation along the borders?

A. I think the policy about that has not changed—about not tolerating the border situation: during the past few days or so there was one incident which is about the average we have been having for a long time; I do not think the incidents have changed and the policy has not changed.

Q. What about the stories that Israel troops like to fight in the dark with no moon, on the assumption that the Arabs do not like moonless nights?

A. Do you think we can do something about the moon? Now we have to wait another two weeks. It's a good idea; I think it is true to say that our troops get training to fight in the dark as well.

Q. Do you feel a reduction of troops on both sides of the Sinai and some kind of check on the border raids can be accomplished through diplomatic channels?

A. I do not really think that through sheer diplomacy—let's say just by asking Egypt to do it—it can be done. Anyway, it did not work. On the important question about the Straits of Tiran I doubt whether Egypt would do this just on the appeal of the United Nations. If they would, they would not have brought their forces there in the first place.

Q. If war breaks out, do you think it will be short?

A. If war breaks out I know we shall win, that is the main thing.

Q. What do you think of the United States-Canadian proposal to put United Nations troops on both sides of the border?

A. The first problem is to have free passage in the Straits of Tiran. United Nations Forces were there and one day, when Nasser did not like it, he just sent them off, so what's the point of putting them on both sides or on one side of the border if, whenever Nasser feels like it, he just sends them home and blockades the passage of the Straits. So what's the point of bringing up such a proposal?

Q. Should war break out can we expect that the military tactics and doctrines that the Government of Israel operated under in 1956 will be similar in 1967?

A. The tactic in 1956 was simply to win, and the sooner the better.

Q. Do you have something to say at this time to the citizens of Israel?

A. I have not said anything to the soldiers or to the Israeli public because I do not have anything to say. I have not yet joined the Government and I do not want to start making any statements now. Before saying anything let me get into the Government, join the other members of Parliament, find out about the policy: then I will know if I have anything to say or not.

Q. Is it correct to assume from your replies that you, personally, have lost confidence in diplomacy and in the United Nations at least in getting the Arabs out of the Straits of Tiran?

A. I would be glad and surprised if they do that. I do not expect or want any people to fight and get killed for us. That is very clear. If anything can be achieved diplomatically, that would be far, far better. What happened during the last weeks is that we have seen the collapse of arrangements made ten, eleven years ago without anyone trying to stop it. But if somebody starts again and succeeds in achieving and getting freedom of passage through the Straits of Tiran through diplomacy I will be very glad, and I think it should be given a chance.

Q. My feeling is that the people of Israel feel that if there is a war it will be a very costly one.

A. I think they have a case; because no matter how the Sinai campaign started, eventually and ultimately British and French troops were at the same time fighting in Egypt when the Israel troops carried on their war in Sinai. So I can imagine that people think that now that the British bombers will not be bombing the Egyptian airfield—somebody will of course have to pay for it.

Q. You just said we are witnessing the collapse of international arrangements without the world doing anything about it. Wouldn't you say the world is trying to do something about it when you consider the statement of the Prime Minister of Britain and those of the maritime nations?

A. What I referred to was the United Nations Emergency Force in Sinai and about taking care of the Straits of Tiran. But when they were called off it was done just like that, in no time, and it was not brought up to the Security Council or the General Assembly: Nasser just asked and the Secretary General agreed, and that was that. Now I understand a new way is being tried, and I think this should be given a chance.

Q. It seems to me that a lot of Israelis feel that if there is a war, this time you will have to strike very hard at your Arab enemies to prevent this sort of situation arising every ten years. Do you feel this to be true?

A. Every ten years sounds very regular. But I think in any war, if you want to fight and win, you have to try to strike very hard.

Q. Do you think you should fight this time to end it once and for all?

A. I do not think there can be such a thing as "once and for all." History—Germany, etc.—have proved you never know what the next generation will do. If we win a war, a new situation can arise. I do not think "once and for all" can ever be applied to war.

The correspondents sent back that weekend exactly what Colonel Nasser wanted to read though I do not know how much they had been influenced by Dayan. Here are two examples of what appeared in the quality newspapers on Sunday from leading foreign correspondents, first from David Leitch of the *London Sunday Times,* the second from Patrick O'Donovan of *The London Observer*. The first ran:

"Moshe Dayan's appointment as Minister of Defense in the newly-formed Israeli national emergency Government is not so much a triumph for the hawks over the doves as for the strong against the weak. The new appointment has electrified a country very badly in need of inspiration but though Israel still teeters on the brink of war she is, if anything, less likely to try to resolve her problems by immediate attack than she was twenty-four hours ago. The army trusts Dayan and is more likely to accept the need for restraint when pressed in the name of the Sinai Victor than from a Government which, in the last forty-eight hours, has vacillated and apparently worked on the principle that by the time all hands had been counted, the war would be over. Some hopeful Israeli hawks may think, almost certainly incorrectly, that the Dayan appointment makes action more imminent. Dayan, a strategist who is strongly against mounting an attack at a time when the enemy is ready for it, may well turn out in his new Cabinet role as a strong partisan, preferring statesmanship to precipitate action."

The second dispatch opened: "In his first public appearance since his appointment as Israeli Defense Minister, General Moshe Dayan said today that diplomatic action must be given a chance, although he was confident of Israel's success if war came."

Now if I said to Moshe Dayan that he had boxed cleverly he would have laughed again in his inimitable way. The fact is, however, that I saw indications time and time again that Moshe Dayan was aware that if a Minister wanted to whisper in the ear of Nasser, the best way to do it was to make a statement to the press on Israel. Not that the press was disloyal. On the contrary. So whether he wanted to or not, Moshe Dayan misled Colonel Nasser.

A well known expert of Middle East affairs with whom I travelled by taxi to our hotel dropped off at an airline office after Dayan had answered our questions. This was thirty-six hours before the war was to begin. "Think I'll go back for three or four days," he said. "Watch it from London. Been here two weeks—everything seems quiet enough now." Several others were doing the same. These correspondents were at home when the radio told them on Monday at breakfast that the Arab-Israel war had begun. Probably the best known correspondent of all was about to leave Tel Aviv on Monday at 8 a.m. "I had my foot on the stairway," he said, "when the air raid sirens sounded." Like everyone else he thought the sirens were being tested. Then they went again. He allowed the plane to go off to London without him.

The correspondents had gone back home, and had no hope of returning for four days because all planes were stopped when the war began; they must have been as angry as Colonel Nasser. He, too, incidentally, told a British ex-Minister that fateful weekend that he had no intention of starting a war. This was the day after Dayan's conversation.

Moshe Dayan had lowered the temperature of the world by several degrees. Cairo, Baghdad, Amman and Damascus were better able to enjoy the weekend. Certainly the news must have relaxed tension on the Arab side of Israel's borders. Foreign correspondents who decided to stay on in Israel used their time on Sunday in various ways. Some of them rented automobiles, mixed business with pleasure and visited parts of Israel they had not yet seen, especially in the north in the region of the Sea of Galilee. It seemed to me that if war came the most dangerous front from the civilian point of view would be the Israeli-Jordanian, in particular on the Jerusalem sector where the border cuts the city in two. I therefore went to Jerusalem. I had crossed many times from Jordan to Israel through the only access, and that a narrow one, at the Mandelbaum Gate. I felt I would like to know how the crisis was affecting the area. There is actually no gate, only the ruin of a house once owned by a man named Mandelbaum. It stands on a deserted road in No Man's Land between the two parts of the tragically divided city. I found that the sentries either side of the access had been heavily reinforced. The atmosphere was very tense. People had left houses in streets on the Israeli side and no doubt the Jordanians had done the same on the Hashemite side. The traditional seven gates of Jerusalem which abut on to Israel were, of course, closed. No one was using the Mandelbaum Gate. The two parts of the city were completely cut off. The inhabitants of new Jerusalem could only look on to the Holy Places from certain vantage points. They were not at all happy with what they saw. In the dreary ribbon of No Man's Land there were ruined churches, houses, convents and shops. Skeletons of rusted cars and smashed gas stations reminded me of the War of Liberation. Where there were walls instead of barbed wire between New and Old Jerusalem these had been built double to provide room for snipers. There was a reproduction in No Man's Land of the ruins in the streets near Kurfürstendamm in Berlin immediately after the last battle. There were the same crumbling walls, exposed, twisted stairways, gaping windows, even the same kind of electric ranges hanging miraculously on to a wall which had no floor. Roaming the littered streets were mangy cats and an occasional wild dog. No Man's Land had always made me shudder for as I had passed through I had sensed the watchful eyes of the rival sentries and felt they were trigger happy. Now, I almost hoped that it would remain just like it was. But the tension. . . . If it had not been for what Moshe Dayan had said in answer to our questions, I would have felt more disturbed about the immediate fate of thousands of people either side the border. If war came this would most certainly be the most perilous place.

I telephoned a few friends in Israeli Jerusalem and found one of them at home. He was a retired professor who used to be at the Hamboldt before the war. I was greeted by the family with great warmth but as in the case of my other friends very little was said about the crisis. After a meal I told my friends what Moshe Dayan had said, hoping that it would cause them to talk about the crisis. They listened intently but without a word. When I had finished there was silence. To break it I added rather lamely that some of the correspondents went off to England to take a rest. There was another silence but some members of the family fidgeted uneasily.

"What's going to happen?" my host asked me as we lingered over table.

"I've only been here two days," I said. "You know better than I."

"We *are* going to war, my boy," he said. "I was told on good authority on the phone that Nasser has shot his bolt. There was a secret meeting of our Cabinet yesterday and this afternoon. The matter has been thrashed out in furious debate. The hawks and the doves divided. Eban was the major dove, as one would expect, although he has no hopes of the United Nations. He pleaded for more diplomatic latitude. General Dayan, the new Defense Minister, came out as a hawk. There was no question of Israel starting war without any provocation. It was decided finally that Israel would no longer countenance the kind of provocation it had been compelled to endure so often lately. It was thought to be too dangerous with whole armies massing on her borders. It was decided that if there was any hostile action on any frontier Israel would act without waiting for an outright invasion."

"But," I said, "Dayan is not yet sworn in. He is only designate."

The old man laughed. "He is a leading Israeli. Do you think a simple matter of a formality is going to make a man of his caliber wait at a critical time like this? Not on your life."

Twenty-one men made the historic decision to go to war. The burden fell on a cabinet of, with three newcomers who were supposed not to be sworn in until Monday, twenty-one honest men violently opposed to war. There were men, under the leadership of Levi Eshkol, such as Yigal Allon, Minister of Labor; Moshe Dayan, Joseph Saphir and Menahim Begin (he comes from Brest-Litovsk). There were others of whom not many Westerners had heard, among them Aranne, Barzilai, Bentov, Galili, Gvati, Kol, Sasson and Warhaftig.

When I travelled back from Jerusalem to Tel Aviv that night, only eight hours before the war officially broke out, I thought I heard gunfire. I stopped my car and got out to make sure my ears were not deceiving me. It was a lovely starlit night, delightfully cool and with a light breeze. The sound I had heard over the engine of the car was not repeated. I learned later that a triple-machine-gun nest on the Jordanian side had fired on an Israeli position earlier that afternoon. There had been shots fired later but so far as was known not around midnight.

5

THE CONTENDERS

The geography of Israel made it perilous to await attack. An unfinished war with the Arabs had been the chance architect of her borders. It had left the country narrow as a rail in the most densely populated part. There was little more space to retreat than to go from the front to the back room of the house. The cities were extremely vulnerable. Israel was outnumbered eighteen to one in troops and two to one in weaponry that was twice as modern. One of the four Arab nations, Egypt had 1,000 Russian tanks and 400 modern planes. Amateur strategists, who remember how during the war they cried out for the opening of a second front in France as the beginning of the end for the Germans, may be impressed by the fact that Israel would have to fight on four fronts. And at the same time. Attack obviously was the best means of defense but only if the attack was like a bolt from the blue, an almighty blow between the eyes that would put the enemy down for a count of ten. Even that would be a reckless gamble, as I realized when looking at a photographic map taken of the Middle East from Gemini II. Israel's 2.6 million people, who had arrived, in the hope of finding peace, from sixty-four countries scattered all over the world, seemed almost pushed to the edge of her 117 miles of Mediterranean coast or to be scattered about the arid Negev. Israel's position seemed absolutely hopeless, wedged in between the sea and four hostile neighbors with a total border, then bristling with arms, of 591 miles. Israel shared 47 dangerous miles with Syria; 330 with Jordan; 49 with Lebanon and 165 with Egypt. To the rear and to the east and west of these countries was the second echelon of the challenging Arabs—110 million of them belonging to fourteen countries. Israel's chances of survival seemed hopeless. She was tiny by comparison.

On the credit side one had to remember that the defense of Israel was the basis of life to her people. It was a religion, a way of life. The Defense Forces were an integral part of the educational structure of the country, the foundation of her unity, the backbone of her hazardous border farming in outlying villages. There was also the fact that if she had to fight, Israel would have a small secure base with no fear of Fifth Columns, even from her own Arab population. She would have interior lines of communication along which were subterranean hangars, concealed factories for the repair of recovered weapons, and easily accessible stocks of fuel and food which Israel had been hoarding there for years. Her lines of communication would enable her, as she demonstrated when reserves were urgently called forth from the Negev to the Jordan and the Syrian Fronts, to transfer forces to surprise the enemy. As Major-General Itzhak Rabin, the Chief of Staff, told the troops just before the battle, the Israeli army might be outnumbered and have fewer tanks but they were close to their base, at times almost on top of it. The Arabs would have to move a very long way from their bases and have long lines of communication. What the Israelis would have to prevent at all costs was any link-up across the narrow part of the Negev through an alliance of Egypt and Jordan. More than anyone, Colonel Nasser realized that to bring about real unity among the Arabs, with himself as the modern Saladin, he would have to take possession of the Negev. The Negev is the only land bridge that connects Egypt in the south with Syria and Lebanon in the north and Jordan and Iraq in the east. Once the Arabs controlled the Negev they would have a common front. They would not only surround Israel in the fullest sense of the word; they would be able to concentrate Arab armies against her from distant places. There was the undeniable fact that the Israelis were a mighty fighting people. This could be a people's war. The Israelis would fight not only for the lives of their people but for their mission in their new-ancient homeland.

Israel was clearly the David to the Arab Goliath. She possessed by far the smallest regular standing army, numbering about 70,000. War-time strength of all services, counting all reserves and National Servicemen, was about 260,000. Men up to 49 and childless women up to 34 were available for call. Men over 49 were enrolled in civil defense. Air Force strength was about 14,000 and there were about 450 aircraft. So far as I could discover all front line combat aircraft were jets, mostly of French make. Four squadrons for certain had 72 Mirage III supersonic multi-mission fighters. Three fighter-bomber squadrons had Mystère Ivas and two had Outragans. Squadrons which did such excellent work at the beginning had supersonic Super Mystères and Mirages. The Air Force also had tactical bomber reconnaissance squadrons of twin jet Vantours, transport squadrons of Noratlas C 47, some swing tail Stratocruiser aircraft, some helicopters and locally built Magister jet trainers. Hawk surface-to-air missiles were in use during the fighting. The total strength of Israeli armored forces was unknown but she had British Centurians and the remarkable 105 mm. gun. It was not possible to obtain any idea even during the war, they were so mobile on the four fronts. Major-General Rabin told me: "I was asked whether it was true that we had between 600 and 800 tanks. I can only say that whoever relied on that estimate was mistaken." Whether he meant Israel had more or fewer it was impossible even to guess. The indications are that they had far more.

Egypt, which maintains a peace-time army of 100,000, with National Guards numbering 50,000, had a possible war-time force of about 250,000 men. She had over 1,000 tanks, most of them of Russian make. Apart from some Mark II Centurians she had at least one regiment of Stalin IIIs. She had hundreds of T 34s, about 250 T 54s and some T 55s. There were also about 350 Soviet Block armored troop carriers, over 430 Russian 120 and 122 mm. field guns and 50 100 mm. self-propelled guns from the same factories. She also possessed 40 155 mm. heavy artillery pieces. Soviet "Guideline" surface-to-air missiles were in use. The most formidable of an impressive array of sophisticated weapons the Egyptians had from Russia was a radar-controlled ground-to-air missile, the SA2, which weighed nearly two-and-a-half tons and had a range of twenty-five miles. Experts said that the same model had been used with considerable success in North Vietnam against American bombers. Egypt had even set up a Missile Command and this had at its disposal at least 75 rockets, the Azafir with a range of 235 miles which could reach Israel's big centers and the Al Kahir which was almost as deadly. They had missile firing torpedo boats. Egypt also had an anti-rocket unit containing four missiles, which the Israel General Staff believed to be in advance of any similar weapon in the West. There were a radar unit for correcting the faulty range of artillery fire on moving targets, a communications command vehicle containing a wealth of radio equipment, an anti-tank recoilless rifle and a rapid-fire cannon. The Egyptians had a howitzer, with a 10-mile range, which was made in Russia as recently as 1966. This fired seven rounds a minute and could outrange any similar weapon in the West.

Egypt's Air Force was largely equipped with planes provided by Russia and Czechoslovakia. It may have comprised about 430 combat type. These included 12 Squadrons of Supersonic Mig 21 and Mig 19 fighters and Mig 17 and Mig 15 fighter-bombers. There were two squadrons of TU 16 medium jet bombers, three squadrons (1 wing) of Il 28 light jet bombers, a number of the latest Sukhoi fighter-bombers, eight Antonov 12 heavy transports, 12 Mig heavy helicopters. There were also many turbo prop An.12s, Il 14s, C 47s, C 45s, Doves, besides Yak IIs and Yak 18s.

Syria's army in peace time comprised 45,000 men, a civil police force of 5,000 and a Bedouin Control Force. Her equipment with technical advisers was supplied by the Russians. The basis of her armor was 200 T 34 tanks and an unknown number of recent models. Syria's Air Force was also equipped by Russia. She had a first line strength of numerous day fighter-bombers, several all-weather fighter squadrons and at least 60 Mig jets. Even her training planes were Russian Yaks.

Iraq had a standing army of 70,000 which had equipment mostly of Russian origin. The Air Force had Russian-made planes, including TU 16 medium bombers, Il 28 light bombers, Mig 21 day interceptors, Mig 17d night fighters and Mig 17c day interceptors. She was also to employ British-built Hunter jets and Wessex helicopters.

Jordan seemed to be the only Arab army not fitted out by

the Russians. Her army comprised four Independent infantry brigade groups with an armored force of two combat groups or armored car regiments. There was also a National Guard of 30,000 men. Jordan's Air Force consisted of two squadrons of Hunter jet fighters, some Star fighters and one squadron of Vampire fighter-bombers.

The most important factor in any war for Israel, however, was not its relative strength in men and arms but the place where the war would be fought. When she attacked the Arabs in 1956 she did not do what was expected—invade Jordan. She would probably make a diversionary move this time towards Syria and attack Egypt. Nitsana, which stands by the side of major cross roads, is the gateway into the Egyptian Sinai. This would be the obvious target if war came; I was sure both armies were concentrating on their own side of it. Israel would invade the Sinai. She would attempt to repeat the remarkable *blitzkrieg* of 1956. It did not much matter that Nitsana, where Israel thrashed the Egyptian invaders in December 1948, had become a demilitarized zone between Israel and Egypt by virtue of the Armistice. The Sinai was ideal for modern mechanized war. The Israeli soldier loved it. The Egyptian hated all deserts. This arid, brutal moonscape might have been provided by nature to test the endurance of men and machines. If it was not empty, the population, except in the north, was nomadic and accustomed to striking its tents and moving rapidly on without notice, taking their few belongings with them. They did not favor the black tents of the Bedouin in Jordan but used low oblong brushwood shelters with an enclosed brushwood compound for their livestock. This cost only time to build. Except on the coastal road, where there is a simple railway mainly for freight from Gaza to the Suez Canal, there was nothing of value to destroy. It reminded me of the Western Desert but its terrain was more broken and uneven and its high mountains are carved into fantastic shapes by the wind. In this vast sunbaked triangle men could fight each other as savagely and murderously as they wished without fear of witnesses.

On the night of June 4th-5th the Israeli army was on the alert. Since May 20th, when two-thirds of all able-bodied men had disappeared from the streets, the army had undergone exhaustive final preparation to defend the borders. They had been mobilized in seventy-seven hours—Israel held the world record in time taken for mobilization—and were then all in position, arms and ammunition and rations at hand. The men understood exactly what was expected of them if the command came. For two weeks they had not for a moment relaxed their vigilance. Now they were more alert than ever. The commander, Major-General Itzhak Rabin, the 45-year-old graduate of the British Staff College at Camberley, who had drawn up the plan of attack, talked to the men in serious tones. He had told them they were in the midst of a campaign in which their military power and the readiness to put it into action were closely coordinated with political moves. The two arms of the campaign, the military and the political, supported and complemented each other. Military preparedness lent force to political activity. It was the prime condition for its prospects of success. He warned them that the transition from one state to the other might be precipitous and sudden. They were capable not only of stopping aggression but also of defeating the enemy on his own soil. They must not delude themselves that the danger had passed or lessened. The effort required of the soldier who had to wait while maintaining high tension was not less than that required in assaulting an enemy. Though Israel's troops might be outnumbered and have fewer tanks, it must be remembered they were close to base, at times almost on top of it. Troops from Egypt, Iraq, Syria had had to move a very long way from their bases. They had long lines of communication.

The Israeli army was created in the midst of battle against the invading Arabs in 1948. It had ever since been confronted by one enemy only, the Arabs, and on a front that never changed. It had been the same for twenty years. It was the same now. Called Tsahal—the initials of Tseva Haganah Leisrael—the army was composed of land, sea and air forces and it had never been so ready for action as it was on the eve of the war. It was full of elation, proud of its origins and its past accomplishments. The army had grown mainly out of the Haganah, the volunteer organization formed during the Mandatory period, and partly out of the Jewish Brigade which fought with the Allied forces during the Second World War. It consisted only of a small nucleus of commissioned and non-commissioned regular officers with the reserve and a contingent called up for national service for between two years and twenty-six months. Because of this ingenious arrangement a little, not very rich country like Israel, surrounded by enemies, could be ringed with steel within a few hours of mobilization. Every village was in communication with every other village and with the commander of the area. Men who an hour before were serving at shop counters, working in factories or garages or in the fields and the citrus plantations were wearing uniforms stamped with the jagged black stencilled mark of the Defense Force. Israel could deploy instantly a force of reservists and National Service men big enough to meet any contingency while avoiding the need to keep a large standing army. Because men went back in an emergency to areas and positions in which they had been trained, no man was a stranger among his comrades.

Morale was tremendously high as exemplified by a story I was told of a punishment unparalleled in any other army. Just before war broke out a reservist's wife wrote direct to a base and asked a sergeant if she could speak to her husband. The man was summoned before his commanding officer and charged with a breach of security for revealing to his wife his location. The sentence was severe. "Go home," said the officer. "We have no place for the likes of you." The man slunk out but he did not go home. He began instead a sit-down strike by the camp gate. He begged everyone who entered to plead with his C.O. to reconsider his sentence and take him back. He was still at the gate next morning. In the evening the C.O. relented and took the man back. The soldier refused after that to answer any question put to him by his comrades. He would not even tell anyone the time.

Young people who had established new agricultural settlements on the borders had joined the army in groups called Nahal. Single women up to the age of 34, organized into Chen (in Hebrew this means "grace"), had been called up to perform duties which would release men next morning for combat service. There was the Gadna—contraction for Gedudei No'ar—youth troops and other organizations who would on June 5th take over essential duties to help the troops. They all knew what war meant. There were acts of war on one front or another throughout the year. It was because of this that the territorial defense system was based on a long linked chain of villages along the border in which people grew crops and now stood at the ready as soldiers. Each village had its local command, was issued weapons and ammunition, and took part in the tense vigil. Positions, arms and ammunition as well as essential supplies were ready for the emergency.

Full mobilization was not officially ordered until 10 a.m. on June 5th, and it was then that another record was created. A military spokesman read out over the radio the code names of the remaining units left over from the partial mobilization when three-fourths of Israel's manpower had been called into action. Code names were: Love of Zion, Close Shave, Men at Work, Alternating Current, Open Window and Good Friends. The men who responded were those in essential civilian occupations who had kept the nation's economy going while their comrades were at the front.

The strategic problems arising from a long front of 591 miles, manned by the Arab troops of four nations, were handled that night by the Israeli General Staff. Under General Rabin, Brigadier-Generals commanded Southern, Central and Northern Commands. Brigadier-Generals in the Sinai, on the three axes, as in other areas, commanded formations. Each Command constituted an autonomous formation which administered all the units within its geographical jurisdiction. It also coordinated the strategy and the logistics of the armed villages, or *kibbutzim,* within its segment of the territorial defense system.

All Israel had pored over old maps of the Sinai campaign of 1956 and tried to guess the strategy of the war they knew would come. Already thousands of Field Postcards had been received by their relatives from men "at the front," and they gave, of course, not the slightest clue as to their whereabouts. On the night of June 4th, D-day minus one, Israel's armored divisions were lying concealed in the Negev near the Sinai border, poised and ready to pounce on Khan Yunis and Rafah; near Nitsana, the gateway to the Sinai, ready to strike at Bir Lahfan and Gebal Libni; farther to the south, two forces were ready to strike at Nakhl, one via Abu Agheila, the other via Kuntilla. Other troops were also in defensive positions on the Jordan, Syrian and Lebanon borders. The Air Force and the tiny Navy were on alert.

Radars all over the Middle East, including those of the British, U.S. and Russian Navies in the Mediterranean, were continuing their long vigil, little suspecting that D-day was at hand. Special spy ships from the United States and Russia lay off the Israeli and Egyptian coasts. One of them, the U.S.S. *Liberty,* which was a top secret vessel dealing with codes, ciphers and communications, was later to be fired on, killing one of America's top secret experts.

Some people were already saying that nothing had changed in Israel's strategy since 1956. True, Israel's objective was exactly the same as in 1956—to attack Egypt to forestall an offensive, and to stop, once and for all, the many acts of aggression on Israel's borders. But though the objective was the same there was one vital difference between Israel's judgment now and in 1956, and this was to have a profound effect on the campaign.

Before 1956, Israel had handed air initiative on a tray to Egypt. She had imposed on herself a crippling code of aerial warfare under which she had solemnly vowed not to send her aircraft across the Suez Canal and not to attack Egypt except in response to Egyptian action. This code was based on, but even stricter than, the Yalu River Rule of the Korean War, and was, in fact, referred to in Israel by the same name. There were reasons why this rule was applied, but if Egypt had taken advantage of it she might have done to Israel what Israel was to do to her. As it happened, Egypt was prevented from striking by air at Israel in 1956 by the Anglo-French air forces, which put the Egyptian Air Force out of action before the war began. It was strange that no one ever mentioned the Yalu River Rule when they discussed the war that seemed now to loom on the horizon. No one seemed to know if it would again operate. All they knew was that the Israeli Air Force was far inferior in numbers to that of Egypt, even without considering those of the other Arab nations. Air attack was the one feature of war that the Israeli civilians feared. No one dreamed that Israel, whether it held to the Yalu River Rule or not, would dare provoke the massive air retaliation that would inevitably follow by making an attack by air on any Arab country, least of all on Egypt. Such strategy, they thought, would be suicidal. There was no Anglo-French Air Force now to put the Egyptian Air Force out of action. What General Rabin and his General Staff had decided in their plan was never the subject of public speculation. The fact was, however, that the Yalu River Rule had long ago been scrapped. The Israeli Air Force, for the first time in war, was completely unshackled, even free to take the initiative and cross the Suez Canal.

The Israel ground forces did not move forward on June 5th as is generally the case in war in the early hours of the morning. The necessary provocation was not committed until later. The troops did not in fact move until Israeli clerks, all of them middle aged, were on their way to work in the towns and cities.

6

ARAB AIR FORCES DEFEATED

The first indication that operation "Nachonim" had begun was just before 8 a.m. on Monday, June 5th, when air raid sirens sounded. No one took any notice. Israel had been lulled into a state of false security by General Moshe Dayan. War was further from their minds that morning than it had been for weeks. People thought the sirens were being tested, as they had been tested before. One or two people looked up at the cloudless sky. They saw nothing, as they heard nothing. The announcement that hostilities had begun came fifty-four minutes later. Before it came, however, the sirens were sounded a second time. The banshee wailing seemed then to be a little more urgent. Planes could also be heard far off but they belonged to Israel. People hurried in disciplined fashion to the air raid shelters. Very soon the streets were clear although a few cars continued to run. People ran out of houses, collected their children, and hurried into their air raid shelters such as have to be built in Israel when the houses are built. The same cry was on everyone's tongue. "*The Egyptians have attacked.*"

When I arrived at Beit Sokolov the Israel Army spokesman made two statements. Since the early hours heavy fighting had been taking place on the southern front between Egyptian armored and aerial forces which "were seen on the radar to move against Israel. Our forces went into action in order to check them." The other was that settlements bordering on the Gaza Strip had been intermittently shelled by Egyptian guns and mortars. They were Nirim, Nahal Oz and Kfar Azza. At once I recalled that the second communiqué in the Sinai campaign in 1956 had also referred to Nahal Oz. Egyptians had then opened up with mortar fire. Shells had hit the settlement and the surrounding area. Then had followed a long communiqué which said in a round about way that the invasion of Sinai had begun. It even said that Egypt had sought to strangle Israel's economy and life by blockade of the Suez Canal and Aqaba. That Egypt had sought to encompass Israel with a ring of steel with the announced purpose of annihilating her. What had just happened was all so very familiar. Although a new Chief of Staff had carried out the planning for war against the Arabs, Major-General Rabin instead of Major-General Dayan, I had a feeling that operations would bear a remarkable likeness to one that had gone before. Israel could fight twice as well as Egypt or any other Arab army in the desert, and in the desert it would be. The build up was the same. Longer had been taken over preparations. Plans were therefore far more detailed and thorough.

Rabin would go through the gestures Dayan went through to deceive Egypt. Last time Dayan appeared to be about to attack Jordan. Rabin would now make not very surreptitious moves to the north, against Syria. The Israeli-Egyptian border had been peaceful for nine years and now it was noisy as hell. There had been no incident of any account, partly because of the presence of UNEF, partly because of the cooperation of both sides.

Overnight, I was now told, as if to justify what had happened, there had been a number of incidents in the Jerusalem area! A light plane had flown over Israel territory. The day before a mine had been planted near Nirim but it was discovered. On June 2nd at 2:30 a.m. at Kfar Hanassi, Syria, two Israeli soldiers had been killed in a clash two and one-half miles from the border by a band of armed Syrians. There had been outrages, infiltrations, sabotage, mining and firing on fifteen occasions since May 15th, ten of them carried out, probably, by Syrian trained terrorists from among Jordan refugees.

It seemed to me, therefore, that there was nothing unusual about the shelling of the *kibbutzim* on the Gaza Strip border. It was not possible to check the report about the Egyptian airplanes sighted on Israel radar, or to get down in the deep Sinai to check movements there. The best I could do was to go to the Gaza Strip. This is what I did in the 1956 war.

As I drove to the Gaza Strip I recalled some of my old friends at Nahal Oz, a heroic village with a history of violence that would make a thriller. There were sounds and signs of real war as we approached it again. Tanks and artillery were concealed in nearby groves. The crunch of shells and the roar of cannon came to us on the stifling air. A pall of dust from the desert churned up by a helicopter hung in the heavens to obscure the sun. The wheat had been set on fire. There were deep trenches and gun emplacements among the citrus fruit, the vines and the general crops. The children and old people had been evacuated. People were in a trench now because there had been more shelling. There had been shelling on a wider front at 8 o'clock, about eighty shells, 35-pounders and 120 mm. and 80 mm. mortars. Some ten cows had been killed and fifteen had been injured. They had been slaughtered a little before their time amid the din of war. Some buildings had been damaged and more fields of stubble were now burning. Luckily, most of the crops had been garnered. There were so far no human casualties.

Israeli troops, armor and infantry (some of them Nahal Oz warrior farmers) invaded the Gaza Strip. Israel was, in fact, about to capture its first Egyptian town in the war—not that we had heard war had been declared. We all assumed so. Guns flashed even in the face of brilliant sun. The noise was like thunder. I learned that the town Israel forces were about to capture was Khan Yunis, at the start of the fulfilment of an objective to cut off the twenty-five miles of Gaza Strip which penetrated Israel like a dagger at its heart. Khan Yunis was general headquarters of the Egyptian forces (mainly Palestinian refugees) of 30,000. Fighting was heavy but my attention was distracted. Batteries in Givet Ali Muntar in the Strip began again to shell Nahal Oz. It was too dangerous to go nearer to Gaza, five miles away. It had clearly not yet been captured. It looked, in fact, quite serene in the late sun, a little like a set in a Hollywood film. Even the cone-shaped hill of Gaza looked like a back cloth. Advance units moved down from Khan Yunis, now flying the flag of the blue Shield of David. Gaza, the old Philistine town founded by the Canaanites and associated with Samson, was now the objective. Gaza was a tough nut but it would be a great capture politically as well as militarily. The Palestine Liberation Army, fanatical fighters who aimed to take over Israel, belonged to the 250,000 refugees in the Strip. They felt they were fighting for the return of their homeland.

Already the Palestinians had set up a Palestine government in exile. They had been waiting with their bags packed for victory to come along so that they could take over Tel Aviv. But the home of the Philistines, whose capital was Gaza, also had a moral significance for the Israelites which I do not believe was lost on any of them. I almost feel that the Strip was put first on the list, instead of last as in 1956, because of the allusive nature of its history. This ancient area recalled the fight between Goliath, the 9-foot Philistine giant (possibly a descendant of Anakims) who was slain by the infinitely smaller David, future King of Israel (I Samuel 17). The biblical context had a religious aspect (I Samuel 17: 43, 45). It symbolized that might was not always right and that virtue could triumph in the face of odds. The victor placed Goliath's sword in the sanctuary of Nob. The Chief Rabbi to the Israeli forces wanted there also to be a religious outcome to the war.

Israel wished even before the war had been going on a day that it had not burdened itself with the Strip. The army found 100 Egyptian tanks intact in the orange groves but they also became aware that there were thousands of light arms hidden for future use by the population. Some of them were used that night for sniping. On my way back along the border of the Gaza Strip I visited Yad Mordechai, a nearby *kibbutz,* from which I looked out to the battle of Gaza. I was hidden from the few Egyptian planes in the sky by the orange groves. I met a learned farmer beside the 12-foot-high, bare chested, ball-fisted statue of Anielevic, the guerilla, which seemed to me as I listened to the strife of war to be a symbol for all Israelis that day. The farmer assured me that shelling had begun before the cocks crowed that morning.

"Maybe," I said, "Nahal Oz saw the very beginning of the war."

"Well it was one of the places that did last time."

So far as I was able to discover the *kibbutzim* along the border, so accustomed to the terrorism of the Strip, were the only part of Israel soil actually hit by the Egyptian army that ill-fated morning. For all we knew the incidents taking place were no different from hundreds of others in the past though there were signs that the settlers were taking events a little more seriously. When shelling began again, everyone vanished into shelters and trenches. The swings for the children behind a high protecting wall were hit. When parents collected the milk and the children's toys and took them into the vaulted reinforced concrete bunker, used only on "special" occasions, it meant that the children would be in the bunkers for many hours. Sometimes the children spent all day below ground in the light of a bare electric bulb while the sun shone brilliantly up above. Babies slept together in home-made cots in a corner fondly thought to be safe. The Egyptian propaganda had had its effect on some of the women. When there was no witness some of them told me openly that they feared because the Palestinians were so near. If someone came within earshot I noticed that the women changed the subject. It would not do for anyone to betray the fact that they did not trust their own troops implicitly to keep the Arabs out of Israel. Women, as well as men, could tell you exactly where the Arab troops were.

I had to hurry back because the military spokesman, Colonel Moshe Pearlman, was going to brief us on the day's events. He performed the function in 1956. No matter how enterprising a man is as a war correspondent, and covering a war is an occasion for the exercise of more than enterprise, it is not possible to learn who advanced, and how far, when and how many tanks and planes had been destroyed or captured or how many prisoners of war had been taken. I came back in a car that was a veteran of Dayan's campaign. It was driven by an immigrant Cossack who sang Russian songs at the top of his voice. In the intervals between he talked violently partisan politics. Luckily the roads were deserted. The traffic lights were out, otherwise we would have had a dozen accidents. The singing nearly drowned the sounds of the air raids, in and out of which we ran the whole way. It was impossible to distinguish the alerts from the all-clears. The Egyptian Air Force was making inept raids on the coastal road. The crunch of bombs and the rattle of ack-ack fire could be heard over the bass voice of the Cossack. Sound was magnified in the dead silence of the first night of war in Israel for eleven years.

Back in my hotel, I was given three sheets of notepaper with my key. One said, "For security reasons we have taken out of your bedroom all electric bulbs." The other: "Please keep curtains closed in your room day and night (24 hours)." A third, from a friend, said, "There's something very mysterious going on. No one at military headquarters will say *one* word. It almost seems that what the Gyppies say on the radio about advancing is correct."

I went to my bedroom and wrote a dispatch in the glow of one cigarette after another, smoked by the Cossack to light up the keyboard of my typewriter.

A retired Israeli journalist who could speak Arabic and English had been given the task by a number of us to monitor the radio during the day. He had prepared three reports from Cairo.

(1) Early in the afternoon Cairo Radio said that Egyptian troops were holding their own in fighting with Israeli troops along the Sinai border. The radio said Israel had attacked all along Sinai this morning "but could not pierce our lines." In the biggest ground battle reported, Egypt claimed that Israel lost most of thirty tanks in the Gaza Strip.

(2) Egypt said Israel planes were raiding airfields at Cairo and in the Suez Canal zone around dawn. Cairo Radio said that seventy attacking jets had been shot down and fourteen pilots captured in the Canal zone. Between them, Egypt and Syria claimed to have destroyed more than a hundred Israeli planes. Egypt said she had lost two planes, but the pilots had parachuted to safety.

(3) According to Egypt, the Suez Canal was also the scene of two incidents. An American tanker is said to have tried to slew sideways and block the Canal, and Israeli planes have allegedly tried to attack a French ship passing through.

I shall never forget the boredom of that night after the excitement of the day. Beit Sokolov was efficiently blacked-out. We had to grope our way in the darkness over a lawn and up and down two flights of steps, which seemed to move, contract and expand. Correspondents lay on the lawn in the dark waiting for a briefing from Colonel Moshe Pearlman without which they could not write fully informed accounts of the day's war. Morning newspaper men from all over the world had deadlines to meet. As they lay listening to air raid alerts and all-clears, with the sound of bombs and guns wedged in between, they complained that these deadlines were rapidly approaching or passing. Many of them eventually had to write personal accounts based on their own experiences on the Gaza Strip front.

The briefing had been fixed for 9 p.m. The hour passed without explanation. The military spokesman was just not available. I remember someone started a rumor when the briefing had been postponed three times and midnight was at hand: something terrible had gone wrong. My friend who had left the note at my hotel was so worried he might have been an Israeli. Communications were good in that tight little country. Even in the Negev in war, the Chief of Staff and the Government must have known precisely what had happened. No one could think of an explanation for the delay. Some of the correspondents who had been heavily engaged all day in great heat sent off incomplete dispatches. They decided to rely on the news agencies for additional details and then groped out in the strange darkness of the black-out to try to find a taxi to their hotel. Sometimes this operation took hours.

What had happened was this. Major-General Dayan, in connivance with Major-General Itzhak Rabin, willfully sat upon the facts of the first day's battle for four-and-a-half hours. Something they had learned about Colonel Nasser had caused them to exercise great caution.

Early in the day Egyptian headquarters in the Sinai and in the Gaza Strip had sent off from their headquarters situation reports of the early fighting which vied in their imaginative content with the more flighty tales of the Arabian Nights. True to the practice of Arabic inferiors they told their superiors what they wanted to know rather than admit distasteful truths. A chain of Egyptian soldiers, officers of higher and still higher ranks, passed on from one to another wholly inaccurate versions of all battles. They left out every unpleasant fact in the forlorn hope that Allah must soon wake up to the fact that his miracles were needed to handle and contain the Infidel. Other facts the Arabs scarcely admitted to themselves. Just as Colonel Nasser speaks in two languages, the language of reason and statesmanship when he addresses himself to a foreigner who is his intellectual peer, and the language of incitement to hatred and violence and war when he speaks to his own illiterate masses, so the Egyptian soldier of any rank is apt to become vague, meaningless, inexplicit, sometimes contradictory in times of military adversity. Colonel Nasser was given to believe that his forces in the Sinai, and in the Gaza Strip, had quickly responded to Israel's surprise attack. They had not only held their lines but actually thrown back the enemy. Colonel Nasser sent pleasant précis of these reports to the Russian Ambassador in Cairo. He also misled President Atassi and Prime Minister Zayiyen of Syria and King Hussein of Jordan. The Soviet Ambassador sent reports to Moscow. Moscow understood that Egypt was winning and did not demand a cease-fire at the United Nations that day.

Israeli Intelligence officers accompanying the advancing army allowed Egyptian communication units to send off a spate of optimistic messages to the Egyptian High Command. Then they set out to execute a plan to cut all communications between the Gaza Strip, and two areas inside the Sinai, with Cairo. Such was their intelligence, some based on information gathered in the Sinai in 1956 and re-checked, and some recently obtained in the Sinai, that they knew all the alternative locations from which Egyptian signals would be operating. As soon as radio operators changed wavelengths Israel jammed them. Finally there was a complete blanket on communications between Cairo and the three areas in which the Egyptians had been defeated. Probes from adjacent Egyptian areas were quickly discouraged. Messages were carefully accepted from Cairo, recorded and re-transmitted to Israeli advance, later to rear, headquarters. These told General Itzhak Rabin, General Moshe Dayan and Levi Eshkol that utter confusion reigned in Colonel Nasser's High Command. Radio messages intercepted showed that Colonel Nasser was highly suspicious of earlier reports of successful Egyptian resistance and completely in the dark about events since. No one could explain to the Egyptian Sinai Commander, General Murtaji, and he could not explain to Marshal Amer, and Marshal Amer could not explain to Colonel Nasser exactly what was happening. Confusion still reigned though it was beginning to dawn on the Egyptian General Staff that some of their forces had been completely overwhelmed and that the Israeli army had managed to sever communications.

Israeli Intelligence then learned that Egyptian Intelligence had been specially briefed to maintain an augmented monitoring service on press cables which left Israel for capitals all over the world. Basing his supposition on Cairo's common practice, Colonel Nasser assumed that there would be a press briefing between eight and nine o'clock at which the army spokesman would summarize the achievements of the day. A corps of Intelligence monitors began to work with the utmost diligence. Colonel Nasser was to be telephoned as soon as a press cable had been intercepted and told of its contents. To the mystification of all there was an extraordinary dearth of press cables from Tel Aviv or Jerusalem to the capitals of the world. From time to time negative reports were sent to Colonel Nasser. He became more bewildered and more angry. So, while the war correspondents waited impatiently at Beit Sokolov, uttering curses against Colonel Moshe Pearlman, Colonel Nasser and Marshal Amer, not to mention General Murtaji and others in the field, were also waiting.

As the hours dragged on, more and more correspondents left. Others dropped asleep, exhausted by a long and heavy day. It was at half past one on Tuesday morning, instead of at nine o'clock on the previous evening, as had been arranged, that I saw Colonel Moshe Pearlman come half running into the briefing room. The depleted ranks of war correspondents shook themselves into wakefulness. Pearlman began to speak with tears in his voice. He was terribly sorry. He had kept everyone waiting four-and-a-half hours but the position was that if he had come any earlier he would not have been able to give them a worthwhile set of facts. He had been with General Moshe Dayan waiting for things to be confirmed so that he would have something big to tell them. Now, he could speak. The journalists sat bolt upright, prepared for good news, not suspecting for a moment they had been used in a matter of top security at a most delicate moment of the war and that the delay they had suffered had done much to frustrate Colonel Nasser and help the Israeli cause.

Then Pearlman went on to tell thrilling news which caused Israeli journalists and their overseas Jewish cousins to rise to their feet and cheer at the tops of their voices. The Israeli army had occupied Der al Balagh in the Gaza Strip. Khan Yunis had fallen. At midnight the Israeli army was heavily engaged in battle on the outskirts of Gaza which would soon fall. Israel had occupied El Arish, Rafah and Sheikh Zuweid and the railway from Gaza along the north coast of the Sinai. In the central sector, Um-Katef was the scene of heavy fighting. But it was the Israeli Air Force which made this splendid victory possible. Some 374 enemy planes had been destroyed, against only nineteen Israel planes lost. The Arab Air Forces had been defeated. The Israeli Air Force had achieved complete supremacy in its "counter strikes" against four Arab Air Forces during daylight hours. Egyptian supply lines would therefore be at the mercy of Israel's Air Force. The Egyptians would have increasing difficulties in maintaining already inadequate food and water supplies. The only piece of bad news was that the Jordanian army had shelled Jerusalem. Already civilians had been killed.

The Soviet Union's radio and television networks and state newspapers on Monday evening gave (from their viewpoint) optimistic accounts of the Israel-Arab war. They were based on early reports received from Nasser predicting an Arab victory. It was not until Tuesday, after Colonel Nasser had learned the truth from the monitored Israeli press cables and corrected to some extent his wholly erroneous communications to the Soviet Ambassador, that Tass, the Soviet News Agency, gave some indication of Israeli successes. The agency's Russian and English-language services even reported an Israeli communiqué listing objectives captured and progress made. It was not until hours later that a note of alarm suddenly crept into the reports being issued to Soviet citizens. News reports from Tass to Soviet newspapers and radio stations began to temper accounts of Arab victories.

The Soviet propaganda machine went into reverse gear. The Foreign Office also changed its policy at the United Nations. Some newspapers began to carry critical headlines. Instead of "Arab Victories in Israel" the government *Izvestia* ran a huge headline: "EXTINGUISH THE FLAMES OF WAR IN MIDEAST" it demanded.

7

WHO FIRED FIRST?

Who fired first and what was the provocation, or reason? This is a question no correspondent can answer precisely. He can give the conclusion he has drawn from the relevant facts he has gathered, or give the facts and let the reader draw his own conclusions. The Egyptians swore that the Israelis had begun it. The Israelis put the blame on the Egyptians.* One might ask, however, if the actual physical act of the first strike was relevant? Colonel Nasser had already perpetuated aggression by closing the Straits of Tiran, by sending an army of 95,000 troops to the Israel border and by the clearest statements of his intention to attack Israel in the near future. He had also recruited Arab allies with the stated intention of destroying Israel. But the question of who started the shooting war, and why, will always arouse controversy in the future.

I had acquired somewhere a small notebook marked "Who Fired First?" and I began to jot in this everything I heard or was told or ferreted out which had any bearing on the question. In the 1956 campaign I had carried a similar notebook into which I made jottings which had any relevance to the question of alleged collaboration between Israel and France and Britain. Once you begin a line of inquiry like this it snowballs. It is amazing how many clues can be gathered.

On my way back to my hotel in the black-out from Beit

* Israel stated later she had captured fifty tons of Egyptian and Syrian military documents, many Top Secret. One was an Operation Order of the UAR which indicated that the Egyptian Air Force planned on May 17th to bomb Israeli airfields and Eilat. It was stated that napalm bombs (according to Order) would be used on one air strike. A document found at GHQ, Hashemite Brigade, Ramallah, was alleged to relate to intention to destroy Israeli settlements and kill all people in them.

Sokolov at 3 o'clock that Tuesday morning, I resolved eventually to reconstruct what had happened between Israel and Egypt early on Monday morning. I knew several people who might be inclined to help though they had to be certain. I would not reveal who had helped me. First of all, however, I decided to hear what the Israeli governmental and military leaders had to say on the point. There was the nation's leader, Levi Eshkol, Prime Minister of Israel. This member of the MAPAI (Labor Party) and head of a coalition formed in 1964 and 1965, and added to a day or so before, was obviously the person responsible for giving the order to fire whether or not in retaliation after an Arab attack. He made this statement in the Knesset on the start of the war.

"On Monday, June 5th," he said, "seven to eight Egyptian divisions, two of them armored, were deployed in front of our border in Sinai. Nine hundred tanks were dispersed along the border—200 of them opposite Eilat, with the aim of cutting off the southern Negev. Along Israel's eastern border stood 60,000 Jordanian soldiers and 300 tanks. The Jordanian army had been placed under Egyptian command and Egyptian commando units and Iraqi forces had entered its territory.

"On our northern border with Syria, 50,000 Syrian soldiers were ready for the assault, and the entire border was sown with guns and mortars—dug in, fortified, and protected by concrete and steel.

"Some 600 Egyptian, Jordanian, Syrian and Iraqi planes were ready. During the days preceding June 5th, Egyptian air sorties took place over Israel skies. *The decisive moment came. Facing the movement of Egyptian forces to the Israeli border, our forces went out to repulse the enemy's aggression, and air and armored battles developed."*

It is noted that Eshkol was scrupulously careful not to state that the Egyptians crossed the border with their land or air forces.

The Minister of Defense, General Moshe Dayan, made the following statement to the Israel Defense Forces at 10:30 a.m. on June 5th:

"Soldiers of Israel. At this moment we are not yet in possession of fully detailed information on the course of the battles taking place on the southern front. Our aircraft are engaged in grim combat with the enemy air force, and our ground forces have moved to silence Egyptian artillery which had heavily shelled our settlements opposite the Gaza Strip, and to repulse the Egyptian armed forces who seek in the first stage of their campaign to cut off the southern part of the Negev. . . ."

On June 5th in Tel Aviv, I asked Israeli Foreign Minister Eban if he could tell me if the Egyptian air and land forces that morning had actually crossed the border or not. His answer was hesitant. He said: "I think you will be shown on which side of the border *the shells fell.* Whether the Egyptians came with their feet or not I don't know. In any case, you will be informed later as to the operative details."

Eban was probably the more articulate of the Israeli leaders. He referred later on June 5th in a statement on the "Egyptian shelling of settlements (those which I have described) on the morning of June 5th, to the early reports of air attacks and armored movements."

"Which precisely was the first move against Israel this morning?" he was asked.

Eban replied: "The difference was not very great in the timing. The first movement was the movement of the Egyptian aircraft, the second phase was the shelling of Israeli villages near the Gaza Strip, the third stage was the Israeli reciprocation of these movements. The fourth phase has been the expansion of the conflict by the Jerusalem aggression. But if I could say something on this point. This is an aggressive assault begun by Egypt in every sense of the word, in the broad historical sense and in the immediate sense." He was again questioned: "First you said Egyptian aircraft came over and then there was shelling of Israeli villages. Was this in response to the shelling in Sinai—is that correct?" "We responded," said Eban, "to the air movement by chasing them (the airplanes) and we responded to the shelling by shooting against those who shelled us. I would rather you wait to get this military report with its military vocabulary."

Eban added, "Let me enumerate the main stages in this process which the provocative action constitutes in Sinai: Hundreds of tanks against our southern border. A large tank force opposite Eilat in a plan to sunder the southern Negev from Israel. The blockade of the Straits of Tiran and the Gulf of Aqaba in defiance of the international and maritime communities. The threat of strangling encirclement which was an important state. The agreement between Egypt and Jordan. The placing of Iraqi troops in Jordan in accordance with the terms of the Iraq-Egypt agreement. All designed to bring about the total annihilation of Israel. Then the Order of the Day of the Egyptian Commander, General Murtaji, calling on his troops to wage 'holy war' against Israel. Then the constant acts of sabotage and terrorism from Syria and Sinai, and this morning's events beginning with the movements of regular troops against Israel, and the bombardment of the Israel villages of Ramat Hakovesh and Nahal Oz. All this amounts to an extraordinary catalog of aggression which has appalled, and must be condemned by, world opinion and all peace-loving countries in the world."

Major-General Itzhak Rabin, on June 7th 1967, speaking in Hebrew, also made a reference to the start of the war. He said: "On the morning of June 5th the shelling of settlements started on the border as did troop movements and the movement of considerable air groups. We had to defend ourselves. Israel is too small a country to defend itself in any other but an active manner. Part of our mobilization preceded the above events, but the rest of our troops were mobilized by radio on the morning of June 5th. Since Egypt was the one to start the attack and also because Egypt had the most powerful force numerically, most of our action was directed against the Egyptians. Our air reaction was, of course, immediate and our land forces entered the action a little later."

Later he said: "Our air force *met the attackers* and destroyed some in the air and some on the ground. In air combat, as you will realize, *there are no borders and no limitations.* The Israeli army was afforded air superiority almost from the start. This, of course, was a particularly important factor because it enabled the army to maintain freedom of movement and action. Air support was attached to each one of the Israeli army formations and in every armored battle the army was assisted by aircraft attacking enemy tanks. The fact that the Egyptian army was especially well blessed with the most modern and excellent equipment was nullified."

The question whether Egypt or Israel started to shoot first is unlikely to be the subject of an explicit statement by the Israeli Government. Israel made the first attack by air, land and sea, but, in the eyes of most reasonable people, she can justify her action by Colonel Nasser's consistent acts of belligerence. If Colonel Nasser was staging a phony war in the hope that the United Nations or the United States, Britain and Russia would step in and give the lead to negotiations that would result in the Palestinian-Arab question being settled, it is his business. He knows now that he made the biggest mistake in his career and one from which he may not recover.

Many Israelis who have studied Arab mentality, and especially that of their arch enemy Colonel Nasser, felt they knew all along that the Egyptian General Staff had no thought of attacking Israel in full scale war. The Egyptian Commander-in-Chief of ground forces, General Abdul Muhsin Kamal Murtaji, who is a man of impressive sincerity, had stated categorically, and in view of the histrionic temperament of his chief, most unwisely, on several occasions that Egypt had no intention of attacking Israel. They did not accept, or recognize, Israel, but they would not attack her. Colonel Nasser himself told a former British Cabinet Minister when the two met in Cairo during the crisis that Egypt would not start a war. He threatened what he would do if Israel attacked. The story I had been told in Jerusalem was true. The Israeli Cabinet decided that if the Arab States continued aggression on Israel's borders, which is something that had been going on for years, an assault would be made. It would be called a preemptive attack. It would be taken in two or three stages, the second and/or third made dependent on the success of the first within a limited time in regard to all other circumstances.

To most people the fact that in numbers the Arabs had vast superiority in the air was disquieting. In 1956 the Egyptians did not attack the exposed Israel towns, even those on the coast, because the British Air Force had attended to Egyptian air bases in a protracted operation linked to the Suez campaign. There had been apparently nothing to prevent the Egyptians showing the Jews, and the world, who was master in at least one element. Because Israel was so narrow, enemy planes could overfly it in a few moments and be out at sea almost before the bombs they had dropped had exploded. Anti-aircraft gunners, therefore, had constantly to be on the alert—they had so little warning of the approach, or the direction of bombers. If you made an error when tuning in to Jerusalem just before the war began you were likely to find some fanatical Arab nationalist declaring that an attack on Israel was now only a matter of days. Because of this eternal fear the Government had long since compelled the builders of all houses to provide air raid shelters. The population had been drilled to heed the alerts and take cover and not to re-emerge until the all-clear sounded. The haste with which people filled bags with sand from the shore at Tel Aviv, erected barricades at the entrances to buildings, and stuck tape on their windows to reduce the effect of blast showed how very seriously the population feared the air threat. If all three Arab Air Forces, with the help of Iraq, attacked Israel by a coordinated plan of flying in from different directions, there would be little chance for Israel to protect itself. The Israeli Air Force would anyway probably be geared, in the event of war, to cover the army on the various fronts.

The Israeli Government knew of this disquiet in the country. They told Brigadier-General Mordechai Hod, commander of the Air Force, that he had to produce some miraculous plan which would eliminate the terrible air threat which would face the country in the event of war. There had been no need to inform General Hod of the situation. He knew the facts only too well. For years he had patiently built up a strong air force of young pilots who almost lived in the sky. He realized that the air force was the one arm of the service which could pave the way to victory by the remainder of the defense forces. He drew up a plan which had the instant approval of the Government, though all its secret features were not spelled out in lay language. In making this plan Brigadier-General Hod was influenced by what the Anglo-French Air Forces did before the Suez Canal operation. The Egyptian Air Force was then immobilized for two vital days.

Israel was the victim of past aggression. She could expect

no help from the United Nations, the United States of America, Britain or France. It was all up to Israel's Air Force. Israel could not wait forever keeping a civilian army out in the desert.

The first move on June 5th was, therefore, made by the Israeli Air Force. It was planned with the same scrupulous accuracy as but with infinitely more speed and efficiency than that planned by the Anglo-French bombers before the Suez Canal operation. In the early hours of June 5th the Israeli radar screens "clearly showed what was thought to be a two-pronged approach of Egyptian planes heading to attack them from Cairo direction." The sightings were immediately communicated to Brigadier-General Mordechai Hod who set in motion the pre-emptive attack by three wings of the air force. What happened to the Egyptian planes "seen on radar" is not known. The Israeli planes do not appear to have encountered them on their way to Egyptian airfields. Egyptian Mig 21s and Tupolev bombers were encountered and destroyed by Israeli Mirage fighters on their way back after accompanying Vautoure bombers to Cairo.

The three wings of Israeli aircraft, piloted by young men of an average age of 23, attacked carefully selected targets in Egypt beyond the Suez Canal, and one wing attacked Egyptian air bases in the Sinai. The strike was swift, brutal, merciless, devastating. It was carried out with such terrible precision that the much vaunted Egyptian Air Force with its Russian planes was smothered while still on the ground. The timetable for the operation was measured in seconds, and every rendezvous, and every move, was made precisely on the second. Targets were found with unerring aim. The planes used a special kind of bomb made by Israeli settlers who worked for an industry set up by the Israeli defense forces to manufacture arms, ammunition and various chemicals. Some of these workers were recent immigrants, experts in the manufacture of arms in Europe. The bombs combined minimum size with maximum destructive powers. They were carried under each wing of needle-nosed fighter-bombers and dropped from record low altitude at record high speed. Accuracy was perfected by an internal guidance mechanism which caused the missiles to home in on the vital part of the aircraft.* Meanwhile gunners raked aircraft lined up as for inspection with 30 mm. cannon and rockets. Israeli planes were hit by small arms fire but the low altitude and speed defeated ack-ack gunners. Stories have leaked out of Egypt about the reckless attacks of the Israeli planes. They came in at supersonic speeds, which did not prevent the pilots' executing complicated maneuvers with superb skill and timing. These Israeli raids were probably the most efficient air strike since the Japanese attacked Pearl Harbor. Israel's first two waves had finished the first of many deadly surprise air strikes on airfields in Cairo and elsewhere in Egypt by 7:45 a.m. Israeli time, and 8:45 a.m. Cairo time. When it was all over, thirty-three air bases had suffered. Egypt alone had lost 374 planes. Egypt's plans for a campaign, if Israel attacked them, were completely in ruins. Every phase of it was adversely affected by the absence of air cover.

Israeli planes carried the latest reconnaissance photographic equipment and the pictures taken of the damage done in Egypt, Jordan, Syria and on Iraq planes were all developed and checked before a statement was put out. I saw some of the photographs and later the planes on Arab air bases. Some of the bombs dropped at low altitude at enormous speed had entered large hangars by the open doors and destroyed the planes inside while only damaging the roofs by blast. It was said that the Israelis placed top priority on destroying runways, but this I doubt. Little damage was done to such large runways as those at El Arish. Almost at the same time as the air strikes, whether by coincidence or not, the *kibbutzim* near the Gaza Strip were, as I have reported, shelled intermittently. This was particularly odd. Egyptian artillery would have been expected to shell Israeli army positions if they had been apprised of the air attack on their airfields and not innocent villages of little military importance.

* The Royal Aero Club's magazine *Flight* reported the findings of Robert R. Rodwell, military writer for that publication, which studied Israeli tactics, that a unique lightweight rocket bomb was the key weapon in Israel's defeat of Arab air forces. The bomb, which he called a concrete dibber, was said to be 8 feet long, a foot in diameter and could be delivered with extreme accuracy from aircraft flying only 200 feet off the ground.

Brigadier-General S. Gavish, Commanding Officer in the Southern front of the Sinai, after telling me that the Egyptian attack started with "movements of planes towards Israel," said: "There was also the sighting of an Egyptian armored force in the Sinai." Anyway, what mattered so far as General Gavish was concerned was that his commanding officer, Major-General Itzhak Rabin, signalled him exactly at 8 a.m. and told him that the ground stage of the war must begin. General Gavish was able to start a complicated move along two axes by 8:16 a.m.

8

VIEW FROM CAIRO

Early on June 5th, Colonel Nasser was overwhelmed with reports from his Intelligence Service, from Cairo Security Police and from the Air Defense Command that the raiders had been British and Americans, and not Israelis. One suggestion was made that the raiders might have been a combined force of all three. The two waves of fighter bombers, which had attacked Cairo and the Canal, had flown in not from the east, which was the direction of Israel, but from due north and northwest, which was most unfair. That meant that they had come from the direction of Malta, where there were aircraft carriers of the British Fleet, and from the direction of Crete, where there were carriers of the United States Sixth Fleet. Some people who had seen the attacking planes leaving Inshas Air Base, Cairo, and Abu Suwier Air Base, on the west bank of the Suez Canal, described the markings as British and American.

It was not long before Cairo was buzzing with the reports. The fact was that Egypt's early warning, and local, radar air defense systems had failed at their first test. In modern countries every area of the sky overhead is covered by radar screens of different systems as a protection against air or missile attack. First there is the early warning system manned by the air force which operates radar, orientated in the direction from which the enemy is expected to come. This radar would be efficient for a distance ahead of 500 miles but only on a narrow beam of some 50-60 degrees. Then there is local radar defense. Each area would be furnished with local radar which would operate the full circle of the screen of 360 degrees but probably efficiently only up to a distance of about eighty miles.

The United Arab Republic is different in a geographical sense from other countries. Although it comprises some 1,000,000 square miles, the cultivated and settled area—the Nile Valley, the Delta and the oases—covers only about 31,000 square miles. The security problem, therefore, was simplified. Egypt did not have potential enemies all round her but only in the east. She was tempted, therefore, to economize on her radar protection and forget the desert approaches by which the two wings flew to their targets. Brother Arabs would be unlikely to come in from the north, or the west, unheralded. Radar systems are costly to purchase. It is not only the capital outlay, as Colonel Nasser discovered, but the cost of training personnel. The staff had to be highly trained. Maintenance was very costly. One could not lock up the radar units and leave them when they were not wanted. They required an enormous amount of maintenance. Specialists in repair work had to be given long and careful training. In a country like Egypt an internal cooling system by fans was important (as in cooler countries, for instance, an internal heating system is needed part of the year). If radars were not scrupulously maintained they would not work.

The early warning radar screen, with a directional cover towards Israel, probably up to 400 miles, obviously did not pick up the two waves of fighter bombers which attacked Egypt. The reason was that the screens were orientated to the east from which Israeli raiders were expected to come. But the Israeli pilots had been specially briefed on their manner of approach. They had flown out from their bases, near Haifa and Tel Aviv, for about 200-250 miles in a direct line to the north. Then they had turned sharply to the west, as if en route for Crete or Malta. They then flew by several routes at record low contour flying over land and sea to miss the radar. The most devastating surprise blows were dealt by planes that came deceptively from the north and northwest from far out to sea. As a result of the contour flying at low altitude the planes avoided being seen on the 360-degree radar screens such as protected cities like Alexandria and Cairo. Some screens were not working. Some were out of order. Some watchers of other radar screens might not have been as vigilant at that hour as they should have been. One must remember also the atmosphere of *detente* which Moshe Dayan's words spread over the Arab lands the day before. If watchers had seen the two waves coming in on their 360-degree radar screens they might have thought they had gone mad. Or at least that they had dropped asleep and were dreaming. Could they be friendly aircraft, they might have asked, of which they had not been informed? Might two waves flying in at about 1,500 miles an hour and at low altitude merely have wanted to take a close look at the minarets as the Muezzins were intoning their call to the faithful?

It was this daring trick by the Israelis of coming in by the back and side doors that provided the element of surprise that made possible the unprecedented success of the raids. It was also this ruse which led to the canard that the attackers were British pilots flying in from Malta and Americans flying in from Crete.

Colonel Nasser found it impossible to believe that Israeli pilots could be so superior to his own that they could triumph as they had done. He found himself in urgent need of some scapegoat. He had to tell his fellow Arabs something to save his face.

Reports continued for hours to be received from people wishing to be helpful, and also to deflect blame for the disaster from themselves. The imperialists were up to their old tricks again. This was a repetition of the Anglo-French air attack which had immobilized the Egyptian Air Force before the Suez campaign. The only difference was that the cursed English had persuaded the Americans to take the place of the French. De Gaulle would not play, of course. The line was created for him! So quickly did Colonel Nasser react that the allegation of Anglo-American air intervention was the leading item on Cairo radio at 6:45 a.m. (local time) on June 6th.

What Nasser did not know, but soon learned, was that the Israeli Air Force had gone on to repeat their maneuvers against Jordan, Syria and Iraq. The leaders of these countries were just as bewildered as Colonel Nasser. Just before 7 a.m. they heard their own radio stations quoting the news from Cairo about the Anglo-American planes. It was only natural that they promptly joined in the witch-hunt. Dr. Nuradin Atassi of Syria, whose National Council of Revolution had seized power in collusion with Nasser in 1963, was the first to jump on the band wagon. He told Nasser that Syrian radar had revealed seventeen Vulcans making attacks on their territory. One British Canberra bomber had been shot down. Unfortunately it had fallen into a deep part of the Sea of Galilee from which it was not recoverable. Radio Damascus reported vivid stories. The Anglo-Americans were bearing the brunt of the war. British planes were reported to have been seen loading bombs at a Cyprus base. One Israeli pilot, named Abraham Shellin, whom the Syrians "had shot down" had "admitted" that British planes were operating inside Israel and from aircraft carriers off Tel Aviv. Later, Syrian radio added that British intervention was not to be restricted to the air. Some 3,000 British troops had embarked on a naval ship at Famagusta in Cyprus and were on their way to Israel. They would be landed at any part of the coast where the Israeli Government needed them.

It was puzzling how the Egyptians had confused Israeli bombing with that of the British. The two air forces had adopted contrasting styles. When the British bombed Cairo air bases in 1956 the attacks were so slow that one Egyptian said, "It was like a nagging headache." The Israeli attacks were so fast that one had no time to think.

Hate for the West had been in abeyance, as hate of Israel, the stooge of the West, was at full flood. Now it broke out again in all its terrible fury. The scenes at Arab air bases were so terrible that they were closed to all but troops detailed to clear away the wreckage. It looked as if a tornado had struck. When I saw the Arab air bases later and took the pictures which appear in this book, I marvelled at the marksmanship of the Israeli pilots. Magnificent Russian bombers and fighters which the Arabs had bought at such a high price were completely wrecked.

Major General Moshe Dayan had shown how to exploit the Egyptian practice of monitoring cables and tapping telephones at the start of the war. Now the Israeli Intelligence demonstrated how Israel could monitor communications and telephones, even those between a Presidential lodge and a royal palace. "The crippling blow dealt to the Arab Air

Forces, and particularly to that of Egypt, set the Arab propaganda machine at work both for internal consumption, to explain the defeat of their air forces, and for world consumption," we were told. It was decided to make the story known far and wide that the British and Americans had come to the aid of Israel.

Israel declared: "Early on the morning of June 6th, when the extent of the military defeat was finally clear to Nasser, he began to act to save his prestige. He claimed that Egyptian forces in Sinai had retreated, not as a result of a clear and sharp military defeat in the war, but because of imaginary foreign forces. As a first stage he coordinated the tale of collaboration with King Hussein by radio-telephone at 4:50 a.m. on June 6th. This conversation was monitored by Israel. The tape of the telephone conversation speaks for itself and makes it clear how Nasser initiated this fabrication of the intervention of foreign forces!"

When the recording was played for the benefit of foreign correspondents at Beit Sokolov one of them took exception to it because, he said, Israel was "managing the news." The recording was played privately for me later because it was known I had held long conversations with both Colonel Nasser and King Hussein. I might be able to recognize their voices. The voices of the men on the tape talking Arabic bellowed at each other across a scratchy and inaudible circuit "between Cairo and Amman." Now and then snatches of the two voices could be heard clearly although there were breaks and interruptions. The conversation, so far as Israeli Intelligence had interpreted it, ran:

Hello—His Majesty is ready? The President is coming.
Hello Amman, is His Majesty ready?
Hello, His Honor the President is ready;
How are you? I hear His Majesty, our brother, wants to know if the fighting is going on along all the fronts?
(There was a pause here and conversation was inaudible.) Then:
Yes. Shall we include also the U.S. Do you know of this, shall we announce that the U.S. is cooperating with Israel?
Hello, I do not hear, the connection is the worst—the line between you and the palace from which the King is speaking is bad.

Nasser—Hello, will we say the U.S. and England or just the U.S.?

Hussein—The U.S. and England.

Nasser—Does Britain have aircraft carriers?

Hussein's answer was unintelligible.

Nasser—Good. King Hussein will make an announcement and I will make an announcement.

Thank you.

Do not give up.

(There was a break in the conversation which was resumed later.)

Hello, good morning, brother. Never mind, be strong.

Yes, I hear.

Mr. President, if you have any idea at all . . . at any time . . .

Nasser—We are fighting with all our strength and we have battles going on on every front all night and if we had anything [this was suggested to refer to early misunderstanding] at the beginning—it does not matter. We will overcome despite this. God is with us.

Nasser—Will His Majesty make an announcement on the participation of Americans and the British?

The answer was not clear. Nasser was heard again:

By God, I say that I will make an announcement and you will make an announcement and we will see to it that the Syrians will make an announcement that American and British airplanes are taking part against us from aircraft carriers. We will issue an announcement, we will stress the matter and we will drive the point home.

Hussein—Good. All right.

Nasser—Your Majesty, do you agree?

Again the tape was not clear, then:

Nasser—A thousand thanks, don't give up, we are with you with all our heart and we are flying out planes over Israel today, our planes are striking at Israel's airfields since morning.

Hussein—A thousand thanks, be well.

I have no more than an ordinary memory for voices but I remember the characteristic nasal tones of King Hussein. I have talked with him for long periods several times at the Basman palace in Amman. I talked with him again last year when he made a state visit to Britain and later listened to him make a speech at the Royal Institute of International Affairs at Chatham House. Now and then I thought I recognized the deep bass tones of Colonel Nasser but I felt sure that King Hussein's voice was not on the tape. I said so to the Intelligence colonel. We had a long argument. I asked him if he could tell me any other facts about the conversation which would give verisimilitude to his claim. All he would say, and he repeated the words time and time again, was: "But I am one hundred percent certain that this conversation was between Colonel Nasser and King Hussein. For obvious reasons I cannot tell you where the phone was tapped." I did not expect to be told that but I thought there was no reason why I should not be told the other subjects Colonel Nasser and King Hussein discussed so early in the morning. The tape was a long one and obviously contained the recording of other conversations.

At breakfast time on June 6th, some hours after the phone had been tapped, Cairo radio opened its news bulletins with the words: "It has now been proved that the United States and Britain took part in the air battles." The speaker said: "An announcement from the Supreme Command of the Armed Forces of Egypt states that it has now been made clear in a full sense that the United States and Britain participated in Israel's military aggression insofar as air activities are concerned. It has been conclusively proved that large scale assistance was rendered to Israel from United States and British aircraft carriers. In regard to the Egyptian front, the American and British aircraft also played the role of an air umbrella over Israel. On the Jordan front, these aircraft carried out an active role against the Jordanian forces. This was proved on Jordanian radar, which clearly showed this air activity in support of Israel. King Hussein contacted Nasser early this morning and told him that he is now convinced that American and British airplanes are playing a serious role in the campaign."

In a news report datelined Cairo, June 6th, British correspondent Peter Hopkirk stated that the Egyptian High Command had asserted that there was definite proof that the United States and Britain were providing Israel with air support. American and British aircraft from carriers were supporting the Israel forces with cover on the Egyptian and Jordan fronts. It again said that this had been proved by the Jordan radar network. According to the communiqué, King

Hussein of Jordan had gotten in touch with President Nasser and had informed him that he was certain British and American aircraft were playing an important role in the war. Both heads of state had agreed that this must be made public to the entire Arab world and "must lead to the necessary consequences." Cairo radio simultaneously called on Arabs everywhere to "destroy American and British interests."

In England, *The Times* on June 9th in a paragraph headed "Jordan Denial" stated that Cairo radio repeated Cairo's accusation that the allegation originated in a message from King Hussein to President Nasser (and not, as the Israelis had said, in a message from President Nasser to King Hussein). But according to the Ministry of Defense in London (*The Times,* June 9th) foreign military attachés in Jordan had been informed in an official briefing on Wednesday (June 7th) that the Jordanians had "no knowledge of any British or American aircraft over Jordan." Both Secretary of State Dean Rusk and Prime Minister Wilson dismissed the charges as "monstrous, malicious and utterly false." This did not prevent reprisals being taken against the Anglo-Americans all over the Arab world.

9

THE MAN BEHIND THE PLAN

The war had no parallel in all history, unless one accepts Kings, Joshua, and Exodus in the Old Testament as history. The disparity in the size of the Arab armies of Egypt, Jordan, Syria and Iraq and that of Israel reminded the biblical student of the time when Joshua with so small an army rose up and smote the Philistines. There had never been a case in which a small country with no standing professional army of size had been completely surrounded by the armies of four enemy countries which fought on all fronts. I could not remember another instance where there was such a discrepancy in professionalism and in weapons. Israel was using old tanks, including some ancient models which dated from early in the Second World War. Egypt and Syria had the most modern tanks, many of them Russian. Egypt had acquired some of the latest tanks even before they had been introduced into Soviet armored divisions. While the war was in progress Israeli engineers were still trying to improve their oldest tanks by clever improvisation. They had earlier installed "better driving gear and better guns." But no matter what the engineers did they could not improve their old tanks so that they could compare or compete with, machine for machine, the most modern tanks in the world. No army was better equipped than the Egyptian except the American. The Israelis had some tanks which had already become obsolescent in the British, French and American armies. There was another difficulty. Israel had a very large range of different tanks and no standard equipment in their armored force as in the Egyptian and even the Syrian army.

The fact that Israel was fighting with fewer men and vehicles, with fewer planes and tanks which were less modern than the Egyptian and Syrian, was only part of the truth. All that mattered, said the average Israeli, was that their men were superior in human quality. They had no doubt about that. The fact had been proved in two conflicts already, even if in the last campaign Israel had had the help of France and Britain. I was inclined to agree. On many visits to Israel I had seen Israeli youth of both sexes engaged in all forms of sport and physical and intellectual activity. I had seen a little already of Israelis at war. I had not the slightest doubt that Israeli manpower was of exceptional quality.

The opposing generals in the Sinai, United Arab Republic's General Abdul Muhsin Kamal Murtaji and Israel's Major-General Itzhak Rabin, had something in common. Both had reputations for quick action and skill in the deployment of armor. Both read war books avidly. Both led simple lives, disliked publicity and cocktail parties and rarely gave press conferences. They were much the same in temperament, age and military outlook. Both were interested in Soviet Russia but for different reasons. Murtaji had been to Russia after he left Staff College and taken a course in army training. He had become deeply interested in Russia's social welfare program. Rabin, who was interested in politics, was associated with an Israeli Marxist group. He was being urged by Israeli Left Wingers to enter politics after operations were over, as his predecessor, Major-General Moshe Dayan, entered politics when he retired from the army in November 1958. After Murtaji returned from Russia he was appointed first to the Army Directorate of Training and then, in 1959, to be its Chief. He was promoted Lieutenant-General in 1962. Two years later he commanded the United Arab Republic forces in the Yemen. Rabin was also deeply interested in training and became a member of the corresponding Israeli body. He was promoted Major-General and appointed Chief of Staff in succession to General Zvi Tsur. Murtaji was not the author of the Egyptian plan which was alleged later to have been found by the Israelis. This was the work of a planning body under Field Marshal Abdel

Hakim Amer. Israel's plan, which had the code name of Nachonim, after Nachon, the leader of Judah, was the sole work of Rabin in conjunction with the General Staff. The plan betrayed something of his British Staff College training in England.

Itzhak Rabin was born in Jerusalem. His feelings for the Holy City were very deep. His father, Nehemia Rabin, came to Israel with the soldiers of the Jewish Legion. His mother, Rosa Cohen, is still known by old people in Jerusalem as Sister Rosa, the nurse who went from house to house during the Arab riots of 1920, looking after the sick and injured.

Rabin did not go to the University as was intended. Yigal Allon, then platoon commander at Kadoorie, had noticed the quiet studious boy and enrolled him in the Palmach. Rabin was sent to a platoon commanders' course. He underwent his baptism of fire—the capture, after a 30 mile night march, of a Lebanese border post occupied by Vichy forces. This task was carried out within the time table without losses. Itzhak was put in charge of the Platoon Commanders' Course at Juwara. During the Second World War Rabin wanted to join the Jewish Brigade but his father advised him to stay with the Palmach. Rabin was charged with the daring operation of breaking into the "illegal" Jewish Immigrant Camp at Athlit and freeing its inmates. He completed the operation and remained in the camp to the last, covering the retreat. On his return he said with his usual spirited calm: "The planning and execution of the action were not too bad." Disguised as an electrician, he entered the British Police fortress of Jenin to reconnoitre the situation for a future operation. He accomplished the task. On his way back his motorcycle hit a truck. Rabin suffered serious leg injuries. He lay in a plaster cast for days. On the "Black Sabbath" of June 29th 1946, when the British conducted a house-to-house search for people on their black list, he was discovered. He was transferred to Latrum. Later he received medical treatment at the Gaza hospital to which he was transferred under heavy British guard.

During the War of Independence, at the age of 26, Rabin

was at first deputy commander of the Palmach's "Har-El" Brigade. He took part in all the fighting in the struggle to break the blockades of Jerusalem, in the battles of Bab el Wad, Sheikh Jarsh and Katamon. He also participated in the desperate attempts to break into the Old City of Jerusalem. Rabin was later seconded to the Southern Front as Operations Officer under Yigal Allon. Israeli forces were trying to discover a route to make an attack on Auja el Hafir. Palmach's reconnaissance units reported finding an ancient secret path from Halutza via Ruheiba and Wadi Abyad to Auja. An officer was sent to see if the route was good enough. He said it could not be used. Yigal Allon sent Rabin to reconnoitre the area again. He returned with a brief report—"It's hard, but possible." Auja el Hafir was taken and the words of that report would be his trademark if he ever had one.

Rabin was present at a truce meeting between Yigal Allon and "Tiger" Taha, the Egyptian Brigadier in command of the Falugja Pocket (where Colonel Nasser fought and where the Egyptian force that attempted a southern break-through into the coastal plain was surrounded). Allon informed Nasser's commander Taha that his men were encircled. The earlier they surrendered the better it would be for them. At that moment a young Egyptian officer and future leader of Egypt, Gamal Abdel Nasser, who accompanied Taha and who had been standing by the whole time, requested permission to speak. When permission was granted he inquired whether the insignia Yigal Allon and his men were wearing—a sword between two ears of corn—was that of the Palmach. Yigal said it was. Nasser smiled sorrowfully and exclaimed cryptically: "That being so, everything is clear to me." History turned full cycle. In the Israeli-Arab war Nasser saw the Israel Defense Army under the command of one of the men who was present at that meeting—Itzhak Rabin. After the War of Independence, Rabin was put in charge of Staff Operations. In 1952 he was sent to study at the British Staff College at Camberley, England. He brought back new ideas. He also ordered that every senior officer should undergo paratroop training. He was one of the first to carry out this order. In the Sinai campaign he was given command of the Northern Front. He was later appointed Chief of Operations of the Israel Defense Forces.

"Israel's Chief of Staff," says Israeli writer Raphael Bashan, "is a handsome man—sturdy, broad-shouldered, with an open face. He has a high forehead, fair hair showing a shade of red, and freckles covering his face, which add a youthful charm to his forty-five years. His speech is sometimes slow, but always quiet, to the point and concentrated. His thinking is fast, analytical and thorough-going. He has clear blue eyes that look you straight in the face. He is not smooth, slippery and flexible—his personality reflects the inner calm of a man wholly dedicated to his job. He usually wears a neat Army uniform with an open-neck shirt and the markings of a Rav-Aluf (Major-General) on his shoulder, as well as the silver paratroopers' wings on his chest. His office is compact in its simplicity and efficiency, with a desk, a few small armchairs for visitors, maps on the walls, encyclopedias and strategic manuals on the shelves of the bookcases, light metal aircraft models for decoration, and in a corner a table with a vase of roses. He is said to have a phenomenal memory. One of his officers reveals that the Chief of Staff stores up a most diversified treasury of information in all fields. Staff officers claim jokingly that, if the electronic computer should break down, there is no reason to worry so long as Itzhak Rabin is around. He is a glutton for detail, and whenever the purchase of new equipment is being considered he is quick to learn thoroughly all the intricate, technical and mechanical details distinguishing one type of tank, for instance, from another. He is capable of sitting down and explaining the advantages and disadvantages of the diesel as against the gasoline engine. He knows exactly the life span of the various gun-barrels in standard army use. While Deputy Chief of Staff, he visited France in order to examine the AMX-30 tanks. The French said that so expert was his knowledge of armored equipment that he might have been a born tank-corps man."

During the tough fighting around Um Katef and Abu Agheila, Rabin flew down to Sinai to meet the command officers. He helped them solve some acute problems. Towards the end of the week of war, he was with the Commander of the Northern Front, ready to help with decision. He was offered a tour of the Western Bank area but declined. The war was still on, he said. His duty was to be where there was decisive action. All through the six-day war he slept on a folding camp-bed in his office. There was a telephone beneath it. He only managed to get home twice for very short visits and then to bring back some papers he required.

Just before the present operation began, he met, just outside Tel Aviv, the pilots who were going out on operations: "I have so much to say to you," he said, "but not enough words! Permit me to paraphrase Churchill's words—Never in the field of human conflict has the fate of so many depended on the skill and courage of so few. It is your manner of fighting that will decide the destiny of our people and our State."

10

MEN IN THE DESERT

War correspondents were allowed a great deal of freedom of movement. Some of them took full advantage of it. A few got far too close to the war considering that they were not armed, and lacked protection as a member of a combat unit, and were killed. After the visit to the Gaza Strip where the casualties had been cows, I visited all the fronts in turn though I spent most of my time in the Sinai. This was probably because it reminded me of the days when I was in Lord Wavell's campaign, and, later, at El Alamein. I wrote part of this chapter in Wadi el 'Amr, a sea of shifting sand in which a grim tank battle had been concluded not so many hours before. I had sat waiting for the road ahead to be cleared, having first whiled away the time talking to Israeli troops who were also waiting to go ahead. To the south of me was the 'Amr Jebel, sprawling hills of sand some 450 feet high. Ahead lay the next objective.

The Israeli Chief of Staff had given his commanders their military objectives, scheduled as clearly as a grocery list. They covered all fronts. They had to take possession of the West Bank of the river Jordan which stretched to a point only nine miles from Tel Aviv. They had to capture the north to south route from Janin through Nazareth and Jerusalem to Beersheba. They had also to capture the slopes of snow-capped Mount Hermon from which so many fatal shots had been fired by Syrian snipers at farmers on the shores, and fishermen on the waters, of the Sea of Galilee. All these, in due time, were to be accomplished. But now, in the Sinai, the objective was to capture a worthless desert in the broiling sun.

The Israelis had gone out to destroy the Egyptians as quickly as they could. The Egyptians had quickly sensed the nearness of death as I, in the rear of this furious Israeli machine of war, could sense it. I could feel it in the air, appalling with its foul, brooding threat in spite of the sunshine. The Egyptians knew with their simple minds, many of them the minds of blameless peasants, that the end was near. They retaliated clumsily as man or animal retaliates when he is faced with overwhelming odds and can hope only to delay the last moment. They knew as soon as they saw the terrifying speed and remorseless efficiency of this brutal colossus that they would inevitably be its victims. There never was such a contrast between two armies on the same battlefield. The Israelis were supermen charged with dynamic energy. The Egyptians whom one saw as prisoners, or wounded, were piteous creatures, shocked rather than ashamed. What Napoleon said in Austria that "in war the morale is to the material as three to one" had never been better illustrated. The Arabs had had so many advantages on paper, in numbers, arms and mobility, but the Israelis showed that indomitable courage, iron will and selflessness could nullify the advantages of steel, technology and Russian aid.

Ahead, the armor was chewing its clanging, steely way through the soft sand, beyond Abu Agheila with its forked roads, one to El Arish, capital of the Sinai, and the other to Ismailiya and the Suez Canal. Ugly clattering ships of the desert, like monstrous creatures from another world, had clashed for hours under the blazing sun. Their thick steel scales had become so hot that waves of heat eddied off them. All around me was a wild world of death and destruction so strange and appalling to one who a few days before had feasted his eyes on gentle swaying cornfields and formal gardens and shaven lawns in the haven of peace which is Shropshire. I thought of it as I looked round me seeing the black charred, tangled wrecks of tanks and half tracks and the riddled transports. It looked as if a multitude of fiery gargantuans had chewed them up, contorted their steel bodies, bitten in two their clanging tracks. It was hard to believe that these machines of death, Stalins, T 23s and the like, had been made far away in the blessed land of proletarian peace, and sent here to meet this fate. It was terrible to see the planes from the same land, smashed up like plywood models. In the distance the skyline spurted, blazed, bellowed. Probably I am the only man ever to have sat in Wadi el 'Amr and written anything. Suddenly word came out of the smoking chaos that the road was clear. The way ahead was like the way to the rear, a sea of shifting sand, all the way to Nitsana, the gateway to the Sinai through which we had driven. We had come through Beersheba, famous from the time Abraham had dug a well and planted a grove there. We had skidded through a wilderness as if in deep drifts of dry powdery snow, swerving and lurching. The wilderness, empty and silent for centuries, was now full of the weirdest vehicles, all filling some mechanical role in this war.

Troops with young faces and forced smiles were on their way up to reinforce the advancing army, to replace the men who lay dead or dying, by the wayside. All of them pretended they wanted to swim in the Suez Canal, as if that would justify everything. Some had the phrase in Hebrew "First Stop Cairo" on their vehicles. This was the world of the warrior in which business was quick death. One could not conceive a bird or an animal, not to mention a Bedouin, ever having been there. The soldiers were goggle-eyed and bearded and masked with the yellow dust of the desert. I felt they could remove the mask and become human again. All around them was nothing but sun baked sand, sand hills, dried up wadis. The only suggestions of life were clumps of dust-covered thorn. Someone said it was the kind used out of which to make the crown of thorns for One who was crucified in Jerusalem.

When silence fell and everything stood unnaturally still, there came the far off chatter of wireless communication, the murmur of transformers. Then an explosion broke the silence as a jet broke through the sound barrier. Sometimes I was startled by the sound of laughter. Masses of trucks full of green cans had come to a water point, like a herd of elephants in some game park in early evening, come to drink at the water hole. Then I knew how much the Egyptian Air Force had fallen out of the picture. Fighter-bombers roamed around looking for concentrations of vehicles at water points as lions roam around a water hole, hungry for the kill. There was now no longer fear of strafing, even so near to the front. How difficult it would now be for the Egyptians without air cover to face this adversary! I had crossed into Egypt at Um Bassat. Strewn about there had been empty Egyptian cigarette packs, old Arabic newspapers and the wrappers and containers of delicacies from Groppis in Cairo. These were of the kind each man on leave from the Western Desert during the Second World War used to bring back with him to augment the eternal canned beef. My mouth watered for them now. The sun was lower. It cast the ridges of the tank tracks into shadow. There were figures of eight to show where the tanks had swerved around in battle with other tanks. In their tracks were dismembered corpses, cut up after death. This was perfect tank country, where the tank commanders of two nations had tested each other and come to a conclusion. It had held good for the rest of this short campaign.

Next day I joined up with the second echelon of the Israeli Army in a forced march along the 150-mile-long inverted base of the Sinai triangle that forms the coastal road along the Mediterranean leading from the Gaza Strip border to Port Said. This road, sometimes within view of the sea and mainly through desert, was the only worthwhile part of Sinai, and that says very little. On it is El Arish, the capital, and guardian to the Mediterranean entrance to the biblical "Valley of Egypt." Early on June 5th El Arish was a thriving town of some 10,000 people who were busy cultivating the date-palm groves each side of one of the world's oldest highways. The road the army was taking, through Rafah, El Arish, then straight as an arrow to Port Said, was the old "Way of the Philistines" along which had come conquerors from the time of the Pharaohs. The road was now Colonel Nasser's Via Doloroso.

Plowing my way through tracks ankle deep in soft sand near the Gaza Strip, taking evasive action to avoid snipers, I saw far more signs of tragedy and suffering than I had seen in the Wavell campaign when the British had advanced from the Egyptian border to beyond Benghazi. Lying off the road were hundreds of long huts made roughly of brushwood which the Bedouin had occupied from time immemorial. Attached to the huts were long compounds for a few poultry, one or two sheep and a goat. The Bedouins had somehow kept themselves alive but on a low subsistence level which made the refugees I saw later look well off by comparison. Now the Bedouin had fled, leaving their few animals and their pitifully few possessions behind them. The livestock and animals in that intense heat were searching frantically for water and could find none, and would soon be dead. Stock which the Bedouin had raised by depriving his family of essential food would soon be no more. Near to the huts there was usually a camel, so emaciated as to look like another type of creature. This, too, was searching among the sand for food. Sheep, goats and camels were at times joining in a piteous chorus which echoed among those waste lands. Some of the owners might one day return, when it was too late to help the animals, but some of them would never return. They lay dead along the road, killed by stray bullets from planes.

Near Rafah, from which clouds of black smoke were rising, I saw new refugees, in this area which has known refugees for years. Women and children, cowering with fear and crying, darted along the side of the road from one clump of camel thorn to another, trying to find someone who would help them. Now and then as they strode over the body of a dead man, they would scrutinize the features to see if they belonged to a husband or brother or friend. Firing broke out from time to time and since it was unsafe to get too near to Egyptian settlements we deliberately took an almost impassable road through the sand.

When later we reached a stretch of tarred road we found it littered with objects that had been hurriedly collected from their homes by the Egyptians when the first sounds of war had reached them. There were old trunks which had burst open as their owners had raced along leaving the contents to scatter over a wide area. There were articles of furniture, photographs, cooking utensils, or some carefully preserved article which had been given to the owner as a wedding present long years before. Among them were the bodies of other civilians, their arms still raised in death, but with looks of peace on their faces. Some men lay in such natural positions in the sand that they might have been resting or sun bathing. Tanks had passed here at top speed and the heavy tracks had cut up the road and smashed the objects over which they had passed, now and then grinding to a pulp some dead body which no one would ever be able to identify.

Where there had been resistance, generally from Egyptians in Russian-made tanks half buried in the sand, there was chaos. Smashed trucks which had apparently been parked lay alongside motor vehicles full of dead passengers who, judging from the odd contents of the trunks, had been on their way to Port Said. A hail of bullets, obviously from their defending troops, had caught them as they negotiated a bend in the road, and the vehicles had run on for several yards until they had crashed into something in the way. Occasionally there was a line of small whitewashed box-like homes from the flat roofs of which flew some emblem of surrender. The walls were splattered with bullet holes, the windows smashed and the doors hanging from their broken hinges. Some of the occupants had apparently been transport drivers. Three vehicles at the doors were smashed. One of them, occupied by the dead driver, had on the windshield precisely in front of his face the perforation hole of a bullet which looked exactly like the fake bullet holes which some half-witted drivers stick on their windshields. Where army supply vehicles had been hit there had sometimes been explosions and the road encircling a burnt-out hulk was littered with ammunition boxes, water cans and packages of food rations.

Now and then the roadside was littered with the dead bodies of Egyptian soldiers who had stayed to fight: more often the soldiers had been killed as they ran to the west, divested of their uniforms and their footwear as if they had tried to discard everything that identified them as troops.

The railroad from Gaza to Port Said sometimes ran along the side of the road. I counted four railway smashes. Engines had either been hit from the air or by artillery fire and had turned over, or they had run full force into an earlier train which had been brought to a halt. One had obviously come off the rails because the engine had been travelling too fast and had jumped the tracks. There was evidence near these trains that they had been crowded with people fleeing from Gaza and other stations along the way. Doors of luggage vans or carriages were still open to show where the passengers who had survived the wrecks had leapt out. Luggage had been left strewn over the line. One man who had been shot still held in one hand his ticket as if he had hoped to catch another train to his destination. Signal boxes, stations, and railroad offices had obviously been used by the defenders, for they were pocked with bullet holes.

The Egyptians had learned lessons from the Italian army in the laying of booby traps. We were warned not to pick up attractive looking new portable objects like thermos flasks because they might explode and blow off our hands. Big black flies haunted the corpses. Sanitary teams had not yet had time to sprinkle the exposed flesh of the dead with insect repellent, which is what is done on a battlefield in hot weather when there is no time to dig graves. Later that day, as darkness fell like a blanket, the flies disappeared suddenly. Then the air was filled with the howls and whines of jackals and hyenas who had sensed the presence of food.

We drove into the outskirts of El Arish near to a railway station, a tall yellow structure of stone decorated with the Egyptian eagle, and the former United Nations headquarters. A football lay between two goalposts and the players, probably men of the UNEF, had rushed to their huts to write in chalk: "Don't Shoot. We Are Still Here." But no one was there. The UN quarters were deserted, like the station buildings and the premises on each side of the road.

After open desert we were surprised to find a vast earth square in sight of the town littered with trucks, half tracks, armored cars, tanks and troop carriers. There were so many, jumbled together with no effort at the customary dispersal which all armies adopt as a precaution against air attack, that I searched my mind for some way of describing the scene. It was as if an entire army were in retreat and had run out of gas. Troops by the thousand stood around in groups holding their Uzi automatics, chatting about their experiences. There was no suggestion of discipline. Men wore a variety of headgear, steel hats, Australian type slouches, funny little cloth round hats, or no hats at all. Some men had stripped to the waist, some had camouflaged uniforms and others wore ill-fitting khaki drill with a bold army stencil mark on them in the

Israel's initial air strike. This Russian-built plane was new on June 5th in a hangar at El Arish air base when it was destroyed along with many others by Israeli planes

Wreck of an Egyptian Mig plane photographed soon after it had been shot down by an Israeli pilot in Sinai

Victors of the Sinai campaign: (*top left*) Brigadier-General Yeshayahv (Isaiah) Gavish, O.C. Southern Command, and his three Divisional Commanders—Brigadier-Generals Israel Tal (*top right*), Ariel Sharon (*bottom left*) and Abraham Yoffe

The opening of an Israeli infantry attack between Rafah and El Arish on the northern coastal road of Sinai

The Sinai terrain was extremely difficult for heavy tanks and motorized troops—soft, velvety sand which resembled deep dry powdery snow

Egyptian tanks massed in the Sinai Desert shortly before the Israeli attack

An Egyptian truck blazes furiously in the Sinai Desert, its crew lying dead or wounded around it

Tough Israeli troops indicate to the author where action is taking place on Sinai coastal road leading to Qantara

A column of Israeli infantry moving up to the front

(*Left*) The author talks to Israeli troops near Bir Gafgafa, Sinai; (*right*) Israeli troops waiting near battle area in north and east Sinai. They were the only troops the author saw "resting"!

The last train from Gaza wrecked on the Gaza–Qantara coastal railroad. On each side of the train are dug-in tanks in perfect order. Fleeing Egyptians from Gaza Strip left the train, took off boots and shoes, and ran

Israeli troops about to leave an Egyptian tank destroyed near Abu Agheila in the Sinai

Spoils of war

most inappropriate places. The men smoked incessantly, drank warm brackish water out of bottles, or went into some not inconspicuous corner to relieve nature. On the skyline, where I could see the minaret of a mosque and a water tower, buildings burned furiously, filling the sky with smoke. "They're staging a counter attack," an officer told me, nodding contemptuously in the direction of El Arish. I could hear the crash of shells, the rattle of machine-gun fire and the distant sound of planes. In half-dozen places on the open square Israeli troops were putting up their mortars so casually that it seemed to me that they were doing it of their own volition. In one corner there were clumps of eucalyptus trees and in the shade of these hundreds of Egyptians lay face downwards in the sand, guarded by a single Israeli soldier. Now and then I saw a girl fraternizing with the troops and, such was my experience, I did not know whether she was Egyptian belonging to El Arish (though this would have been most unlikely) or an Israeli girl who had come along as a nurse or to do some chore.

If an American sergeant had seen the Israeli troops he would have died of shock. This army thinks nothing of being properly dressed, or being smart on the barrack square. Being in the army was not a social affair even for the officers but mainly a part-time occupation in which the business was killing the enemy. The army had one badge and there was no question of regiments with an order of precedence based partly on class and wealth. There were no formations exclusively made up of people of power. Everyone knew the main elements of his job which he carried out with dispatch, rigorous self-discipline and amazing efficiency, in spite of the fact that soldiering was not his career. The Israeli part-time soldier was the toughest, most reliable, most aggressive, most indefatigable soldier in the world. He was capable of long feats of endurance. He suffers the most terrible conditions for long periods without a word of complaint. In the course of fighting, he sometimes performs acts of bravery which would earn him in other armies the highest decorations, but which here often go unnoticed. The Israeli has no time for ceremonial parades or ceremonial duties, which he regards as so much nonsense. The tradition of the army is the tradition of fighting in battles in which he has always been outnumbered and out-gunned. He has never lost a major battle in three wars and if he had done so no Israeli would write a poem or a book about it, or try to make it look like a victory. The Israeli is a realist with a clear idea of what is defeat and what is victory. In general he does not believe in surrendering. He sells his life dearly. When the war was over he removed his uniform and took it to be stored. There was no ceremonial uniform. When I asked a colonel if he ever wore parade dress in peacetime he said: "No, but do tell me about them."

The sounds of counterattack were dying down. We managed to attach ourselves to a convoy of infantry on their way to the front and we followed them out of El Arish, passing en route still another train accident. We arrived at El Arish air base where we saw Egyptian Russian-made planes of many kinds destroyed on the ground. Some of them had been wrecked although they were well inside large hangars, as if the Israeli pilots had landed to toss the bombs inside, and with unerring accuracy. There were signs of absolute panic in offices ranged around the field. I could imagine the Israeli jet planes flying out of the sun to destroy everything within sight. I inspected some of the planes and found that the bombs had struck them in approximately identical places as if the missiles had been guided. When I suggested this to an Israeli officer he smiled and shook his head. "It's perfect aiming," he said.

The sandy loam to the east of El Arish provided the land with soil suitable for crops, and judging by those which had been gathered and placed in sacks and left, the crops had grown in abundance. The agriculturalists must have been very proud of them. Now the fields were plowed up by the tanks.

Amid signs of death and destruction along the way the thundering dust-covered monster of an Israeli tank halted beside me. The tank commander was young. He could speak English. He may have come from England for all I know. He gave me a measure of warm water and some Passover biscuits. We ate and drank as we talked. He and I relished the meal as the noon sun shone mercilessly from directly above. That snack, I thought later, was symbolic. I remembered that the Passover was instituted to commemorate the events recorded in Exodus 12 which tells of God's deliverance of Israel from Pharaoh's oppression. Many of the troops now were nibbling at Passover biscuits. Israelis had paused by the desert roadside 3,500 years ago to eat their Passover on the Exodus. Now they ate it as they travelled triumphantly in the opposite direction, into instead of out of Egypt. It seemed to me that that incident was indicative of the continuity of the Hebrews who had survived so many calamities and would certainly survive Colonel Nasser.

At such times as this I felt angry that, because of the criminal actions of the Germans, the Jews had been set down in the heart of the Arab lands where they had constantly to defend themselves.

The Jewish population of Continental Europe west of Russia had been reduced from about 6,500,000 to 1,500,000 by mass extermination carried out in cold blood. The survivors had fled to Palestine where their early ancestors had had a home. Many of the Jews had escaped death in the monstrous destruction factories in which the Germans asphyxiated as many at a time as they could. This mass slaughter had indirectly inflicted suffering of another kind on the innocent Arab third party, the Palestinians, who had lived in that land as long as anyone. The Arabs cared nothing for the suffering inflicted on the Jews by the Germans. All that mattered to them was that because of the action of certain countries in the West, their homeland was being used without their consent to help solve a problem which they had done nothing to create. The result had been one war after another in an effort to correct what was seen as wrong. The Palestinians had left their homeland to fill the role of refugee, which was exactly the same as that which had been filled by the Jews before, and during, the Second World War. The situation had been complicated because an ambitious Arab leader who had wished to become a second Saladin had exploited the refugees for political purposes instead of trying to launch a scheme of resettlement. The refugees had been discouraged from leaving their camps so that these miserable places could be used as wanted, as a political weapon against the Israelis and against the West.

As we moved on I saw Israeli infantrymen bringing back a

group of Egyptian prisoners and I saw on the faces of captor and captured looks of unmistakable contempt and hatred. It seemed to me that I had been a little superficial in my thinking. This contempt and hatred surely went far deeper than something which happened but twenty years before? I felt that it had its origin in the Old Testament. Was it not the continuation of an ancient conflict between the two sons of Abraham, a conflict which had never been forgotten no matter what calamity had intervened and would never be forgotten until the end of time? Abraham's sons, Isaac, to whom all Jews traced their origin, and Ishmael, from whom the Arabs said they were all descended, were fighting again. This was indeed a holy war, as the Arabs said it would be. It was a fight between the descendants of Isaac, who swore by the Bible, and the descendants of Ishmael, who swore by the Koran. Each of these people thought they had been promised by God that they would be dominant. Each of them believed that God had given him all the land of Canaan (which the Arabs call by its Roman name, Palestine, and the Jews call Israel). These two people, closely related thousands of years ago, and since grown apart in hate, nationality and status, now fought each other again for possession of their homeland. The war was just another example of the curse of professional religion which had always caused bloodshed and heartbreak, and set one people against another.

Ahead, the fighting was furious, but the Israelis were advancing at top speed. I had looked around for some time to try to find a field commander. Based on my experience in the Western Desert, I looked for a Command Vehicle in which the Commander worked and lived in a certain degree of comfort in the rear. I had not seen one. Now, as we advanced, I met the very man I sought. He should have been leading his men, he said, but he had had to halt for a while to settle some important detail. Israeli officers up to the highest rank in the field, like Israeli shepherds with their sheep, led rather than drove. The officer could not talk to me then but promised he would have plenty to say later.

When I met the man again, a kind of greatness emerged from the stinking garbage of war. I can shut my eyes now and see the officer and hear his soft casual voice. "Our troops are a little fewer than those of the enemy. On the one hand the enemy has most modern equipment, the most up-to-date tanks, the most modern artillery. On the other hand, there is the matter of troops. I must tell you when you look at them that they do look like a mob. Yet they are wonderful soldiers and make wonderful commanders. True they are not well dressed and use all kinds of civilian vehicles which we call *tnuva* lorries, or milk trucks. I sometimes wonder what the Arab prisoners think when they see our vehicles and our soldiers. But these men have a wonderful spirit, probably because in our army we do not use the command 'Forward.' We use, instead, the words: 'Follow me.' I think that this example set by all the officers, from the top commander through the divisional commanders to brigade down to company commanders, makes a lot of difference. The officers always run ahead of their troops.

"These troops of ours, quiet shopkeepers, farm workers, teachers or factory hands one day, are attacking the next day like devils. I don't know how to explain it. I haven't been able to explain it to myself ever since I started in the army during the War of Independence as a platoon commander. I still could not explain it later, in the Sinai campaign when I saw a lot more of men. Now, as a divisional commander, I am still unable to explain it. There is something in this nation's spirit which makes it possible. Just consider this. The operation of a modern tank is a very complicated affair. In the Egyptian army all the armored personnel are regular soldiers serving terms of many years. Our tank personnel get only very short periods of national service in which to learn the difficult art of tank management in war, to reach the high standard needed to be better than the enemy."

I had wondered many times how Israel, even allowing for the superiority of its men over the Arabs, had managed to compensate for the deficiency in numbers, in material and equipment. I now learned that the General Staff had gone out of their way to discover new and unconventional methods of operating, especially in using tanks and planes, so that the disparity in numbers would not count. In regard to tank management, the method devised, taught and used was a secret element in the amazing success of the Israelis in this war. The method was devastatingly simple and yet remarkably effective. Tank men in Israel had always been told to penetrate deeply into the enemy lines without paying attention to their unprotected flanks, whereas the Egyptians used the Soviet method of successive lines in depth. The enemy was generally confused, lost his equilibrium, and was the easier attacked from behind and inside. The method can be taught easily in the lecture room, of course, but it is possible only to practice it in the field on the basis of an ingenious precept. Even then only superior tank men can put all this, and other, theory into practice. The fact is that the Israeli troops, although they were civilians with so few hours in tanks, were able to do exactly what they were taught. The Egyptians just could not produce the right sort of tank men to equal the quality of their machines, especially at night. The Israelis had splendid techniques of night fighting, even better than in the Sinai campaign, and the Egyptians were soon dislodged from positions which they had carefully prepared.

11

VICTORY IN THE SINAI

Brigadier-General S. Gavish was O.C. of the Southern Command of the Israeli army, which meant the Sinai, in which the Jews were so outnumbered. He had under his command three other brigadier-generals, Tal, Yoffe and Sharon (the Three Musketeers someone called them), to cover the three chief axes in this vast area. Each commanded a division, and they had opposed to them over seven Egyptian divisions. Gavish was confronted with a stupendous task but he was optimistic from the start. He knew he had the best possible three commanders under him, and the best men he could have chosen. When Gavish took command, the Egyptian army was deployed all along the border, and included fighting units which had been hurriedly brought back from the Yemen.

General Gavish very kindly explained his strategy and his accomplishments after the four days of hard fighting were over. When he said at the opening that the enemy "started to attack" I took out my little book containing clues as to who started the shooting war. I wanted to know where. The explanation the general gave was not very clear. He reiterated all that had been said by the other leaders about the radar, the *kibbutzim,* but that was not enough. Like the other speakers he did not say whether or not the Egyptians had crossed the border first. Nor did he say how far they were away from it, if they had not reached it. When he came to his own theater of operations he was more precise, however. He said, and I record it, that: "The Egyptians also started battles in the area of Mitzpe Ramon with a large armored force

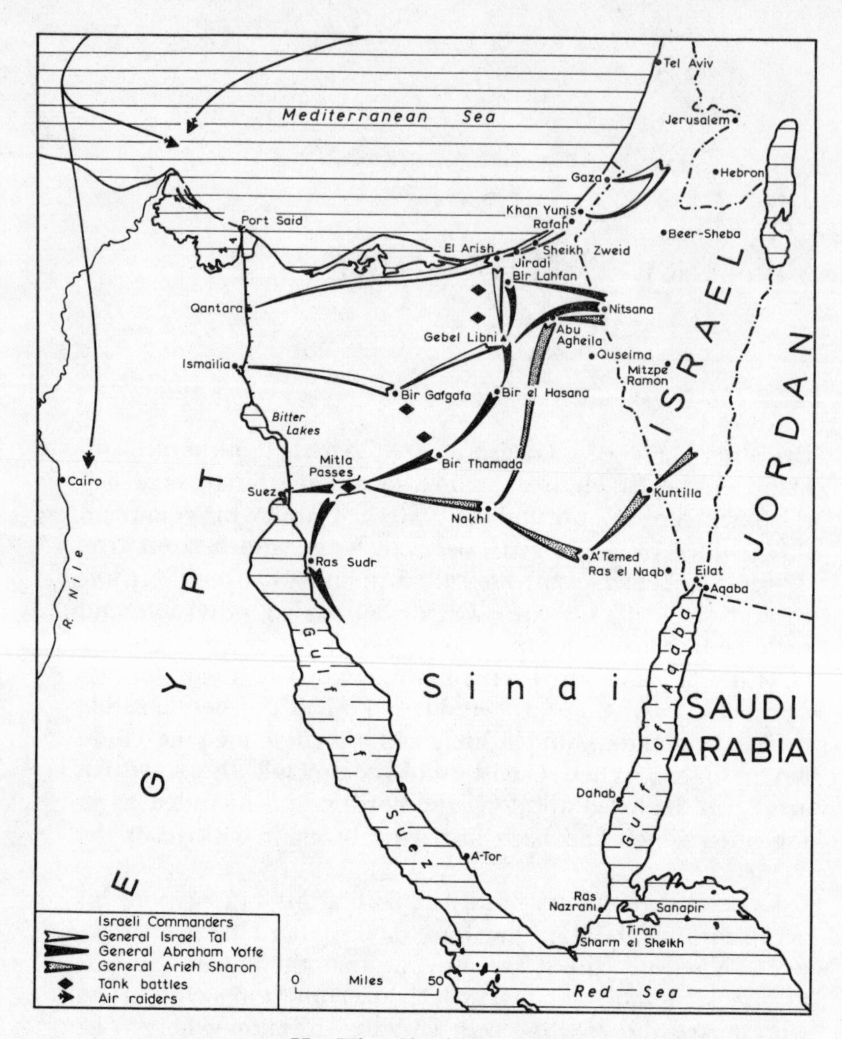

II The Sinai Campaign

which moved across the Israel border." Nothing could be clearer. He added that the movement towards the desert town of Mitzpe Ramon, on the road that links the north with Eilat, indicated the enemy intention to cut off the Negev and isolate Eilat, already cut off by sea by the blockade at the Straits of Tiran. This was supplemented by the additional information that the Egyptian armored force of divisional strength was in the Qreya Pass, "facing Mitzpe Ramon." I was very puzzled. Maybe I was one of few non-Israelis in the room who happened to have been to Mitzpe Ramon. In 1960 I had walked from 'Avat to Mitzpe Ramon, a distance of about fifteen miles. Together with an Israeli pioneer I had plowed southward under a scorching sun through the desolate Midbar-Tsin, otherwise the Wilderness of Zin, where the tribes of Israel had wandered about three thousand three hundred years before on their way from Egypt to the Land of Canaan. My friend had told me how this was mentioned in the Torah: "And the children of Israel, even the whole congregation, came into the wilderness of Zin in the first month . . . and there was no water for the congregation, and they assembled themselves together against Moses and against Aaron. And the people strove with Moses. . . . Why have ye brought the assembly of the Lord into this Wilderness, to die here, we and our cattle, and wherefore have ye made us to come up out of Egypt, to bring us to this evil place?" When he had finished reading I said much the same to my friend. I felt I was going to die of thirst. I began then to see my first mirage. I recall it was of a small inn in the village in which I live in Shropshire, "The Seven Stars." But when I reached the promising spot I saw only a heap of rocks.

With these recollections came the remembrance that Mitzpe Ramon was a fairly remote town amid the canyons and craters of a lunar landscape. It was *not* by any means on the border near Qreya Pass but midway inside the narrowing part of the Negev. It must be about fifteen miles as tanks would have to ply from Mitzpe Ramon to the Egyptian border, and the going is very rough. There are forbidding hills in the area, some of them rising to 4,500 feet. I wondered how the Israeli look-outs were able to see the Egyptian armor cross the border so far off. True, Mitzpe, in Hebrew, means look-out, and it was possible to see a long way from nearby cliffs. I wondered where such Egyptian tanks in the pass would have joined up with Jordanian tanks on the other side of the Negev, for obviously that would have been the tactic. Later, I was unable to get any evidence of there having been such a plan by the joint command. The Egyptian commander could not have known as much about the terrain as I did. Perhaps he had not sent out his spies as Moses sent his spies to Canaan (Numbers 13,21). If he had, he would have discovered that it was still an unattractive place. It was certainly not a place of seed, or of figs, or of pomegranates. Mainly dust-covered camel-thorn, stones and great rocks marked the way. . . . But then the Egyptians do not read the Torah.

General Gavish was more precise when he talked about the action. The Sinai Peninsula had three principal axes. One was the coastal axis of Rafah–El Arish–Qantara on the Suez Canal, along which I spent quite a long time. The second was Nitsana–Abu Agheila, to which I also paid a visit during hostilities; and the third the Kuntilla–A'Temed–Nakhl-Port Fuad-Suez. This axis, along which I flew at very low altitude in the DC3 Israeli military plane, links the Suez Canal, Suez and the road to Cairo with the approaches to Eilat. As there were three axes, so there were three aims to the Israel campaign plan and three stages in which to carry it out. The three aims were to destroy the Egyptian army, and to do so once and for all; to capture Sharm el Sheikh and thus open the road to Eilat; then, as the result of the second aim, there was the intention to conquer all of Sinai as the Israel army had done in 1956. The three stages in which the campaign was to be carried out were to open two chief passages into the peninsula and thus destroy the Egyptian forces on the Eastern line; to push forward, hit and destroy the second defense line; and then to engage the armored divisions in open battle and destroy them.

Of the seven divisions which Colonel Nasser sent to the Sinai two were armored. One was a division of Palestinians in the Gaza Strip, an area of 100 square miles on the Mediterranean and adjacent to the Egyptian border. This was the 20th Division, made up of desperate men who felt they were fighting for the return of their Palestinian homeland, and one that distinguished itself by stubborn fighting. Then there was the 7th Division which I saw in action between Rafah and El Arish. There was the 2nd Division which did not give a very good account of themselves along the Abu Agheila-Queseima line. There was also the 3rd Division, positioned along the Gebel Libni-Bir Hasana line, and the 4th Division, which was armored, mostly with Russian tanks, and which saw heavy fighting between Bir Gafgafa and Bir Temedeh. The 6th Division of Infantry gave a poor show between Nakhl and Kuntilla. There was also the mysteriously placed special armored force of about a division "in the Qreya Pass facing Mitzpe Ramon" which apparently believed in keeping store-hours with their wars even in a stifling climate at a hot part of the year.

I do not, of course, know exactly what happened in Mitzpe Ramon, apart from what Gavish told me, to influence the Israeli Chief of Staff, Major-General Itzhak Rabin, to take the decisive step, but Rabin signalled Gavish and other commanders two minutes before eight o'clock in the morning and told him that the first stage of the campaign was to begin. "The enemy has started the assault," he said. General Gavish was so keyed up that his divisions were able to move out to attack along two axes in sixteen minutes in spite of the difficult terrain. I have never heard of such anticipation and efficiency. One line of attack was via Khan Yunis in the Gaza Strip and Rafah in the direction of El Arish. The second line of attack was along the Nitsana-Abu Agheila line. The two forces which General Gavish used were of divisional strength. The third force, also of divisional strength, broke through over the dusty earth roads to the center of the Gebel Libni-Bir Gafgafa-Bir Lahfan triangle. Two augmented brigades of the Israeli army entered the fray, one in the direction of Kuntilla and the other from north to south of the Gaza Strip. The Israelis fought these first battles excellently. They ended ahead of a tight and demanding timetable the following morning (Tuesday) with the demolition of the 7th Egyptian

Division along the northern axis. Tanks were everywhere burning or had heeled over with tracks broken and torn by shells. Prisoners were being rounded up but many had gotten away in the dark, and divested themselves of uniforms and boots. The field was littered with dead and wounded. Israel had captured, in under twenty-four hours, El Arish and Abu Agheila. Israeli troops, according to plan, had reached the center of their operational area intact. The Gaza Strip, with its 250,000 Palestinian refugees from which raiders had been recruited, had been completely occupied, though it was still dangerous, as I found later, for small groups of men to travel through the Strip. Egyptian commando troops, who had escaped and hidden after the fighting, emerged and sniped on all who passed. The same happened in Rafah and El Arish and all along the road towards the Suez Canal.

The second stage of the plan began at greater speed. Israeli troops advanced to demolish the second defense line from Gebel Libni to Bir Hasana. It had been decided not only to demolish this line but to try to lure the Egyptian armored divisions to mount a counterattack. Unless this was done there was no early chance of making contact and the Israelis were difficult to hold back. The Egyptian divisions seemed for one moment to be about to oblige but they held their fire. They moved back in a cloud of dust to regroup.

It was just about at this stage that the central force on the southern front, an armored mobile division, began to advance speedily in the direction of the Gebel Libni-Bir Hasana line. The force was commanded by a mountain of a man of remarkable personality, Brigadier-General Abraham Yoffe, who, until three weeks before the war, was engaged in the gentle pursuit of nature conservation. His personal story of what happened in this attack is a moving one and I will tell it later. As Yoffe started to advance in a sand cloud his colleague, Brigadier-General Tal, moved his division through the Bir Lahfan area, broke through the Egyptian lines and struck out with lightning speed as if he had wagered with some other commander that he would be first to take a swim in the Suez Canal. He reached Nasser's waterway next morning, very early, when it was too dark to bathe if he had been able to, and cold with chill of the night dew of the desert.

The third commanding officer in Gavish's command, Brigadier-General Sharon, took his division at high speed to break through in the direction of the area between Queseima and Bir Hasana. In fact he captured Queseima.

The third stage of the plan was a dramatic clash of tanks, great clattering monsters which the young crews maneuvered magically in spite of many obstacles, natural and Egyptian made, which stood in the way. The object now of the Israeli armored forces was to surround the enemy tanks by moving more skilfully at higher speed and to force him to fight.

Brigadier Tal's division reached Bir Gafgafa and blocked the Egyptian retreat route to the Canal. Brigadier Yoffe's division bottled up the southern exit after taking Farq'r near the Mitla Pass. Brigadier Sharon's troops cut off the Egyptian forces to the east.

In a vast desert, its surface carved deeply by tank tracks, it seemed as if hell had been let loose. Over the noise of the great machines of war, and out of the thick fog of choking sand they kicked up, there came the thunder of guns and flashes as of lightning. The Egyptians at this stage could do nothing but carry on a running battle in two directions. As they fired they tried to avoid being encircled by the ever-growing ring of steel and to reach the Suez Canal. Israel tried to block the passes leading to the Canal along three ways, Ismailia, Jirdi and Mitla. The arena of battle widened and narrowed as if according to a rhythm. Nothing stood still. Everything moved at a hideous pace and with ear-splitting noise. The sky was hidden by dust yet the heat of the sun came through the haze to make men sweat copiously. The sweat caused dust to clog round goggles, fill nostrils and cover teeth and lips. Everything began to assume the same drab khaki color. The morning passed in hard fighting. Though unseen, the sun climbed directly above. The heat was unbearable but no one thought of the conditions.

The battle raged on all day. If an Israeli could crunch a Passover biscuit or take a mouthful of water, he was lucky. With the sun sinking the battle still continued. The young Israelis were stripped to the waist, at times nearly naked. From time to time there were outcries scarcely audible above the thunder of battle as one after another Egyptian tank burst into flames or came to a grinding halt. Over one thousand tanks took part that day in one of the most dramatic and uneven battles of all time. As dusk began to gather so that dark and dust were indistinguishable, the battle took on the eerie aspect of a vast pyrotechnic display in the wilderness. Guns flashed in all directions and exploding tanks suddenly lit up the area in which they stood as fuel ignited. Men tried to get out, their clothes blazing. The desert was now strewn with wreckage of all kinds, of guns, tanks, trucks and scattered ammunition. And among it all were the dead and dying. Here and there was a foot or a limb or a torso or a head in the deep tank tracks in the sand. So the battle continued into the following night. It was all over before midnight. Then in the strange quiet that followed, the dust began to clear and the stars to glimmer. From the distance there came the cries of hyenas and jackals whose terror at the noises of the night had been overcome by the scent of food. The Israeli tanks re-formed; they did not tarry. By 3 a.m. on Friday all the Israeli forces had reached the Canal. Men were being allowed to form bathing parties so that they could wash off the sweat and the grime of war.

Activity was not confined to one part of this desert. Night was as busy as day. On Friday, for instance, Israeli forces landed by helicopter and by torpedo boats at Sharm el Sheikh. A land unit reached Ras Sudar by way of the Mitla Pass, the place where Israeli paratroopers had landed at the opening of the invasion of Egypt in 1956.

An Israeli officer said he believed that one of the reasons for the success of Israeli units was the feeling that their function was to find the enemy and destroy him. Troops did not move to carry out this operation by command. They acted on their own initiative. It was often the case with other ranks, as with officers, that they showed far too much initiative. The commando units of the Egyptian army apart, the Egyptian was wanting in initiative and would rarely have to be restrained in this respect by his superior. Officers in the Israeli Army had been known to overhear a private soldier asking an NCO for permission to go along a track, or road, which the formation was not taking. When asked the reason the soldier would reply, "Oh, I thought I saw a few tanks over there," or "I'm sure I saw a group of Gyppies on that slope." The commanding officer had to tell the man to stick to orders and to explain to him, since he was a civilian, that if everyone went off on his own to do what he thought was best there would be chaos and probably no army left to face threats as they arose. But in the end the men did the job as it needed to be done, although, if they got half a chance, and no one was looking, they slipped off to engage the enemy, to destroy him. On one occasion a high-ranking officer signalled back for permission to bathe in the Suez Canal. The officer commanding the Southern Sinai did not know until then that this officer and his men had reached that point. He refused permission. One particular formation, commanded by Brigadier Abraham Yoffe, soon reached the Canal at three points, and they were definitely not swimming resorts. On the way they had knocked out 157 Egyptian tanks, many of them technically superior and more modern than his own. All this had been done in four days.

Brigadier Gavish pointed out that concentration of forces, speed of movement and a constantly maintained impetus had had a decisive effect at the start. Israel was able to concentrate its strength at any point it wished and thereby incline the relation of forces in its favor. The next relevant fact was that the Israeli Army was able to maintain its original impetus while fighting continuously and without rest or much food for four days and four nights. The next important factor was that the commanding officers led fearlessly in battle. Because of this a very large proportion of Israeli casualties were of officers in command, not only of platoons and companies, but of battalions, regiments, brigades. Then there was the fighting quality and spirit of the men both in the regular and in the reserve units. They all fought with an awareness of the fact that the war would be decisive for the fate of the country whichever way it went. Because of this, coupled with the deep love all Israelis have for their country, morale was continuously high no matter what setbacks or difficulties had to be overcome. Israel had known for ten years that the war had to come sometime. They had prepared for it in every way. They were able to prepare more effectively because they knew there would be only one enemy, on fronts known to them. They studied the Arab mentality, had lectures on Arab methods of fighting, Arab weaknesses and strength. They studied the topography of borders on which they knew they would have to fight. They carefully chose the plan of battle which would be economical in manpower. They adopted the tactic of unusual penetration in depth so as to immediately undermine Egypt's fighting capacity.

The Arab armies, and especially the Egyptian, were mostly on the defensive. On only a few occasions, and then when ordinary troops were strengthened with commando forces from among the refugees, did they try to penetrate deeply into Israel's lines. From what I learned in 1956, and at the end of the present campaign when I talked to Israel troops and to Egyptian prisoners, it was never the practice in Nasser's army, in spite of his own brave action at Falugja, for an officer to lead his men into action. The officers of higher formations most certainly operated from a safe distance, through staff officers. There was an indication of this in the low proportion of Egyptian officers and other ranks who were killed in actual fighting, as distinct from when they were taking evasive action. There was a clearer indication in the proportion of officers who were taken prisoner compared with the number of other ranks. There is enough evidence to assume that the Egyptian officer was quick to see when he was faced with overwhelming odds. He had a distinct aversion to laying down his life. His relationship with his men was not based on mutual respect. The Egyptian officer and man knew each other too well.

It is a strange fact, since Egypt for so many thousands of years has possessed more than its fair proportion of desert, that even Egyptian soldiers who have had to train there hate and loathe deserts. When I was given the task in the Wavell campaign of bringing important parties of Egyptian officers from Cairo to show them that all Italians had been driven off Egyptian soil it was necessary for them to be accommodated in the open on the Libyan side of the border. Each of them pleaded with me to provide tents and ground sheets. Some refused to sleep on the ground and spent the night on the tops of various trestle tables in messes. Incidentally, they fell off these in the commotion caused in the early morning when a convoy of heavy trucks on its way to Bardia was mistaken for an enemy counterattack. Egyptians, far more than foreigners, are afraid of snakes and scorpions. They can talk for hours about the terrors of such creatures.

As for speed, I defy anyone who has been with Egyptian officers on any kind of operation to tell me that they have any sense of urgency. It is not only in this respect that the Egyptian Army is like the Italian Army. When I have been present on purely Egyptian organized maneuvers, I have noted how frequently the timetable is overrun and how rarely anyone, even the officer in charge, comments upon it. Unlike the Israeli, who is like a fanged dynamo in war, and who can go without food or snatch a bite as he is carrying out another operation, the Egyptian officer detests haste in culinary matters. He is particular about his food. Although the Egyptian Army has improved considerably under the critical eye of Nasser and his former deputy Supreme Commander and relative-by-marriage, Field Marshal Abdel Hakim Amer, the President of the United Arab Republic was only too well aware of the limitations of his men. He thought he could make up for these by giving them the best Russian arms he could buy. But a jet plane or a fast tank or a piece of artillery is unfortunately only as good as the men who operate it. Colonel Nasser learned this lesson too late. The Egyptian organization for the supply of fuel, munitions, water and repairs was good, but not good enough. The Egyptian Army had its supply troubles days before operations began. That is another reason why I doubt if there was any planned start to the war by Egypt. The supply system in the Israeli Army was excellent although its lines of communication were not so stretched as those of Egypt. Israel had so taken time by the forelock that there was enough of everything, even fuel (of which they were denied supplies by all Arabs for a long time), for the divisions to act independently during the three days and nights. The same could be said of reinforcements. On the day the war broke out, there were enough troops in the assembly areas to supply every demand during the early fighting. In fact reinforcements were needed only on the last day.

There is another comparison which is sometimes ignored. The Arabs have armies which are largely professional, and the degree of professionalism, at least in peace time, is high. The Israeli army is almost wholly amateur. Brigadier Abraham Yoffe, commander of an armored mobile division, was fond of saying during the war that all his divisions, from the commander down, were civilians. And they were civilians until two weeks and five days before the war began. As I have already commented, his normal occupation was nature conservancy for two years after leaving active duty. "From nature conservation in Israel," he said with a laugh, "I had to go and start protecting, not nature, but the country." This was the drill in Israel. You are a soldier one day and a civilian the next. Or vice versa. You are never a soldier long enough for it to become a habit, and let us admit it, it is not always a good one. The Israelis will not even allow their wars to last longer than a normal exercise. They have a strangely ambivalent attitude to the army. They give every appearance of loving it and dance and wave about their weapons as if they were ribbons on a maypole. Yet, demobilize them, or let them go off for a day, and they shed their uniforms in a second. You never see an Israeli officer moving socially about Israel in his uniform. This in spite of the fact that the army uniform is honored more in Israel than in most countries. For a people accused sometimes of being boastful and bossy, the young Israelis from sixty-four countries all over the world who make up the new country are aggressively modest, self-deprecating.

How well a civilian can handle civilians when all are dressed as soldiers was demonstrated best of all by Brigadier Abraham Yoffe. He was given at the start the impossible task of penetrating through very difficult terrain and surprising the Egyptian's defensive positions by coming up at the rear. Then he had to stop reinforcements going into the main defense and try to catch those who looked as if they were going to try to run away. He got his men together—shopkeepers, oil workers, mineral workers, railway porters, machinists, quarrymen, and farmers, and told them the position. He did not talk unnecessarily in military terms, but as one civilian to another, adding a quick aside to amuse them and giving not the slightest inkling that it was going to be sheer murder to get through the sand dunes to the back of the Bir Lahfan area. The young men nodded. That was enough. They began a nearly hopeless operation full of hope. Hope prevailed. They did what no Sandhurst man would have thought possible if presented with all the facts. They penetrated the soft sand dunes with the same deliberation as if they were plowing a field on the Syrian border with Syrian guns pointing down at them all the time. They reached the back of the Bir Lahfan area to the amazement of the Egyptian commanders who had also decided that this was impossible. Yoffe helped his friend Brigadier Sharon in a vital respect. He not only stopped two brigades from reaching the defensive positions but he also put out of action all the tanks which escaped Sharon's troops.

Mobilization is, as I have said, as secret as are locations after mobilization. In a little country like Israel, which insists on fighting its wars in an incredibly short time, friends from the same town or village, or even street, are apt to meet for the first time as they are about to go into battle. I saw them respond quite naturally in a civilian way, exchange familiar comments about people and places. It was the same in all battles. So it was in the move on Bir Lahfan. I don't know why but when Brigadier Yoffe, in his natural way, illustrated this with an anecdote tears came into my eyes. "With both forces linked," he said, "and we were about to go on to Gebel Libni, where the Egyptians twice tried to stop us but with little success, all of a sudden I heard a shout 'They are coming.' In one of the first few tanks moving up I saw my brother's boy who is a tank commander. I can tell you it was a very moving moment as we saw each other and recognized each other." Yoffe and his tank commander relative had no time to speak. The general had to coordinate matters as quickly as possible to make sure that the force led by Brigadier-General Tal, which was rumbling up, did not, in their high momentum, start shooting up a battalion of Yoffe's armor. He waved goodbye and carried on with his tanks along the main road to Gebel Libni, at times fighting his way through. Gebel Libni has seen many actions between the Egyptians and Israel and they have generally been won by Israel. It is not so well known, however, as the Mitla Pass, a strategic opening amid the mountains some 23 kilometers long, which Brigadier-General Yoffe's armor went at all speed to take over.

The Mitla Pass played a prominent role in the Sinai campaign of 1956. In landing troops by parachute near the spot flanked by high rocky mountains pocked by caves the Israel High Command showed brilliant anticipation and leadership in the deployment of troops. In its execution the move was a classical example of how paratroopers could be landed behind defenders' lines to create confusion among them and to sever enemy lines of communication. The Pass was then taken in a short time by troops under the command of Brigadier General Sharon, who, eleven years later, kept the Mitla Pass well in view. The Israelis knew that whoever commanded the opening to the Mitla Pass would be actually in command of all access to the Canal no matter how strong were the assaults made. Brigadier Sharon's friend Yoffe had received orders to race to the Pass, to strike hard and encircle it and to stop any Egyptian movements towards the Suez Canal. The venture met with success. The troops took the position. They were there for a day and a night and then another day, on the defensive all the time, trying to capture all the armor and all the columns which tried to get through only to find the passage blocked. At times this put a great strain on the brigade which performed the task the whole time although they had started out at the opening and had gone all the way through. They stopped the gap. They held on to it like a bulldog. The men, one might almost say boys, were nearly asleep on their feet, ravenously hungry, some with minor wounds they chose to disregard. On Wednesday most of the brigade had been fighting continuously and furiously for seventy-two hours, against overwhelming odds. Some collapsed from exhaustion, revived, and took up their positions again. The heat, the dust, the flies, the terrific new demands made suddenly on men who had been used all their lives before to work union hours in peaceful occupations, all these facts together were proving too much.

In the middle of the confusion of battle, with guns firing in all directions, and with tanks waltzing around as if they were electrically operated toys, Brigadier-General Yoffe knew that he had to do something for his fellow civilians, and do it quickly. He was not the only commanding officer to be faced with this problem in the thick of this amazing *blitzkrieg*. But he was the only man to put into action a brigade to take over a running battle carried on by another brigade and yet see to it that the tanks kept on firing all the time until the position was consolidated again. The tanks kept their guns firing furiously as the complicated changeover took place. The gunners took great care as they moved into withdrawal, or advance, not to fire on each other. For some time the situation was dangerously complicated. The Egyptians, if they had been accomplished in the art of tank warfare, could have taken advantage of the position. The initiative and the imagination not only of the Irsaeli commanders but the crews in those rolling furnaces contributed equally to the accomplishment. The changeover was carried out without any mishaps. The men of the brigade which had held the Pass for so long were able to collapse on their blankets in the desert and sleep with the certain knowledge that the Egyptians would not pass. There were many heroic episodes in the fighting in Sinai which made maximum demands on those who had never seen the desert before, but this changeover at the height of a running battle must surely rank very high in the records of the Israeli Army.

The battle, as in the case of the longer tank engagements, had been a test of human character, fighting spirit, human determination and endurance. The Egyptians were always superior in numbers, in hours spent in training, in equipment and especially in tanks and guns. But they showed weakness where the Israelis showed their strength. They displayed fear and indecision where the Israelis showed indomitable bravery and instant action. They quickly tired of the same movement many times repeated while the Israelis came up every time like giants refreshed.

One thing can be said of this war. It was fought in an arena made for war. Since there had to be a bloodletting after so much hate, it was best that it took place there and not in populated places. In a way it was like a game played on a field with defined limits, the obstructions being the wadis and sheer unscalable mountains. This peninsula, with its four Wildernesses, all of which featured in the Old Testament narratives of the years during which Israelites made their way to the Promised Land, was only peopled, if at all, by Bedouins.

Each of the Israeli formations realized that its success meant a huge problem in the form of thousands of prisoners who had to be fed and watered and guarded. As in Sinai, when the Egyptians realized that the Israel Army treated them well and did not maim them or murder them as they had been led to believe by Arab propagandists, they came forth in still greater numbers. As in the 1956 campaign the men often divested themselves of every article of uniform, whether because they wished to be regarded as civilians or wanted to indicate that they had had enough of Nasser, I do not know. They were often parched and famished and so weary that they lay down and went to sleep, disregarding the flies that pestered them. The task was to separate officers and NCOs from the ranks. After formal interrogations the officers, who included in some cases colonels and generals, were taken to POW camps in the rear. The other ranks were helped to reach the Suez Canal, which had been their objective since the war began. When transport and fuel were available, Egyptians were packed into trucks and driven as close to the Suez Canal as operations permitted. Both these, and others who were considered near enough to the Canal to walk or who could not be transported because of lack of vehicles, were given maps, shown the way home and furnished with water and food.

Some of the Israeli troops who drove prisoners towards the Canal or who guarded them on the way saw the Egyptian Army shoot down with machine guns a large number of Egyptian refugees as they approached the Canal. Some of these refugees were thirsty, hungry and weary. They waved white articles of clothing to make sure there was no mistake as to their identity. Why this shooting took place I do not know. I do not believe that the Egyptians did not want the refugees to disaffect the Egyptians on the west bank of the Canal, from whom the worst news had been withheld. I believe the firing was the result of nervousness. They might even have thought that the refugees were Israeli soldiers in disguise who aimed to cross the Canal.

The exact number of Egyptians taken prisoner in Sinai will never be known because of this decision to release other ranks. But other Egyptians who did not formally surrender but took the first opportunity in the confusion of battle to escape, probably exceeded the number of prisoners. I saw some of these stragglers from my low-flying DC3 as I flew over the battlefield in the direction of the Canal. Some were stumbling along, falling, then rising, only to fall again. They were nearly blind and lost. They were without food or water. They were sometimes walking in the wrong direction, towards vast empty spaces where there was no shade. Some 15,000 tattered stragglers were sent across the Canal by the Red Cross and the Red Crescent at Qantara.

Earlier, during the fighting, Egypt had turned off the water supply that came over the Canal to Central Sinai. This had made it difficult for the Israelis to provide water for thousands of unexpected prisoners. They had no pipeline and had their own water problems. They were strictly rationed. The Israelis gave water to Egyptians where they might not have given it to me unless I was in dire need of it. Israel had to bring up water for hundreds of miles in storage cans. Appeals were made to the Egyptian authorities to turn on the water again and this was eventually done when the gravity of the situation was realized. Days after the fighting there were still thousands of poor wretches lost in the desert, still crawling or limping in the wrong direction, still seeing mirages of streams and making for them only to find the same monotonous outcrops of rocks. There was an area of about seventeen square miles, from which there were limited views in all directions, where, I was told, vast numbers of Egyptians staggered about in circles. Some were trying to help others but many were left to die. Medical officers with the Israeli army declared that men engaged in the hot deserts required up to seven quarts of water a day. They had none!

Brigadier-General A. Tal, Commander of the Armored Corps, had achieved great things. The objectives he had been given were to penetrate the fortified lines of the First Egyptian Division (reinforced by a Palestinian Brigade) in the Rafah area, and to cut through the concrete fortification positions at Sheikh Zuwaib and Jirdi to capture El Arish. Then he had to continue, on the one hand along the northern axis to the Canal, and on the other to cut through another line of fortifications at Bir Lahfan to advance in the direction of Bir Gafgafa, and from there, to the Suez Canal. The main objective was not, of course, to occupy as much territory as possible. It was to destroy the enemy's divisions.

"We knew," he said, "that the first breakthrough action at Rafah would be a trial of strength between us and the Egyptian Army, with which we had not clashed for more than ten years. This was clear to all our soldiers and officers. They knew that the action would be carried out regardless of losses. We attacked the enemy line stretching back in depth in both directions for ten miles, with fortified positions on each side, including anti-tank guns, tanks and mines. We effected a frontal attack on the right flank next to the sea coast not far from Rafah. On the left flank, we broke through. We came out of the sands and on to the enemy's rear positions to find they were reinforced mainly by artillery. The moment the first breakthrough on the western flank was effected, our tank force, without waiting for the final outcome, broke through the Jirdi position with its concrete fortifications and reached the gates of El Arish. On the first evening we had attained our first decisive success. The enemy's 7th Division had been totally destroyed before we moved our tanks into El Arish."

The Egyptians reorganized their forces in and around the Jirdi position. Israeli tank units in El Arish were cut off. Instead of waiting until dawn Israel put in a night attack with mechanized infantry. The struggle for Jirdi was resumed. Israel broke through. The whole Israeli division cut its way through to El Arish and then split in two. The northern force turned in the direction of the Canal, and the southern one went on towards Bir Lahfan.

Speaking of the tank action centered around the El Arish airfield, Brigadier-General Tal said, "The outcome became obvious only after a couple of hours." A new force went on to break through the last Bir Lahfan fortified positions. A hundred tanks on the field of battle as well as hundreds of cannon had been destroyed. From Bir Lahfan the armor advanced along the central axis in the area of the Gebel Libni, where an attack was launched in connection with Brigadier-General Yoffe's division. Yoffe's men were pushing through in the direction of Bir Hasana while Tal penetrated the Egyptian lines in the direction of Bir Gafgafa. The two groups protected each other's flanks. As they reached Bir Gafgafa, the Egyptian delaying action increased in intensity. The Israelis took up positions to block the enemy's escape route to the Canal. The Egyptians, understanding the critical nature of this move, attempted to counterattack in the direction of Bir Gafgafa. At the same time they coordinated their attack with air support. The assault was repulsed, and then Israel moved on to counterattack. One of the Israeli forces was at Bir Gafgafa and another on the southern flank. In the counterattack Israel destroyed an Egyptian mechanized brigade which had massed for still another counterattack. At this stage, additional Egyptian forces, mainly T 55 tanks, were brought up from the Canal Zone to attempt to pull the "cork" out of the Bir Gafgafa bottleneck. However, an Israeli regiment took up a position along the possible line of advance to prevent just such a contingency. This regiment, which was furnished with light tanks, engaged in bitter fighting for over two hours with an Egyptian force of over sixty T 55 tanks. It was here that Israel incurred many casualties. By a stroke of ill luck, the supply of mortar-shells and other explosives was blown up right in the midst of one Israeli regiment. In spite of this grave set-back the regiment held its ground. The troops succeeded in maintaining their position and blocked all passage to the T 55s until reinforcements reached them.

After the Egyptian brigade had been liquidated, Israel started moving all its force towards the Canal, with the enemy attempting constant delaying action with a force of a hundred tanks—mainly T 55s. Israel's advance was slower than it had ever been at this stage. It took Israeli armor six hours to cover four miles. They managed, however, to destroy some forty enemy tanks. Finally, Egyptian resistance was broken. Light reconnaissance units supported by a small number of tanks quickly reached the Canal. There was a battle along a very narrow axis which did not permit free maneuvering. The sand dunes hemmed in the Israelis on a narrow front. Only three tanks led all the time, but their gunners were excellent. At ranges of 3,000, 2,000 and 1,000 feet they hit enemy tanks every time, even though the Egyptians were always the first to fire. They had positioned themselves in such a manner as to be able to sight the Israeli tanks while the Egyptians remained hidden. During the second half of the advance, Israeli tanks met a type of resistance similar to the one encountered along the central axis, and adopted a similar manner of progress. For three hours there was bitter fighting between Russian-made airplanes and Israeli land forces. The Egyptians managed to hold up the Israeli advance for a short time, but finally Israeli planes intervened and turned the scales in Israel's favor.

The final stage of this battle saw the junction of two advance axes. At this point the Egyptians opened artillery fire and sent in airplanes from across the Canal. This action took place after the cease-fire deadline. Israel returned artillery and tank fire, directing it towards Egyptian forces on the other side of the Canal. The Egyptians also fired missiles from their bases on the farther side of the Canal and from missile sites located in the Ismailia area. Since this action took place after the cease-fire, the Israeli commander ordered the artillery to return two shells for every shell fired at them. The Egyptians tasted for the first time what Israeli border settlements on the Syrian line and near the Gaza Strip had suffered until not so long before. The Egyptians took the hint at once and stopped firing.

Brigadier-General Ariel Sharon was the only other commander on the Sinai Front. He had been in the War of Liberation as a platoon commander, in the Sinai campaign as a brigade commander and now he was a divisional commander. His task had begun about two weeks before the war when his division took up position in Nitsana, infantry in the trucks and armored troops behind. On the day of the attack between 8 o'clock and 8:15 a.m. Sharon, like the other commanders, received an order from the Southern Commander describing an Egyptian attack. He was ordered to launch an assault which had been planned ahead for any contingency of that kind. His task was first of all to break through the defensive positions at Abu Agheila in order to make possible the passage of Yoffe's force.

"Abu Agheila," he said, "was held by more than an Egyptian brigade group and about ninety tanks. From there I was scheduled to advance southwest towards Queseima and the road linking this site with Bir el Hasana, proceed to Nakhl, and then also advance to the Mitla Pass. When I reached this pass, I wanted to cable Defense Minister Moshe Dayan my greetings, but I did not manage to obtain the connection. It took us three and a half days to break through this position from Abu Agheila. It was a hard battle under very heavy artillery fire. We managed to cut off the enemy in the area of Temed and to destroy more than an armored brigade. I do not know how it happened, but after the three days we still could have moved to the Northern Command to help our troops in the fight against the Syrians. The Israelis in the north, however, were able to manage without help from the south.

"We did not have many prisoners of war, maybe because we were not so close to the Canal," commented Brigadier Sharon. "I talked to several prisoners of war, and they were very disappointed. They were promised that in a few days they would be in Tel Aviv. They were going to kill the men and rape the women. But in spite of this I would say the

Egyptian is a good soldier, a disciplined soldier. I think the commanders are very poor. I would not trust them. We do not think they have any fighting spirit. They are very good where everything is very simple. They are well organized. They are very good in shooting. I must tell you one story I heard. We attacked an Egyptian battalion at Sabba near Nitsana, and managed in a few minutes to destroy the position. Later we attacked the Syrians and we put the prisoners together, the officers separately. The Syrians asked the Egyptians how it could have happened that a battalion in a fortified defensive position, mined, etc., and having artillery, was defeated in a few minutes. The Egyptians answered—'Those Jews don't attack according to the book.' That's what really happened here in this war. I think again we did not attack the way it is written in the books. I think the speed, the momentum and example of the commanders again really showed that they are more important."

Brigadier Sharon described the battle in which he broke through the positions in Abu Agheila. "We operated many troops together—armored troops, paratroopers, infantry, artillery, engineers," he said. "I think this particular battle, of the many fought, was most interesting because it shows our maneuverability against enemy position. The enemy had an infantry brigade and about ninety tanks, and six regiments of artillery holding the area of Abu Agheila. We opened with the paratroopers, who attacked the artillery positions from the rear. Then with infantry who attacked the first lines, and with tanks penetrating from the northern side and attacking from the rear of these positions. Then with other armored troops, who attacked from the front. This operation was carried out between 10:30 in the evening and six o'clock the following morning under very heavy artillery fire. We managed to break through and enabled another division to move its troops through us. On Monday evening at 8:15 p.m. we captured the forward positions. We moved our infantry about twenty kilometres on foot to these positions. We moved our paratroopers, and moved our artillery forward, and then attacked around 11 p.m. and finished around six o'clock the next morning."

While the Israelis had been advancing on the third day of the war, June 7th, in three parallel thrusts, one beneath the other, right across the Sinai to the Suez Canal, Israelis in torpedo boats from Eilat and parachute troops had taken on the most distant point of the war and the place where it started, Sharm el Sheikh, which the Egyptians had taken over from UNEF in order to blockade the Israeli port. When I went there in a DC3, the nearest contrivance I have ever seen to a flying Turkish bath, I was flown very low over the battlefields, some of which I had traversed in the rapid advance. Why anyone should want the Sinai, excepting for strategic reasons, I cannot imagine. It is a 260-mile-long triangle at whose southern apex the Gulf of Aqaba joins the Gulf of Suez at the head of the Red Sea. Its broad end stretches for 150 miles along the Mediterranean and here there is some advantage in holding it. The Sinai has a 15-mile-wide band of sandy dunes reaching south from the Mediterranean. It has a high plateau of limestone and gravel riven by dried-up wadis, and it has a mountainous mass in which a division could lose itself and die of thirst. The only animal which can live centrally is the camel.

I saw Israeli troops about two-thirds of the way down on the west side of the peninsula in the first of the four wildernesses of Sinai, the Wilderness of Sin (not to be confused with another, the Wilderness of Zin), the Wilderness of Paran which reaches the Arabian, the rift which extends from the Sea of Galilee to the Jordan Valley and on to the Gulf of Aqaba, and the Wilderness of Beersheba. There were no signs of animal or bird life but there were army columns in places where no Bedouins had ever been. I saw a column crossing the middle of the peninsula on what was probably the old caravan route which passed from Memphis on the Nile to Ezion-geber, the port and refinery of Solomon at the head of the Gulf of Aqaba. I saw a second and third column on one of the traditional routes of the Exodus which took the migration near to Mount Sinai, with the Monastery of St. Catherine, which has been occupied for the past 1,500 years. Many were the ancient settlements I saw, cut off completely from the world. The few nomads, with their camels, who had lived there had had, until they heard the sound of distant guns, no idea that their alienated cousins were fighting out again their ancient quarrel. There was no thunder when the sun shone so brilliantly.

As we approached Sharm el Sheikh I found myself in a world of magic and color. The mountains, which reared their jagged heads to spike an azure sky at 8,000 feet, were pink, turning to orange, and so beautiful in line I could only stare and weep. Some of the mountains, carved and sculptured by the eroding wind, assumed shapes of grotesque beauty. Now and then the sun, which lit like lamps the sharp many-sided flints strewn on the desert floor, revealed for a second or two in the mountains veins of green or gold or sometimes white. The Gulf of Aqaba and the Gulf of Suez were startling. Their translucent waters of Reckitts' blue, flanked by saffron sand, had the iridescent allure of submerged coral.

We left the plane in the open desert, its wings affording the only shade visible anywhere, and we were driven over the stony land in a small truck that threatened to brain us every yard. The victorious Israeli troops, haunted by the perpetual mirage of a brewery, cheered us as if we, instead of they, were the conquerors. Partly encircled by a wildly lunar landscape of sun-baked mountains, these young warriors managed to maintain their high morale although they lacked the conveniences of a war-time camp. Their only beverage was warm water, and not an abundance of that. The only pleasure they had had, and this they enjoyed with their visitors, was the sight of the first ship flying the Israeli flag, the *Dolphin,* to travel uninterruptedly through the Straits of Tiran since May. Their only company in that inhospitable place were many thousands of Egyptian flies which, judging by the insistent way they explored my every feature, were trying to identify their former Egyptian hosts. The commander of the Sharm el Sheikh area, which measures some 220 square miles, told me that the Egyptians had not waited to fight. They had taken to their heels, or to the water. They had first removed and hidden the breechblocks of the four guns which had illegally dominated the Straits. A few had fled into the mountains but they had been forced out into the valley by thirst. Some had surrendered, some had fought.

Israeli troops loaded us with army field postcards to mail in some civilized place to wives or sweethearts they had not seen for some weeks. Judging by the identical length of the messages, and other parallel features, it seemed to me that the Israeli army, like the British when at war, relied on a group letter writer who sold rights in a master love letter full of sweet endearments for part of the cigarette ration. Anyway, he made a lot of women very happy. When I left the troops to return to civilization they were trying to make work an oil-fired refrigerator left behind by the United Nations. "It's like everything else about the United Nations," one wiseacre said, "it just won't work." As I got into my flying Turkish bath I told myself there was nothing half so bad as this in the Western Desert during the last war.

I was surprised a little later to see how Eilat had developed since I first saw it after the Sinai war. In eleven years a scattered, dusty border post of unfinished shacks had become a flourishing port of 10,000 people. A second, larger port had been built south of the first with a capacity of 500,000 tons, instead of 200,000, in addition to accommodation for 2,000,000 tons of bulk cargo. The new port was opened in 1964 but work was still going on. Soon Eilat would have docks measuring 4,200 feet (compared with 450 feet in the old port), anchorages 38 feet deep and berthing capacity for ships up to 30,000 tons. One new warehouse could accommodate 40,000 tons of potash and 30,000 tons of phosphates. Since 1957 export of phosphates to Asia had grown from 300,000 to 1,000,000 tons. Eilat had been joined to the Mediterranean by major roads and an oil pipeline had been laid from Eilat to Haifa, with a branch to the new harbor at Ashdod. The bulk of Israel's oil had flowed through the pipes until the Egyptian blockade. Then hundreds of sailings under dozens of flags had dwindled. Plans had now been made to extend the Haifa-Beersheba railroad to Eilat and to make the port the southern terminal of a Mediterranean-Red Sea canal.

The sailor in a boat in which I travelled down the treeless coastline in a temperature of 102 degrees told me how Britain had disillusioned the sailors on the Red Sea by allowing Egyptian gunners to fire at the British ship *Empire Roach* in

July 1951, when it was en route for Jordan. Maybe, it was thought, the British Navy did nothing because the Egyptians didn't hit the *Empire Roach*. Later, however, on April 10th 1955, the British ship *Anshun* was fired on at Tiran and actually hit because it failed to stop to be identified. Again the British did nothing. Now they had done nothing again to keep an international waterway open. Israel had had to act on its own. "Things have changed!" he said.

As a result of these operations in the Sinai, the Egyptians lost between 500 and 600 tanks destroyed and over 100 which were captured still in running order. Some 3,000 Egyptian prisoners of war were taken and tens of thousands who were not rounded up took to their heels in the direction of the Canal.

According to Brigadier-General Gavish, four Egyptian divisions of Colonel Nasser's proud army had been totally destroyed while a further three divisions had been almost smashed. In the confusion of battle after dark some mobile units managed to escape. A ground-to-air missile launching base was captured intact between the Mitla Pass and the Suez Canal. A number of SA 2 ground-air missiles were found ready for launching. Egypt lost between 7,000 and 10,000 men killed. The number wounded and in hospitals was unknown. Israel lost 275 killed, 800 wounded and some slightly injured in the Sinai. She also lost 61 tanks.

Brigadier-General Samuel Eyal, head of "A" branch, General Headquarters Israel Army, told us after the war that nobody knew how many Egyptians were left in the desert.

"I can only say exactly how many prisoners we have in the cages. Any number I could give of those in the desert would be plucked out of the air. If we knew where they were, and if they were wandering along the axes, we would put them on vehicles and take them towards the Canal. If they were wounded we would treat them. There are 5,495 prisoners of war—4,500 Egyptians, 483 Jordanians, 333 Syrians, and 179 wounded of all the armies together, now in civilian hospitals. There are 90 wounded prisoners of war in the camp who are being cared for by the Army Medical Corps. The prisoners of war are in our central camp at Athlit." Some 300 identified themselves as officers, but several officers had removed their insignia of rank. Prisoners included nine Egyptian generals and ten colonels. The others were majors and below. They had released Egyptian prisoners of other rank in Sinai and sent them home. For three days they tried to collect prisoners to transport them back on Israel army vehicles towards the Canal. The Israeli Army also used loud-speakers to ask the Arabs to give themselves up, telling them that they would be treated in accordance with the Geneva convention.

There were very few Israeli prisoners in Arab hands, only nine in Egypt, two in Iraq, two in Syria, one in Lebanon and two in Jordan. Wounded prisoners who died in the hospital were given a military burial. Those who died on the battle-field were buried in the field, in accordance with Convention rules. First action had been to Israel's own wounded and those of the enemy. After that they had buried the dead.

Here are the answers to some pertinent questions asked of General Eyal:

Q. Was the water pipeline in the Sinai cut off by the Egyptians or by the Israelis?

A. It was cut off by the Egyptians.

Q. Is there a plan now to release all prisoners?

A. A Red Cross representative arrived a few hours ago (June 14th) from Kantura and there is a permanent representative here from Switzerland. We have already held meetings with them and I shall be meeting them again. I hope we can come to an arrangement for the exchange of prisoners.

Q. Are all the Israeli prisoners air force personnel?

A. There are three pilots and six soldiers.

Q. How do Egyptian soldiers manage to continue to move about the desert with arms?

A. During a battle when the soldiers run away from their equipment or leave the tanks or their artillery, they take with them small arms and they hide about one or two kilometres off the main roads, hoping that something will happen which will enable them to come back to their own equipment. This has happened in the past.

When the tanks were not destroyed, the crews have returned and have fired on convoys. Or they hope they can reach the Canal on foot or by any other forms of transportation. Only when they are near the roads and desperate do they give up their arms when asked to do so. A prisoner of war is a man who gives himself up and surrenders his arms, but if he keeps his arms and hides himself somewhere in the hundreds of square kilometres we cannot find him.

Q. Are there any non-Arabs among the prisoners?

A. No.

Q. Has any water been air-dropped to the prisoners?

A. The water to the Sinai was cut off and during recent days we have been forced to air-drop to our soldiers. Units which had prisoners in their possession of course shared this water with their prisoners, but as for Egyptians wandering about the desert—we do not know where they are and we therefore cannot give them any water. You must not forget this is war and if they disperse about Sinai this is an immense area—complete divisions get lost there. It's impossible to know how to get to the men who ran away. I asked the Red Cross representative who came today from Kantura by helicopter whether he had seen any stragglers. He said that although he had looked for them he had not seen any, he had only seen those who had reached Kantara.

Q. Would you deny that you hold any Russian prisoners?

A. It is categorically denied that we hold any Russian prisoners.

Those of us who had been in the Sinai campaign of 1956 could not help but compare it with its 1967 counterpart. Eleven years ago the Israelis, with the cooperation of the French and the British in Suez, and led by General Moshe Dayan, conquered most of the Sinai and demolished the Egyptian army in five days. Acting alone and led by General Gavish the Israelis had broken Egyptian resistance in three days. In 1956 the main thrust in the Sinai was through Nas el Nagb and Kuntilla with a parachute drop at the Mitla Pass that completely demoralized the Egyptians in the area. On October 30th, the thrust through Kuntilla passed Nakhl and a second developed in the direction of Abu Agheila. On the third day, October 31st, the Abu Agheila advance split into two and reached the center of Sinai. The Kuntilla advance stayed where it was as Britain and France made air attacks on the Suez Canal. On the fourth day, November 1st, the Israelis made four independent thrusts, one from just south of Gaza, aimed at that town, one through Abu Agheila, which approached the Suez Canal in two places, one through Kuntilla, which remained in the same place, and a fourth from the apex of the Negev aimed at Sharm el Sheikh. On the fifth day, November 2nd, the thrust on Gaza remained stationary. Another advance along the Sinai coastal road reached within striking distance of Port Said. So had the move through Kuntilla. The fourth thrust reached Sharm el Sheikh.

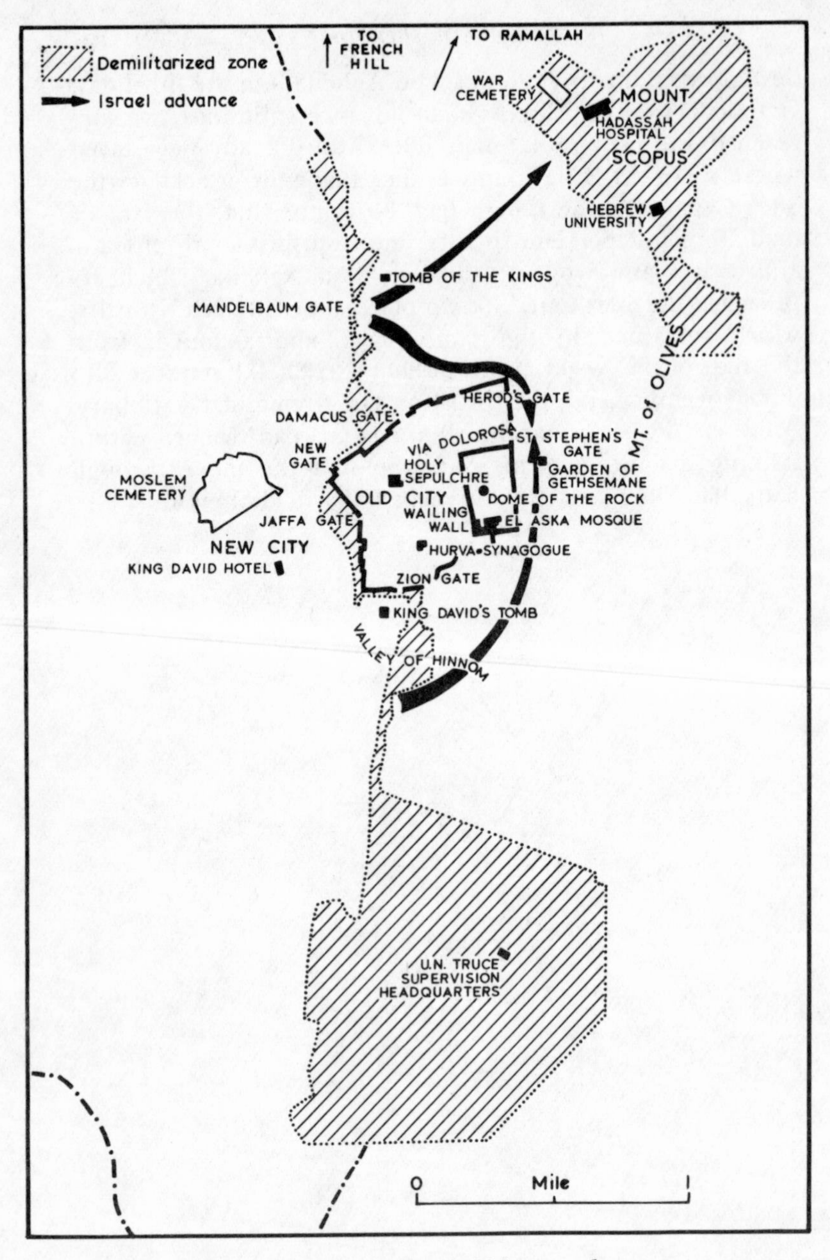

III The Capture of Old Jerusalem

12

BATTLE FOR JERUSALEM

A careful watch was kept on the number of reserves in the various assembly areas from the time the second war began on June 5th. Israel knew that her population was small and all forces had to operate within narrow limits. Aggregate demands for reinforcements in the Sinai battles were not so high as had been estimated. There were few demands for reinforcements after the destruction of the Egyptian Air Force. The reason was that the battles were fought mainly by the armor and relatively few tanks were put out of action from the air. Infantry played a secondary role in the desert, in skirmishes, in and around captured towns and in mopping up activities after the tanks had passed on.

The first alarm that there might be an unexpected demand for reinforcements came from the front with Jordan soon after the battle had started. Israel had hoped that it might not have to fight on more than one front. The General Staff had been urged to cooperate with the Government and go to all possible lengths to avoid a situation in which Israel would have to fight on the Northern Front as well as the Central Front with Jerusalem, a distance, in all, of 377 miles. The only way Israel could be defeated, according to strategists, was for the country to be subjected to simultaneous attack by four Arab nations on their borders in maximum strength, and with air cover. Even without massive air cover this could be touch and go. Intelligence reports stated there would be no trouble from the Lebanese. The Syrians could be expected to attack ferociously since Syria had been the major cause of provocation for a long time. Syrian Prime Minister Zayiyen had told the Arab Chamber of Advocates on May 29th: "This is but the beginning of the way. The Palestine people will make good its national right for the liberation of their homeland. It deserves every support from Arab progressive forces. This struggle will be the overture to the spread of the popular war of liberation. . . ."

Some Israeli observers did not attribute much importance to the military pact which King Hussein had signed with Colonel Nasser. Jordan was surrounded by enemies. The dramatic reconciliation between the young king and the Egyptian President was seen as still another effort to save the twenty-one-year-old kingdom from extinction. They recalled how Jordan, which became an independent kingdom as the result of a gesture by Winston Churchill, had developed since 1921 from a wild, desolate country which no one wanted into a promising land which was eyed greedily by its neighbors. All of them would gladly take part in its partition. Even some Israelis, though they were officially opposed to the annexation of territory, would not have been averse to taking over the Old City of Jerusalem or the West Bank of the Jordan to improve their security. Since the Anglo-Jordan treaty had ended by mutual consent in March 1957, there had been occasions when the Hashemite throne had seemed in extreme danger. It was still in danger following trouble with Syria. King Hussein had somehow managed to resist a succession of attempts at subversion by Syria, Egypt and Iraq. In 1958 he had been compelled to call for the support of British forces to maintain his regime. The latest of many perils came now from the Palestine Liberation Organization composed mainly of Palestine Arabs from Jordan. Its leader aspired to form a Jordan Army independent of King Hussein, for the express purpose of attacking Israel. King Hussein had no time for the organization which he knew Colonel Nasser had inspired and for which Nasser had chosen the leader. Israelis believed that if King Hussein could see a chance of removing all danger to Jordan he might hold fast. It may have been partly because of this thought process that the Israeli General Staff decided that the Central Command, which had a responsibility for the Jerusalem front, should be organized on purely defensive lines.

General Rabin, the Chief of Staff, more than anyone, was anxious to avoid full-scale battle with Jordan. He had seen battle many times, but the fighting in which he had been engaged in Jerusalem had made an indelible mark on his mind. He remembered with horror the action in the War of Liberation which aimed at trying to break through the blockade of Jerusalem. He once said of this: "Many of us fell. In fact half the men in my unit were killed. Men were tired, wounded and indignant, for we had almost no ammunition left and little protection against the enemy's fire. The men objected to attempting the breakthrough in open civilian trucks, but when I agreed that anybody unwilling to do it would be excused, not even one yielded his privilege of dying in order to secure the road to Jerusalem. During the fighting over Beit Mahsi, boys of seventeen and others not yet of military age went up as reinforcements. Half of them were mown down by Jordanian fire before they could fire a shot. The fighting was terrible. It lasted for five days."

The Israelis were prepared to go to greater lengths than national pride would normally allow to prevent a full-scale war against all four Arab nations. Fighting in the Sinai, in a largely empty desert, was one thing, but fighting on the Central border, especially in the Jerusalem sector, was quite another. Casualties and damage to property, the Holy Places included, would be heavy. Already the troops on the Israeli-Jordan line had been given strict instructions that they must at all costs avoid damage to the Old City and the Holy Places. To do this, they would first, before going into the city, have to surround the Old City completely to cut off support from outside, and then prevent shelling.

This was recognized as a hazardous operation and likely to be costly in lives. Jordanian units were known to be secreted in hidden pockets within the walls. Only with infinite care would the Israeli infantry be sent into the narrow, high-walled and twisting, stepped passages and alleyways to eliminate snipers and guerillas. This was made difficult because they would be indistinguishable from ordinary civilians. Old Jerusalem might have been designed for ambush. This operation would be infinitely more difficult than, for instance, a breakthrough to the Syrian plateau where huge concrete and steel defenses, the work of years of construction, were known to have been prepared to prevent flanking operations. It was the Jerusalem sector to which the Israeli Government had given most thought. The city was sacred to the Jews, as well as to Moslems and Christians. The Israeli population would react violently if, for instance, the West Wall of the Temple (the Wailing Wall) were damaged.

A number of secret moves had been made to try to persuade the Jordanians to see the folly of warfare in a densely populated city like Jerusalem. Israel hoped Jordan would remain on the defensive. Rabin was determined to remain on the defensive unless forced to act otherwise. It was rumored that one highplaced personage with the knowledge of Levi Eshkol had been in touch with the Basman Palace in Amman to try to dissuade King Hussein from initiating full-scale war.

Prime Minister Levi Eshkol made a radio broadcast a few hours after hostilities broke out between Israel and Egypt on June 5th and hoped this would have a restraining effect on Syria and Jordan. He said: "We shall not attack any State so long as it does not wage war against us. But anyone attacking us will meet with our full power of self defense."

The Israeli Government had reason at one stage to feel certain that King Hussein would not carry out the obligations arising from his agreement with Colonel Nasser. Had this been the case it would have had a profoundly beneficial effect on the Israeli position. Jordan had at its disposal on Israel's eastern border 60,000 troops and 300 tanks which had been placed under Egyptian command. The Jordanian troops were also supported by a number of Egyptian commando units which would prolong any fighting that took place. There were also Iraqui troops in position. It was stated that Colonel Nasser promised King Hussein proportionate help from his air force of modern Russian-built planes. This, he said, would mean that Jordanian troops would have complete air cover. It was officially stated in Jordan that Nasser repeated this promise of air cover in the early hours of June 5th, when he knew that his air force had been destroyed, mostly on the ground, in less than three hours. The Jordanian military commander, though he had no idea of this, refused to launch full-scale attack in accordance with the terms of the pact without the presence of air cover. Jordan had only twenty-eight British-built Hunters and five United States Star Fighters. In another radio-telephone message in the early hours Colonel Nasser told King Hussein that his air force was then raiding Israeli air bases to destroy their planes. This was, of course, a lie.

Brigadier-General Uzzi Narkis, Israeli Commander on the Central Front, set out in the early hours of June 5th "to play it by ear" on the Jerusalem Front. He knew as well as any military man who had ever toured Jordan that the area north of Jerusalem, between the Holy City and Ramallah, would be the place to attack, and at once, although the operation would inevitably be bloody. Whoever held the area would hold the whole of the West Bank of the Jordan. The Old City was like a rabbit pen. The Jordanian army, which the Israelis had fought in Jerusalem in 1948, was a tough force. They did not always have a second line, but they dug themselves in well. Their positions were always well fortified and they clung to them.

"First move," Narkis commented later, "was to hold fast, bite our lips and not answer fire even when the Jordanians opened up."

This was to enable King Hussein to satisfy himself with a "salute" and thereby fulfil his obligations to the Pan-Arab Agreement.

What happened came as a terrible shock to many Israelis. In spite of all the efforts to dissuade King Hussein from launching an attack (and let it be admitted his army was completely unprepared for this) the young monarch sent his army, under the overall command of the Egyptian General Riadh, into the attack along the whole border of the West Bank of the Jordan.

When this dramatic news reached the Israeli General Staff it was decided that the Central Front had to be reinforced with well seasoned troops. In the past, the Arab Legion, trained by General Glubb, had been tough fighters, especially in built-up areas which they knew intimately, and which the Israeli troops did not know at all. The Sinai front was going well and it might be possible to make some modification of the plan to open up new fronts in the Sinai.

The Chief of Staff, Major-General Rabin, had his attention drawn to a parachute brigade, commanded by Colonel Mordechai Gur, which was even then in fields adjoining a main air base awaiting orders from the General Staff to become airborne on an important operation. The parachute troops had a fine reputation. They had carried out the initial daring move in the 1956 Sinai campaign by a drop near the important strategic Mitla Pass. They had been expecting to carry out a similar operation, though they did not yet know where, in the present campaign. They had been keyed up for hours awaiting orders. Colonel Gur had been hanging grimly on the phone and the men had shown signs of impatience. As he hung on the telephone waiting for General Rabin to give the command, he could see that even his officers were beginning to get bored. To fill in time Colonel Gur ordered instructors again to inspect all parachutes. After a while the men were handed instruction sheets which kept them quiet again for a short time.

Meanwhile General Rabin had decided reluctantly that he had to cut out the proposed airborne operation and substitute another role. Men of the caliber of that brigade were needed in Jerusalem more than anywhere, although they had not been specifically trained for that kind of fighting. General Rabin probably thus consoled himself, as did General Keightly in Operation Musketeer (Suez) when he found he could not send all his paratroops in on an initial stage. Once paratroops are dropped they are "used for good" as far as the assault and the initial advance are concerned.

General Rabin informed Colonel Gur that he needed one of his battalions for another function. This, later, he amended to two battalions, and later still, to the entire brigade.

Colonel Gur was patient but bitterly disappointed. He told his men that the airborne operation to which they had been looking forward so keenly was cancelled. The brigade had to go to Jerusalem. The parachutes were collected from the men now scattered all over the field. Soon it became known that the brigade had been chosen to carry out a task of great responsibility fraught with tremendous danger and difficulty, to break through into a built-up area on the Jerusalem front. They had to connect up with Mount Scopus and create a situation on a front which was easily defended and from which they could break through into the Old City of Jerusalem.

Unit commanders conferred in anxious groups. None of them knew the area in which they were to operate and which was contiguous with Israeli Jerusalem. All kinds of fears were expressed about an attack in strange territory in the dark. For many of the disappointed paratroops this would be their first visit to Jerusalem. As it happened it was to be their last!

Colonel Gur had managed to visit Jerusalem earlier, together with other commanders. He had studied the area closely in case he ever had to command an operation there. He knew, without being told, that his unit commanders were not familiar with it. Gur decided, therefore, on an unusual move. He sent all his unit commanders on to Jerusalem in trucks ahead of their men so that they could get a quick look round, if this were possible, before dark. Next came the problem of moving the brigade to Jerusalem. This was solved by acquiring a fleet of public buses which had been taken off the streets to be available for troop movements. The brigade followed their officers along the narrow, twisting roads to Jerusalem, not all of them singing as troops usually sing in such circumstances. Many were deeply disappointed about the last minute change in a role for which they had undergone severe special training for years.

The battle was in full swing when Colonel Gur's unit commanders arrived but they were able to approach the boundary line and take a look at positions ahead. They were able to fix the axis of the movement they were to make, and determine the various stages of the action.

It became still more apparent when the brigade arrived and moved into the area of Beit Hakerem that many of the men were complete strangers to the area. Even the few who had been there before had never realized the extent of the sector. Nor had they looked at the sector with the eyes of potential attackers. Brief and improvised instruction sheets were handed out amid the clamor of battle when it was almost too dark to read them. Maps were frantically inspected under the light of shielded flashlights. Then, without any delay, the troops began to move. Many things had to be improvised. The additional loads to be carried, the extra ammunition and the exact makeup of the force groups for this entirely new operation had to be worked out while the men were in movement.

The brigade had planned to start the attack at midnight, June 5th, but this was found impossible. The attack had to be held up. Difficulties arose from unfamiliarity of the unit commanders with the area and with the adjoining built-up sector in Jewish Jerusalem. It was realized as the Jordanian artillery heavily shelled the area and the place rocketed with machine-gun fire that they would inevitably have heavy casualties. It was decided, therefore, to prepare in advance an even better evacuation system for the wounded, so that they would be taken to the central hospitals as rapidly as possible. Time dragged on. It was finally 2 a.m. The brigade had not moved. The question arose whether to attack that night or wait until morning so as to get more support, particularly air support.

Colonel Gur gathered the battalion commanders together in the dark and asked for their opinions. Every single officer expressed the desire to launch the attack immediately in spite of the difficulties of recognizing the terrain. They preferred to traverse the area from what was formerly Jewish Jerusalem up to the area of the barricades and the fortifications in darkness. So the final decision was made. The attack was to begin at 2 a.m. on June 6th. Colonel Gur climbed up on to a roof in the center of the sector just before that hour in the midst of heavy shelling to take a last look at the situation.

As soon as the brigade opened fire the Jordanians intensified their bombardment. The brigade suffered casualties even before they had made contact with the enemy. The area was very familiar to the Jordanians and it had been marked out in advance. The Israelis suffered heavily in casualties from the first shots. The wounded, in their agony, complained that if they had at least succeeded in "lifting the 'Uz zis' (automatics) or in throwing grenades" they might have been spared. To be hit and have to go back to the hospital before they accomplished anything meant they had not taken part in the battles. This was what happened to scores of Israelis. Upon advancing still further artillery fire had at once been directed at them. The brigade's very first operation was to evacuate the wounded to the rear. At 2:20 a.m. the brigade began to get artillery support. Tanks rolled forward down a nearby slope and took up positions. As soon as the noise of the tracks was heard, the Jordanians opened still heavier fire along the entire length of the line. From then on the battalion commanders carried out their tasks and shelling increased in intensity.

Israel's Brigadier-General Narkis, although he had been instructed to be patient, had understood that if Mount Scopus, which had been held by an Israeli police post for years, was attacked he was to wait no longer. Mount Scopus was known to be threatened by a whole armored brigade of 88 Patton tanks, sited on Jericho Square, as well as by the 27th Jordan Infantry Brigade. The General kept the mount under view. Israel could not allow such a disgrace that Scopus should be taken by Jordanian troops.

Mount Scopus (which dominates Jerusalem from the northeast) had played a decisive role in many battles for the Holy City from the beginning of history. It was here that the Roman Legions of Titus camped in A.D. 70 and the Crusaders in 1099, and the British after they entered Jerusalem in 1917. The Arab invaders, also from Mount Scopus, had tried in vain to subdue the forces of New Jerusalem during the War of Liberation in 1948 and had been appropriately dealt with. To the Jews, Scopus was more than a rocky mountain. It was a mountain of prestige. Since the War of Liberation the mount, with the Hadassah hospital and the Hebrew University, had been cut off from Jerusalem proper because the road leading to it lay in Jordanian territory and it had thereby acquired legendary fame. The buildings were guarded by Israeli police. Under the supervision of a United Nations observer a convoy travelled proudly once every two weeks under the Israeli flag from the temporary premises of the Hebrew University to Mount Scopus through the Mandelbaum Gate. The Israeli police, in off duty moments, had looked over New and Old Jerusalem from their vantage point on the mount. Some of them had uttered silent prayers that one day the two parts of this living organism would become one under Jewish jurisdiction. The sight of the two parts of the divided city and of the surrounding mountains must have recalled to pious Hebrews the words of a psalm: "As the mountains are round about Jerusalem, so the Lord is round about his people. . . ." The area of the summit of Mount Scopus was two miles long and sixteen hundred feet wide, and General Narkis decided that every effort was to be made to capture it. The troops went speedily into action with the minimum strength needed to reach the objective.

Jordan's offensive along her border with Israel had begun earlier with a bombardment by 25-pounders, 120 mm. mortars, and even 155 mm. "Long Toms." The aim was to reach over the border and hit Israeli settlements from one end of the Central Command to the other, southwards to Mount Hebron. The points attacked in the first hours included Eyal, Ramat Hakovesh, Kfar Sirkin, Yad Hannah, Raanana, the Kaplan quarter and even Tel Aviv itself. Israeli Jerusalem was attacked along its length and breadth. Nathanya, Kfar Saba, Sirkin and several crossroads were also bombed by enemy aircraft. When General Narkis had seen that the Jordan action had exceeded what was expected of a "salute" and "meeting an obligation," he gave orders to reply as required in each sector. Jordanian action quickly developed. Government House, which had been in the possession of the United Nations, was taken by the Jordanians with the apparent intention of holding it and from there advancing on Israeli Jerusalem. The whole of the Central Command went into action. The war raced on at a frantic pace.

Preparations for the Israeli assault had been made by the Commander of the Israeli Jerusalem Area, who knew the enemy terrain. At midday, June 5th, Brigadier-General Narkis was sent one battalion for support from Area Command and told he might get additional forces. It was about this stage that the Israeli Parachute Brigade, commanded by Colonel Mordechai Gur, burst into the most difficult area of Jerusalem and through it to Mount Scopus; they also moved on to the Police Training School and the Sheikh Jarrah district containing the Mandelbaum Gate (which I inspected on the evening before war broke out). The very presence on that Front of Gur's heroic brigade suggested to all a radical change in the tactical plan of the offensive.

"The fighting was of a sort," Colonel Gur remarked later of one action, "I had *never* experienced, both as to intensity and duration. The men had to break through at least five fences before they reached the emplacements."

The paratroopers managed to enter the Jordanian trenches and fighting became intensely fierce and confused. There was fighting in the trenches, on the roofs and parapets and in the cellars—everybody and anywhere. The battle in the trenches lasted four hours, from 2:20 a.m. to 7 a.m. It was considered by many commanders to have been one of the most extraordinary examples of fighting for a fortified position. The Parachute Brigade actually fought in all for seven and one-half hours without a pause and captured most of the difficult objectives in the Old City.

The resistance in the trenches indicated the bravery of the Jordanians. They fought far better than the Egyptians in the Sinai. As the battle continued ammunition was rushed up from the rear. The Israeli unit commanders did most of this work as if they were laborers. They felt in duty bound to be in the forefront of the mopping up operations in the trenches. There were many instances of bravery. On one occasion the Israelis had reached a bunker containing two heavy machine guns. The Israelis did not know about this as it had been hard to pinpoint by air-photograph. The commander was on top of the bunker before he realized there was a bunker there. Just then a soldier jumped up, climbed above the bunker, and dropped a grenade from above, although he was completely exposed. The grenade exploded, but the firing from the bunker continued. Then other Israelis threw to him three charges of explosives. The first soldier jumped to the other side of the trench and exploded the three charges. Only three Jordanians were killed. Two continued to fire. The soldier then rushed up again and flung another grenade into the bunker and silenced the firing. Some unit commanders, who did not ask for reinforcements, finished the fighting with four soldiers left in every company.

The Sheikh Jarah quarter of Jordan Jerusalem, which is dominated by the Mandelbaum Gate, was the second sector in the battle. "We continued to advance from fence to fence, from house to house, until at last we crossed the road and entered the American section where we proceeded with our mopping up operations," Colonel Gur said. "By this time we already had quite a number of casualties. Some of the doctors had been hit. At this point a civilian girl orderly came up to one of the evacuation points with an ambulance. Seeing what was going on, she refused to turn back. She stayed with us until the end of the battle dealing with the wounded. Our two regiments continued to advance. The Ambassador Hotel fell into our hands. The whole of the American sector fell to us a little later. Some of the Jordanians retreating from the front line took cover inside the buildings, and so there was house to house fighting. Sometimes it was necessary to deal with the same house twice. Here we suffered casualties in the streets. The Jordanians continued to fire from those houses which had not yet been dealt with. Some of our men were shot from behind. As dawn broke a little after 4 a.m. (June 7th), we engaged our tank battalion. We distributed the tanks between the regiments. Fighting went on in the inner courts while we went on mopping up along our main lines of advance up to the Rockefeller Museum. We now threw in our third regiment, the one that had been fighting in the Mandelbaum Gate area. Its orders were to reach Herod's Gate —a very important point, since it was through this gate that we planned to pour our infantry into the Old City. . . ."

At the same time the Israeli armored brigade had continued northward in the direction of Ramallah. Another brigade captured the Abu Tor section of Jerusalem during the night and advanced along the Mar Elias-Bethlehem axis to the final clean-up of Mount Hebron. The armored division captured Ramallah on the evening of June 6th, then continued to move northward in the direction of Nablus. The troops quickly descended into the valley to capture Jericho. There were, of course, additional axes on which two other forces moved—one took Latrum and then proceeded up to Ramallah, and a second force moved along the Qalqiliya Tulkarem axis and arrived north and west of Nablus. When the Jordan cease-fire went into effect, the entire West Bank of the Jordan was within the Central Command's jurisdiction.

Another armored brigade, commanded by Colonel Uri Ben-Ari, which, according to plan, was to be used for a counter-attack within the Command had been earlier instructed to go immediately to the Jerusalem area and to penetrate the vital terrain between Ramallah and north Jerusalem. Ben-Ari's brigade had to pass along three axes, Radar (named after the radar opposite Maale Hamamisha), Sheikh Abdul Raziz and Beth Aksa, all of them mountains about 2,100 feet high with narrow twisting paths. They had been sown with mines as fields are with oats. Colonel Ben-Ari's brigade went into the attack within four hours of having left the plain, providing a startling example of the speed with which Israeli troops operate. They received the order to attack at 1 p.m. The order had been carried out by 5 p.m. Ben-Ari, who had known the area well twenty years before when he had attacked its concrete posts and fortified villages in the War of Liberation, was full of admiration for his men. All of them were reserves over normal military age. Some of them were grandfathers. As an officer commented later, the way the men completed the task proved that it was not the vehicles or their armaments which were the fundamental factor in success but the commanders and the men under them. The brigade had confronted two enemies: the Jordanians, who had fought with determination (and with skill traceable to British training), and the terrain, which was as bad as any the brigade had encountered.

Sheikh Abdul Azia and the Radar opposite Maale Hamamisha were in Israeli hands just before 1 a.m. on June 7th. They next took a fortified locality called Biddu after a heavy fight with many casualties. This was in the hours of darkness, and the people in nearby dwellings first tried to escape and then cowered in cellars and shelters. The back of the mountain ridge between Ramallah and Jerusalem was reached by 4 a.m. The brigade gathered on top of the mountain to breathe in the cool morning air and to watch dawn break. It was almost like a miracle as birds began slowly, then in a chorus, to sing as if all were peaceful. As the sun began to rise the brigade look-outs watched the important road from the river Jordan to Jerusalem. It was not long after this idyllic interval that a tank battle developed with thirty Patton tanks of a Jordanian crack brigade on the heights dominated by a place called Tel Poul where King Hussein had built a palace. Seven Pattons were destroyed. Some thirteen thought discretion the better part of valor and rumbled off on the road to Jericho. Where the others went in the heat of battle no one knew, but Colonel Ben-Ari made a note to keep a look-out for more Patton tanks along the road when he advanced later.

The Israelis had been given the order to take a rise called, for some strange reason, French Hill. The Israeli armor moved south, unaffected by sniping. The battle that followed the easy conquest of a place called Sha'afat was unexpectedly tough.

Colonel Ben-Ari was a commander of experience and little surprised him. He had been in the thick of night battles in the Sinai and much had been later said about the murderous fire. The battle near French Hill was several times worse. His men did not take the hill at first attempt. They had to retire, which is what Israelis hate to do, re-form, get a talking to as if they were civilians pretending to be soldiers (which is often what they are) and then attack again. Then French Hill fell more easily. Two battalions then advanced.

For the first time in the experience of Ben-Ari, or of the brigade, they had to try to capture a city (Ramallah) in the dark. They approached Ramallah with a battalion of tanks, shooting on all sides as they went. They crossed and re-crossed the city several times in the most un-military-text-book style and waited for it to fall. There was resistance from bazookas, but within less than an hour all resistance had ceased. The brigade did not waste time. This round of battle was like a Cook's tour headed by a guide who had to get home to his new wife. The brigade continued on to oasis-like Jericho, which, owing to the depression below sea level in which it is situated, is seen only when one is nearly on top of it. There was no resistance en route, but the outposts and look-outs, which moved ten miles in advance of the brigade, discovered the rest of the Patton tanks. The entire Jericho landscape and the Dead Sea were revealed, lush and silvery in the hot sun.

The brigade moved along two lines. One battalion attacked the police station—the most important part of Jericho—and another battalion used the "Ramallah method" of attack (which may find itself in the Israeli text-books) of going through Jericho and back again, wiping out all resistance on the way. Sniping and enemy movements continued throughout the night. When morning came the brigade "mopped up" the town which suddenly fell silent. The brigade then went down to Beth Ha'arava (on the shores of the Dead Sea), but not to take a look at the place where Christ was baptized. This move actually completed the operations of the division. One battalion went north and seized the Chabara camp which lies before Nablus, where it linked up with other units which had taken the town.

Colonel Gur's parachute brigade, which this narrative left outside the gates of Old Jerusalem, was mopping up the exterior walls, the tops of which have afforded protection for snipers ever since the rifle was invented. They had nearly finished all the areas allocated to them by 10 a.m. on June 6th.

The most dramatic moment of the war for Colonel Gur's men, and the entire Israeli army, was fast approaching. The Jews would soon enter the high gates of the Old City of Jerusalem, from which they had for so long been excluded. They would see with their own eyes the Holy Places, including the most sacred western wall of Solomon's temple, the Wailing Wall, of which they had heard in legend, in stories at the knees of their fathers, or seen in sacred pictures. The Jews had been expected suddenly to be vitalized, as if inspired, by this prospect of entering the mysterious, forbidden city of the Arabs, but instead many of the troops became suddenly lethargic. The impetus of the attack declined. The Jews had been engaged in a series of minor actions for many hours and they might have been tired, but they were more likely to have been overcome by emotion and awe. The

Arabs seemed to discern hesitation. They crept onto the high parapet again, just as in Hollywood films Arabs always do when their walled cities are assaulted. They sniped all along the gate. Soon it was impossible for the Jews to move without being hit. Jerusalem was as sacred to the Arabs as it was to the Israelis. Until the attackers had captured the walls it would not be possible to move inside or along the streets outside to reach Augusta Victoria heights, seen inviting them from a distance. A tank battalion which had recently come into action, and had suffered many losses, was ordered to regroup. The attack was resumed towards evening. At nightfall the Israelis employed two reduced tank battalions, one for cover and one to advance straight up the road to Augusta Victoria. Anti-tank fire hit a tank which went up in flames, as did some reconnaissance jeeps. The Israelis had casualties from the very first moment. They decided to make slight changes in their schedule.

The Israelis adopted in this action unconventional moves which in ordinary circumstances would never have been used. One regiment drove straight uphill from Mount Scopus to Augusta Victoria. Another regiment conducted a daylight frontal attack while Jordanians on the wall in their rear continued firing at them. Troops advanced through built-up areas. Colonel Gur decided to take whatever risk there might be. The third regiment pushed on along the wall from Herod's Gate, regardless of fire from the wall. All that mattered now was that the Israelis had to break through the wall and reach the Temple Mount.

"Not knowing for sure what the enemy position was," Colonel Gur said after the battle, "we decided to disregard our lack of information and go according to plan. We brought in the air force at 8:30 a.m. Although the Mount Scopus regiment asked for another fifteen minutes to prepare I could not let them have it. I gave orders to attack at once. I instructed our tanks to start moving up to see where contact would be effected with the enemy, so that I could determine the battle plan. We laid down a heavy artillery cover. Our tanks advanced and fired in every direction. After them I sent a mechanized unit with recoilless guns. Now everything broke loose. We jumped into the command half-track and pushed forward, giving the Mount Scopus regiment its orders to advance at top speed and the second regiment to start its frontal attack. As we reached the crossroads we saw that matters were far simpler and easier than we had imagined. We knew there were tanks farther up and in the direction of A-Tur and the Eizariya junction. We turned our column left along the ridge and swept it with heavy fire. During the mopping up operation we found plenty of enemy ammunition. Eventually our column was in the square facing the Old City. The Temple Mount was before us, with its gold and silver cupolas, and all the New City beyond. At this point, I ordered my brigade to attack the Old City. The plan called for a tank advance along the road to a gate. Three infantry regiments were ordered to move as far forward as possible—whoever came first, well, that would be his luck."

The Israelis began to shell the Moslem quarter of the Old City which bordered the wall; otherwise defenders might have prevented Israeli forces from breaking through Herod's Gate. The shelling lasted ten minutes and was effective. All the tanks opened fire, and so did troops with recoilless guns. The whole wall was swept but not a shot was directed at, or hit, the Holy Places. The breakthrough area came in for concentrated fire. The wall shook and some stones were loosened to the right of St. Stephen's Gate.

"When I saw the tanks advance towards the Wall," said Colonel Gur, later, "we got into our half-track and went on to catch up with them, while ordering them to proceed at a faster pace. The infantry were also ordered to keep up with the tanks. For a moment I stopped the artillery fire, but after our tanks had spotted the enemy positions, we renewed firing and continued our advance up to the bridge beneath St. Stephen's Gate. The tanks found it more difficult to maneuver at this point, but it was by this time impossible to check our impetus."

Colonel Gur ordered his sturdy driver, Ben Tsur, a bearded fellow weighing some 210 pounds, to speed on ahead. They passed the tanks and saw the Gate before them with a car burning outside it. There wasn't a lot of room, but the Colonel told Tsur to drive on. They passed the burning car and saw St. Stephen's Gate half-opened in front. Regardless of the danger that somebody might drop grenades into their half-track from above, Tsur pushed on and flung the door aside. The half-track crunched over the fallen stones, passed a dazed Arab soldier, turned left, and came to a third gate. Here, a motorcycle lay blocking the way. In spite of the danger of booby-traps Tsur drove right over it. So Colonel Gur reached the Temple Mount. There was no more firing because it was a Holy Place. The Israeli tanks could not, unfortunately, get there but the infantry regiments raced along. So the operation was completed. There only remained mopping up to be done.

At this point the Governor of the City came up to Gur, together with the Kadi (a Moslem religious dignitary), and informed the colonel of the solemn decision "not to defend the Old City." The Governor assured Colonel Gur that the troops had all left. There would be no further resistance. Colonel Gur promised him that the Israelis would start mopping up without shooting. They would only shoot if they met resistance. The Governor replied politely he could not be responsible for snipers opening fire but there was no more resistance. Thus had ended the battle for Jerusalem. One regiment occupied the Nablus Gate area, another held the corner of the wall facing Yemin Moshe, a third occupied the Dung Gate area near Mount Zion.

In the battle for Old Jerusalem, Israel lost some 180 dead from the three brigades involved.

It was at the Wailing Wall in the Old City that I later witnessed a ceremony which will enter Israeli history books and religious works as one of the greatest events of all time. I saw all the Israeli Army Commanders, who had come there, as if on a magic carpet, with Major-General Moshe Dayan, the Defense Minister, and Major-General Itzhak Rabin, the Chief of Staff. The two great heroes stood together in that sunken place where voices echo against the wall of Solomon's first temple and where material things fade almost to insignificance. This was the great emotional climax of the whole war. The troops, muzzles of their Uzi automatics still hot after hours of firing, actually wept at the sight of it, as if they were children. Men who had seen so many buildings destroyed by war in the past week that a ruin was an entity in itself, looked at the sacred surviving wall of Solomon's first temple without realizing that this was the actual relic of a previous war when the Temple was destroyed by the Babylonians in the sixth century B.C. They saw the Wall complete and perfect as a shrine with its sacred meaning for all Jews. They prayed God that it had not been damaged in the fighting. They did not even realize that the second temple was destroyed by the Romans in still another war which turned Jerusalem into a holocaust and sent their early ancestors into the *Diaspora.* Mount Moreab, on which the Wall stands, was, as they all knew, intimately associated with the life of Abraham (it was the place where he offered up his son as a sacrifice). They did not know, however, that it got its name from Mora, which in Hebrew means awe.

If ever I saw awe on the faces of people it was to be seen on those of the unique congregation before the Wall. All who were there stared for seconds, which seemed like hours, at the high structure before them, built by King Solomon in 960 B.C., its stones smooth as silk through being stroked. They remembered how in the old days Jews had made pilgrimages there the occasion of a fast in memory of the Temple. They remembered the old legend that at night the stones of the Wall are covered with little drops of dew, the tears which the Wailing Wall sheds for all Israel. The men there assembled, strong, open, masculine types, with chests like barrels, hirsute and burned brown by the desert sun, put their weapons aside for a moment as if they were walking sticks and wiped tears from their eyes with the backs of sweating hands. One burly sergeant in the infantry, who must have been an unholy terror to his men, sat with tears trickling unashamedly down his cheeks. It was only then that I had the slightest idea what the Wailing Wall meant to Jews. In all the wanderings in exile, Jews who had come to Israel from sixty-four countries all over the world had cherished the fond hope that they might be spared to make at least one pilgrimage to the Wailing Wall. Men who had been severely wounded and had died in the attack earlier, had begged comrades who had given them succor in their last moments to go to the Wailing Wall and deposit between the stones written prayers for them and their families. Even those soldiers who had come to Israel from thousands of miles away and had found a home and work in New Jerusalem had doubted this moment would ever materialize, that they would ever see the Wailing Wall of which their fathers and grandfathers had told them so often. The shrine, to them in New Jerusalem, had seemed so near and yet was so far. They had worried that it was in the hands of Moslems who knew nothing of its meaning. Arab children had played football in that sunken place and chalked goalposts on the holy stones. Now, after sixty hours of furious fighting, the two parts of Jerusalem were united under the Star of David which already flew in the passage high above the Wall. Two bleeding halves of an organic whole had been put together again in the hope that they would unite.

I looked around from the top of a flight of steps that led down to the Wall and saw first the solemn gathering of the commanders below and then, to the left, the Arabs who were looking dismally at wrecked houses or smashed cars which had been parked in the street while the fighting took place. The Chief Rabbi began to recite the blessing. Suddenly my mind was brought back to the scene with a fearful jolt, by the penetrating blast of the Shofar or ram's horn. It made my blood run cold as it did that of the Moslems who heard it. The sound echoed for some seconds in the silence that followed. It seemed to awaken the ghosts of Old Jewry of long departed days. More soldiers came to the top of the steps and stared down to see what was happening. To their amazement they saw all their leaders uttering silent prayers of thanks for the miracles which had made the great transition possible. Some soldiers swore that they would never allow this shrine to go back to Islam. The Arabs had contaminated it. A soldier with a bayonet that still had upon it stains of alien blood shed in close combat climbed up to remove the name which the Moslems had given to the Wall—El Baraq, the name of Mohammed's horse "which bore him to heaven." Someone donned the Tallith and prayed aloud. Someone else, a veteran far too old for the combatant's uniform he wore, flourished a Sefa Tora which had been used in the 1956 Sinai campaign.

In the moments that followed I had the opportunity of seeing close together and for the first time two great men,

Moshe Dayan, the victor of Sinai, and Itzhak Rabin, the victor of the war that had nearly ended. They were a curious pair. The sight of them filled me with reverence, yet they seemed to suggest some truth in a rumor I had heard that the two men were professional rivals and likely to become keener political rivals. This was not a time for light gay chatter, but I felt that even if these two men had been standing together at a cocktail party, instead of before that Wall, they would have found little to say to each other, apart from talking shop about the war. The two men seemed in one sense to be far apart, to be different in personality and outlook. I could imagine them being irritable with each other over trifling details. The rumors of the rivalry between these two men, who, between them, had saved a nation from extinction and won a victory, may be entirely unfounded. They might have been based on errors made by well-intentioned journalists in dispatches to foreign newspapers. Some of them had given credit for the planning of the present campaign, which was a work of genius, to Moshe Dayan, although he had retired from the army years before and occupied himself since in agriculture and in the law. Some had written long articles and ascribed to him details of planning which had the signature of General Rabin written all over them. When friends had drawn the attention of the two generals to these articles they had treated them lightly. Moshe Dayan had later dissociated himself from the information which some had contained. Itzhak Rabin had only smiled. He had replied quietly that he did not anyway take much notice what the press said about him. There was, however, a fundamental impediment in the relationship between the two personalities which prevented their becoming intimate friends. Some newspapers had also suggested that General Rabin was being schooled for a political life as a "counter balance" for Moshe Dayan, and this I think was true. It was inevitable that Dayan should have been sensitive to this. The actions of Rabin concerned him if only because he (Dayan) was the former Chief of Staff and Rabin was his successor. He knew all the difficulties of the job. He would have been less than human at times, if, as Rabin's boss, he had not thoughtfully reminded him of some of the snags of the Sinai or some of the military aspects of the

Egyptian Army. Rabin looked far more affected by the gathering at the Wall than Dayan. The reason was obvious. Rabin was born in Jerusalem. He had fought there in the War of Liberation. When he had entered the Old City a short time before in the Company of Dayan, through the Lions' Gate, he had been filled with emotion. He admitted later that that day was perhaps the most important one in his life.

When the two leaders spoke to the assembled commanders they also addressed a far wider audience. Dayan addressed the Defense Army of Israel. Rabin went further and added the words "on land, at sea and in the air." "We have defeated the enemy," Dayan said, readjusting the patch over his lost eye. "We have crushed his forces and frustrated his plot but the price we have paid is a very heavy one: [the loss of] the best of our comrades, the bravest of our fighters, the dearest of our sons who have fallen in action. The sands of the desert and the rocks of the Sea of Galilee are drenched with their blood. Victory is ours—and so is bereavement. The battle is over but there is no end in sight as yet to our struggle. Those who rose against us have been vanquished but have not yet made peace with us. Return your swords to your scabbards, but keep them ever-ready, for the time has not yet come when you can beat them into plowshares."

Major General Itzhak Rabin addressed "The Defense Army that had liberated the Sinai, taken the Western Bank and broken the blockade leading to Eilat." They had, he said, smashed the threat to Israel's security and had protected her citizens.

"It is with affection and pride," he went on, "that the whole nation salutes you today for the decisive victory you have brought us. It was not handed to us on a silver platter: you have achieved it after heavy fighting soaked in blood and sweat. You have shown the most extraordinary leadership and valor. As in the past, so today, the Defense Army of Israel has shown its mettle in carrying out faithfully with the utmost determination the task with which it was charged. As in the past, so today all of us wearing the uniform—soldiers of the regular army and members of the reserve units—have stood shoulder to shoulder, sharing the blood brotherhood of love of our country with the members of the border settlements along all our frontiers, with the citizens of Jerusalem and the inhabitants of the towns and villages of the north, east and south. Ready and prepared, the Defense Army of Israel has met the enemy face to face and has defeated him unaided and alone. The fighting was savage and hard [it still went on in the North]. Many of our comrades in arms have fallen in action. Their sacrifice shall not have been in vain. To the bereaved families I say—it is the supreme courage in battle of your dear ones that has enabled us to achieve victory. The countless generations of Jews murdered, martyred and massacred for the sake of Jerusalem say to you—comfort ye, our people; console the mothers and the fathers whose sacrifices have brought about redemption."

All Israel heard those brave words from Dayan and Rabin. Those who were not bereaved celebrated quietly and in a dignified way the Sinai and Jerusalem victory over their enemies, and those who were bereaved found consolation in their great sorrow. There were no speeches later, no boastful eulogies on *Kol Israel.* The Israel newspapers were for once allowed to speak the thoughts of the entire nation about the capture of Old Jerusalem. Here are a few extracts from what was written:

Davar (Histadrut) wrote: "Two thousand years have not diminished the yearning in every Jewish heart for the Holy City of Jerusalem. For two thousand years the Jewish people in all its wanderings through exile, has preserved the vision of returning to Israel's eternal capital. Yesterday the vision of many generations has come true."

Ha'aretz (non-party) wrote: "There are no words to express the feelings throbbing within our hearts at this hour. Jerusalem is no more divided, but united under the flag of Israel. . . . All of Jerusalem is ours. Rejoice and be merry, people of Zion."

Hayom (Independent): "Thank the Lord for He is good, for His mercy endureth forever. This is the day we have been longing for. . . . Millions of Jews for many generations have been dreaming of this great day. Coming generations will be proud of those of us who lived in these glorious historic days."

Hatzofeh (National Religious Party): "When the Lord restored Jerusalem-within-the-Walls to Israel, we were as dreamers. Happy is the Generation, the flower of whose youth, the soldiers and commanders of the Israel Defense Forces, have enabled us to reunite the Holy City."

Al Hamishmar (Mapam): "The campaign forced on Israel is not over yet, but the sixty hours, beginning from Monday morning, have not only changed the position and status of Israel, but the face of the entire Middle East. Great events have taken place in our lives. . . . But from the Jewish historical point of view, the greatest of them all is the unification of Jerusalem, under the flag of Israel."

She'Arim (Poalei Agudat Israel) wrote: "Holy Jerusalem, Old Jerusalem, the site of the Temple and the Wailing Wall, is again in the hands of Israel. With God's help we have liberated her from alien captivity and hoisted on her walls the flag of free and liberated Israel—after she had fallen to Edom two thousand years ago, and nineteen years ago to Ishmael."

Omer (Histadrut) wrote: "The greatest day of all has come: Jerusalem, Israel's eternal capital, is not divided any more. . . . The heart overflows with joy and humility. . . . In humility and gratitude we shall put Jerusalem above our chief joys. The Lord has brought about this day."

Lamerhav (Achdut Ha'Avoda), instead of an editorial, printed excerpts from Isaiah, Chapter 62: "For Zion's sake I shall not be silent, for Jerusalem I shall not keep my peace. . . ."

13

JORDAN AND SYRIA

The quarrel between President Atassi of Syria and King Hussein of Jordan continued even after war began. News reached Damascus and Amman almost at the same time from Colonel Nasser in Cairo stating that hostilities had begun with air raids and that they must all fight together. Colonel Nasser knew of the quarrel between the two countries over the explosion of a Syrian bomb which killed fourteen Jordanians, but he hoped that this would not prevent the two Arab enemies of Israel on the same sensitive northern front from entering into close military liaison to bring about the enemy's downfall. Colonel Nasser was enough of a strategist to realize that if Syria and Jordan threw all their joint weight into a broad attack on Israel it would prevent the Jews taking risks on the Sinai front. Israel had a small army and if all the Arabs synchronized their attacks the impetus would be taken out of any one Israeli thrust. The Egyptian President had one fear, and that was that he would be left to fight Israel alone as was the case in 1956. He had moved heaven and earth to make sure Israel would have two fronts at least on which to fight. He also sent to Amman, to take up the overall Egyptian command provided for in the treaty with Jordan, General Riadh, a man of forceful personality and determination who would brook no half measures from the Hashemites.

The fact is that there was no liaison between the Jordanian tanks and infantry and the Syrian tanks on the joint northern border, just as there had also been no mutual acknowledgement by the General Staffs of Jordan and Syria that the two Arab countries were allies in war with a common foe. There

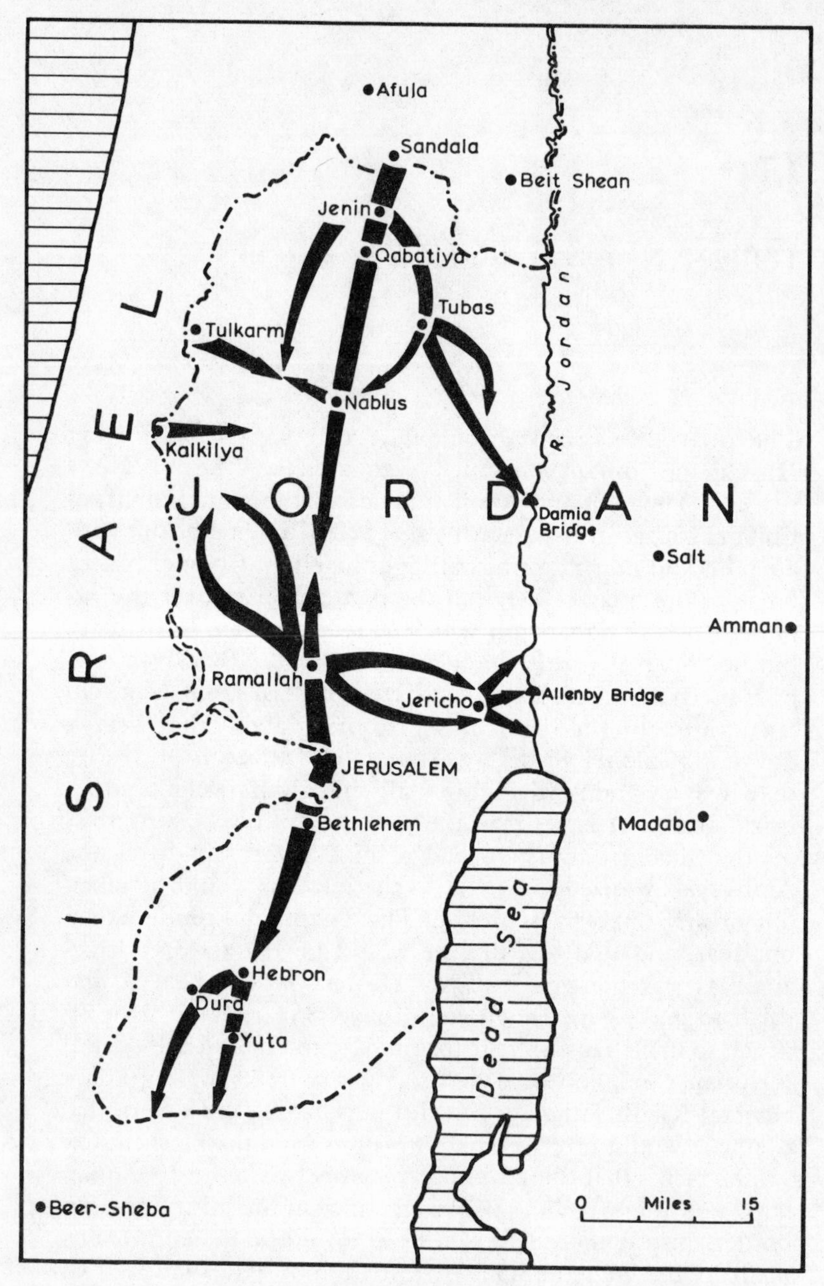

IV Operations on the West Bank of the Jordan

was also no communication between President Atassi and King Hussein. Israeli Intelligence, sensitive to anything that might affect the burden of the Defense Forces in the north, learned by intercepting messages that the two Arab countries were still uncoordinated.

There had some time before been joint planning to cover such an eventuality. Arrangements had been made for liaison officers to make contact on the joint border south of the Sea of Galilee. There had also been some optimistic conjecture about what the Arabs would do to the Israelis in their major tourist area to which millions of foreign tourists came to visit the Mount of Beatitudes where Jesus is said to have given the Sermon on the Mount; the Sea of Galilee, where Christ is reputed to have walked upon the water and where his disciples fished, and the monastery near to the well-known miracle of the loaves and fishes. They had decided, when Israel had been cleared from the area, to make their headquarters in Tiberias, Herod's city.

Israel feared that when news came of the air disasters, all Arabs would at once sink their differences. Nothing of the kind. Syria and Jordan did not unite even after their air forces had been demolished. They did not join forces in the effort to put the blame for the air attacks on Britain and the United States. Syria confined herself to artillery bombardment, mainly on Israeli settlements, and did not send her infantry or armor over the border. Israel took advantage of this and remained on the defensive. Fire was directed at the Israeli Command from the Jordan front from the early hours of June 5th but there was little ground fire from Syria. Obviously, Syria was going to let Jordan take the full brunt of the Israeli-Arab war on that sector. If Jordan got the better of exchanges Syria would at once join in and collect the spoils of victory, but if Israel began to teach Jordan a lesson so much the better so long as it did not jeopardize the Syrian front.

Jordanian fire hit, with some accuracy, Tirat Zvi, Mukeibla and Sandala as well as the posts of Mazat and Gilboa. At noon, the Israel General Staff considered something should be done on the Northern Jordanian front, but without (if there was any danger of this) Syria being caused to attack.

Brigadier-General D. Elazar, O.C. of Northern Command, had the dual responsibility of defending both the North Jordanian and the Syrian fronts. His aim, obviously, was to take the two opposing Arab forces one at a time, preferably Syria second, by which time, if he needed them, he no doubt would be able to get plenty of reinforcements of men free from Sinai. He did not know, but guessed, that Syria and Jordan were not going to work out a common plan of action. He could have been faced by three Arab armies, if Lebanon had fought, but Syria had not stimulated Lebanon into action for strategic reasons. Syria had by now mobilized some 115,000 men, of whom 60,000 were regulars. Syria was a sleeping dog Elazar would very much like to let lie. When Ramat David airfield seemed to be in danger from North Jordan fire, Brigadier-General Elazar was ordered to open attack on the Jordanians.

Because the Israeli attacking forces were not in the frontal sections but in distant assembly areas when the order came through, the brigade went into armored attack, forming while in movement.

The first Israeli force did not cross the North Jordanian border until after 6 p.m. The plan of attack was on Jenin, but this, as was anticipated when it was drawn up, developed later into an attack on Nablus also. There was a concerted assault on Jenin with the aim not to make a frontal attack on the Jordanian lines but to outflank them, and then attack Jordan's dispositions from the rear. The plan succeeded after hard fighting. One of Israel's two available armored forces accomplished the move. The other armored force opened up a second line at once. The Israelis broke through on an additional sector on the Yaved side of the front. Jordan had here one infantry brigade forward in battalion formation ready to take the full force of the attack. It also had one force which held two lines—one in the rear and one near Nablus. Three battalion lines were held by two battalions from the brigades on the coastal plain. There was also a battalion of Jordanian Patton tanks and the American equipped 40th Armored Brigade as well as two battalions of Patton tanks and a battalion of armored infantry with M 113 armored troop carriers.

During the night of June 5th–6th two breaches were made

Israel has reached the Suez Canal and one of her soldiers is searching an Egyptian straggler carrying a makeshift white flag and seeking to cross the Canal from the Sinai battlefield

Egyptian prisoners at El Arish show signs of shock and bewilderment

Israeli naval vessels in the Straits of Tiran after the Egyptians had been driven out of Sharm el Sheikh

The first ship flying an Israeli flag to pass through the Straits of Tiran since the Egyptian blockade. The 4,000-ton S.S. *Dolphin* from Massawa (East Africa) seen from Sharm el Sheikh

(*Right*) The man who planned the campaign, Chief of Staff Major-General Itzhak Rabin addressing a conference. Brigadier-General Mordechai Hod, Commander of the Israeli Air Force (sitting right) is among the listeners. (*Below*) Brigadier - Generals Uzzi Narkis, O.C. Central Command (Central Jordan front and Jerusalem), and David Elazar, O.C. Northern Command (Northern Jordan and Syria)

Israeli troops looking across the Jordanian sector of Jerusalem towards Mt. Scopus just before hostilities with Jordan broke out

At the same time thousands of Palestinians demonstrated in Jordanian Jerusalem calling for a "Holy War" against the Jews

General Moshe Dayan, Israel's Defense Minister, walking through the captured Old City of Jerusalem

Israeli troops shortly after capturing the Old City of Jerusalem

Scene at the Wailing Wall the day after Old Jerusalem fell

Israeli rabbi and soldier pray at the Wailing Wall

Israeli soldiers advancing in the captured Syrian town of Kuneitra

The war is over and Syrian Arabs are being rounded up to be searched

by heavy fighting. Jenin was captured by the morning of June 6th and then Nablus fell. This enabled the forces to join up with Central Command which came up from the south from the direction of Ramallah.

The Jordanians were later reported to have had, in all, 8,000 casualties on the Central and Northern Fronts. Two brigades of infantry were destroyed; three quarters of a tank battalion and part of the 60th Brigade's armored infantry battalion in the Jordan depression were put out of action. The Iraqi troop which tried to reach Israeli Jerusalem was smashed and the remains retreated across the Jordan. The Israelis captured 36 of 90 guns which were on the West Bank, some thirty-six 105 mm., eight out of sixteen "Long Toms" of 155 mm. One tank battalion in full working order was captured in the Hebron hills. Some twenty-two Hunter planes, some Star fighters and seven transport planes had already been destroyed on the ground. Jordanian authorities said later that 6,094 Jordanian soldiers were killed in the war. Syria stated her losses were 145 in dead. The Egyptian newspaper *Al Ahram* claimed the four warring nations had a death toll of 20,000.

While Brigadier-General Elazar had been fighting on the Jordanian Northern Front he had one eye all the time on the Syrians. When Nablus fell on the West Bank of the Jordan and the heights were captured after a fierce battle on June 7th, he heaved a sigh of tremendous relief. The Israelis on the Central Front to the south had broken into the Old City of Jerusalem between ten and eleven o'clock in the morning to reach the Wailing Wall. Then, and then only, was he able to now turn his exclusive thoughts to Syria.

During the whole of the afternoon and night of June 5th through to June 8th (the day after the Jordanian surrender), and partly on June 9th, the Israelis had patiently borne a ceaseless hail of artillery fire on settlements along the border. Considering that Syria knew that starting June 5th the Israelis were fighting Egypt to the limits of their powers in the Sinai, which involved extending lines of communication in a way that made great demands on the supply system, and were also deeply involved in fierce engagements on the West Bank of the Jordan, she did remarkably little to take advantage of the position. For nearly five days and four nights during which Israel's army had sat there, drawn up for defense, and particularly anti-artillery defense, Syria had taken no risks and played for time. True, the Syrians had shelled some 205 settlers' houses and some 21 chicken coops, recreation clubs, tractor sheds and barns. They had also hit some 45 tractors and other vehicles. They had set fire to some 250 acres of orchards and grain. But they had not engaged in serious war. They had caused only eighteen casualties in all and of these sixteen were wounded superficially. When one remembered the bloodthirsty threats of the Syrians for months before the war their actions and the damage they had inflicted were amazingly light: It was not as if they had not considered themselves at war with Israel. Damascus radio had made three announcements on June 5th which were tantamount to an admission, indeed a boast, that they stood in this relationship—at 11 a.m., 12:30 p.m. and 1:15 p.m. In all of them they had claimed that their planes were bombing Israel cities. The claims were partly true. The announcer said: "Syria has joined the campaign. The forces of the Arab revolution will not retreat before they have totally destroyed Zionist existence on Arab soil." This seemed a little premature. Since the Syrians had not even advanced, they could not very well retreat!

The Israeli Northern Command had been patient for two reasons. As in the case of Jordan at the beginning Israel had been prepared to give Syria a chance of making a noisy demonstration and then remaining on the defensive. It was known that the Syrian Government was on unfriendly terms with their neighbor, Jordan. A little earlier the two had nearly broken off diplomatic relations. Syria had looked on in more than disapproval when King Hussein flew to Cairo and signed a military pact with Colonel Nasser. So unpredictable was President Atassi that he might have resolved to let Jordan take the full force of Israel's Northern Command. He knew this command had joint responsibility for roles against Jordan and Syria. In fact there seemed no other clear explanation, but Syrian action in the circumstances had not been sufficiently serious to provoke Israel into attack before the morning of June 9th.

Major General Rabin, pleased that the Jordan Front was finished, as well as that of Sinai, gave Brigadier-General Elazar the order to attack Syria. Elazar's forces were in distant assembly points outside the range of Syrian artillery. He brought them up to the grouping points and then went into battle.

Israeli Intelligence knew more about the Syrian positions than they had known even about the Egyptian. The pro-Communist Ba'athist Government of Syria was said to have revealed these positions with pride to some of the hundred Soviet officers who are still stationed in Syria. They admired all the defense positions along the heights from Mount Hermon to the southern end of the Sea of Galilee. The Russians may have been prejudiced. The positions had been planned according to a contemporary Soviet idea of defense. Syria had two not very parallel lines of defense with communication trenches between gun positions. One unusual feature was that the National Guard was in the forward position to take the brunt of the assault, and the regular army units were comfortably ensconced in the second line. Syrian defense was based on the supposition, supported by the "best" military opinion, that the Israeli tanks would be put out of action before they reached the first Syrian line of arms.

There had been doubts about the tanks making the lines even among members of the Israeli General Staff. The tanks had been tested out in a mountainous area in the eastern Negev. The gradients and natural obstructions were steeper and greater than in front of the Syrian lines.

If the Israeli tanks had failed to negotiate their inclines the Syrians would have gone immediately into the attack. Syrian armor was concentrated for this very purpose on the line from Kuneitra, headquarters of the Front. A Syrian plan of attack, and other evidence of aggressive intentions, had been found by an Israeli Intelligence sergeant at Kuneitra. Maps showed indications of a planned advance through Lebanese territory (although that country was not fighting) towards Acre and through Mishmar Hayarden towards Haifa, then by one divergence to Nazareth and by another through the Jordan Valley turning in the direction of Affula. The assault force had also been planned. The Order of Battle was found. This consisted of several brigades of infantry, a strike force, and one armored and mechanized brigade concentrated near the Customs House in Mishmar Hayarden.

The Syrian defensive force with which the Israelis had to deal on June 9th were the 11th, 8th and 19th Infantry Brigades, all of which had manned the lines since February. To the rear were the 90th and the 32nd Infantry Brigades. They covered the north and south of Kuneitra. Each of the Syrian infantry brigades had a battalion of T 34 and CU 100 tanks. There were also about twenty-five tanks in the forward positions as they had been during reconnaissance made by the Israelis in the past several months. The armored striking force was composed of two armored and two mechanized brigades. Two other brigades, one armored and one mechanized, held the road to Damascus.

Brigadier-General Elazar's plan, as he revealed it just after the cease-fire, was to make a breakthrough at what was considered to be a comparatively "soft" place near Givat Ha'em south of Tal Azaziyat. From there the plan was to send in an armored force to take up a position on the ridge near Ein Feit Ze'ura with the eventual task to advance south towards Zuwaib el Meiss Kalah. An infantry force belonging to the "Golani" Brigade, with tanks, was then planned to take the posts of Tel Azaziyat, Tel Faq'r and Bourj Bravil, and, afterwards, Meiss Kalah.

The battle began on terrain that was hard and steep, but everything went according to plan. At one place only, Tel Faq'r, did it look for a time as if the Syrians were going to hold out, if not win. The battle at this point on the Syrian Heights on June 9th will be remembered for many a day as one of the fiercest, most vicious and bloodthirsty that has ever taken place in Syria. The troops fought not as men of the twentieth century, but as near savages of long ago when the only weapons were clubs and bare knuckles. The troops fought in the open, then on the parapets of the trenches, finally in the trenches. There was terrible hand to hand fighting by men who had either dropped their small arms or who had been deprived of them. The fight went on for three breathless hours. It might have been the high point in some incredible Hollywood movie. The men fought with fists and feet, with knives, rifle butts and any instrument that came at hand. The men even bit each other like savage dogs, tried to gouge out each other's eyes. The warriors of an atomic age bled from the most unexpected places. Battles in the Sinai had been indecently impersonal. Tank had fought tank from a distance. There had been no emotion. No hate. But Tel Faq'r provided enough hate for the whole war. At the post, and in the trenches, at least sixty bodies were soon spread out on the ground when the victors were able to look around. Wounds were of the kind that had never been inflicted anywhere but in a street brawl or at a political riot.

Another infantry force had earlier than this opened a number of additional breaches in the areas of Gonen, Darbashiyeh and Jelabina to provide more breakthrough points. An additional armored force came in from the direction of Gonen, via Kfar Awiya, and reinforced the attack.

The Israelis crossed the border into Syria at about 11:30 a.m. on June 9th and continued to advance all afternoon. Towards evening, they had scaled the heights as far as Bakala, taking enemy positions at Azaziyat, Faq'r, Bourj Bravil and Darbashiyeh. The Israelis had by dark won two bridgeheads on the heights which was more than had been anticipated in view of the steep and narrow roads.

Next morning, June 10th, with heavy air support the Israelis attacked along the heights in the direction of Kuneitra with the help of an additional armored force. After the breakthrough, which was accomplished quickly, the Israelis attacked towards Nass'ada to the north. One force advanced towards Ruweyeh along difficult mountainous country and dealt with anti-tank emplacements and then pushed on towards Kuneitra.

Syrian units which held out were destroyed by a force commanded by Brigadier-General El'ad Paled, whose infantry climbed the cliffs of Tawafik, whose armor pushed on through ground not initially prepared, and whose paratroop force, flown in by helicopter, attacked the enemy's positions in the rear. Kuneitra fell at 2:30 p.m. on June 10th, twenty-eight hours after the operation began. The road to Damascus was open. The Israelis say they could have been in Damascus in thirty-six hours.

Brigadier-General Elazar disengaged his troops long before the cease-fire deadline at 6 p.m. on June 10th. He swore that stories disclaiming this were utterly fallacious. There was no need to advance any further; they had attained all objectives in the time limit set, before the cease-fire deadline. The Syrian army might not have been totally destroyed but it had suffered serious losses. About one-third of Syria's tanks were lost. Of 300 with which Syria had been fighting some forty were taken over by Israelis. Some sixty or seventy tanks had been put out of action. Over half of Syria's artillery, or eight regiments, was lost. Half of it was in Israeli hands and the rest destroyed. Two brigades of infantry suffered heavy losses and fled in utter disorder. Infantry regiments suffered heavy losses. One of four Syrian armored brigades was badly mauled.

Northern Command casualties on the Syrian Heights were 115 killed and 306 wounded and on the North Jordanian Front 107 killed and 322 wounded, which is considered some indication of the ferocity of the fighting in view of its short duration.

The Syrian Government reeled under the crushing defeat and so did the Russians, but they were by now used to reeling. The army and air force had been crushed; the strongly fortified positions from which the Syrians for years had fired at Israeli settlers on the plain had fallen in an unexpectedly short time. Contrary to Syrian radio claims that Syrian troops had advanced into Israel, they did not put one foot across the Israeli border. On the contrary, Israeli tanks penetrated some 28 miles into Syrian territory.

14

CEASE-FIRE

The Syrian Army had largely escaped along the road to Damascus, but it had suffered severe casualties. The battle had fallen into three stages—the breakthrough by the Israelis, the fighting, and the exploitation of the Syrian collapse. The fight had been the more difficult because of the steep inclines the Israelis had had to climb under fire and the Syrian positions of reinforced concrete bunkers and covered stone emplacements from which it was difficult to expel the defenders.

Brigadier-General Elazar said the actual fighting following the breakthrough was brief. The Israeli ground troops had been helped considerably by support from the Israeli Air Force which had been freed from obligations on the other fronts and been able to devote its full attention to Syria. But even this would have been in vain if the initial impetus of the ground units had not reached such a speed that it completely threw the Syrians off balance. Syrian officers were the first to realize that their army was no match for Israel. They turned and fled. It was this flight which accounted for the fact that while hundreds of prisoners had been taken there were very few officers. The Syrians collapsed and were routed. They left behind them on the heights most of their heavy equipment.

The Commander went out of his way to deny reports presented to members of the United Nations Security Council on June 10th in New York that Israeli forces on the Front had continued to thrust deep into Syria after the cease-fire had been fixed and that they even were prepared to encircle Damascus. United Nations observers, whose statements from

Damascus were read by U Thant, had been misinformed, he said. Israel had not launched an attack around Damascus, nor had their planes raided Damascus. United Nations observers, he thought, must have been the victims of the alarmist reports in the capital, which was for a long time in a state of bewilderment and alarm.

The United Nations staff in Israel proposed that the Cease Fire should take effect at 4:30 p.m. on June 10th, but the actual time when Syria accepted the Cease Fire was 6:30 p.m. on June 11th. The Council had been called together as a result of an appeal an hour before dawn by Dr. George Tomeh, who had become alarmed, but all that had happened was that Israel had taken Kuneitra nine miles inside Syria and forty-two miles south of Damascus. Some tanks had meandered on and Israeli planes had gone ahead of the armored forces, retreating to the capital "to have a look around." There were reports in weekend newspapers that Israeli Centurion tanks had led a drive deep into Syria and were on their way towards the capital. These, too, were said to be "a little exaggerated."

The six-day war was over. In so short a time the Israelis had broken through the blockade of the Gulf of Aqaba, liberated the Temple area in Jerusalem, captured the hills overlooking longsuffering villages in Galilee and the Jordan Valley, taken the West Bank of the Jordan and cleared the Sinai. The Arab armies which had for so long boasted that they would eliminate Israel in a holy war lay conquered at their feet, defeated, humiliated and sometimes destroyed.

From Sharm el Sheikh in southern Sinai up to Kuneitra in Syria, the last place to fall, there lay on the ground an amazing quantity of arms of all kinds which only a week before had been the pride of four armies. There were wrecks of planes, huge hulks of tanks and half-tracks, twisted skeletons of troop carriers and broken guns as well as hundreds of weapons of tremendous value which had been left intact by fleeing armies of Egypt, Jordan, Syria and Iraq. If Israel wished to go into the scrap metal business and recoup the cost of the war to her economy, then now was the time to do it. But although the war was over, apart from a few alarms in Syria and some fighting at the end of June and during July near the Suez

Canal, great struggles lay ahead to overcome difficulties, economic and political, which had to be settled soon.

The Israelis are an efficient people, as the war had shown. They were united and successful and joyous that their beloved Jerusalem was liberated. They would not neglect to do their duty. As Itzhak Rabin told them later, just as Israel's Defense Army had gone out to protect Israel on the field of battle so they would all know how to consolidate and maintain Israel in the days of struggle and hardship after the battle.

The Arab-Israeli war (Part III) was over, this time in six days, by 2:30 p.m. on June 10th, with the fall of Kuneitra in Syria, 28 hours and 4 minutes after operations had begun against the Syrians. The world had become again at peace with itself except in Vietnam, and that war had become a habit, almost a way of life.

Looking back on the week that shook the Middle East I could not help but admire the feat of Israel. On Sunday, June 4th, the long sandy beach at Tel Aviv had been crowded with, mainly, women and children enjoying themselves in the hot sun. Then on Monday morning, like a bolt from the blue, Israel was at war. The air force had struck its crippling blow at the Arab Air Force and changed the political complexion of the Middle East in 2 hours 51 minutes. The unparalleled success of the youngest air force in the world (but with a record of the longest time spent in the air) had led to the greatest victory in any short war in history. Probably Israel's greatest achievement off the battlefields had been in making it seem to the world that Egypt had started the war. That she had actually invaded poor little Israel which was in danger of being completely over-run in a few hours. Instead, after the attack on Cairo and the Arab air bases by Israeli pilots, Israeli armor had smashed through into Egypt, overwhelming the Egyptians, who were taken completely by surprise. The Israelis knew that the Egyptians lacked air cover, the very thing they had been promised by Nasser before hostilities began. Air cover to them in open desert was as the Maginot line had been to the French in the Second World War. When the news circulated that Egypt's planes lay wrecked on their own airfields, the Egyptian Army, and especially the officers, were numb. The troops were completely demoralized. They never recovered from the shock. There was a conspiracy of silence, for reasons I have given, by Israel not to reveal for eighteen hours what the air and land forces had achieved. There was also a conspiracy of silence by the Arabs who could not admit even to their allies that they had been so thoroughly defeated. It was not known that all the air forces had suffered the same treatment. When this fact leaked out the Arabs began to look for someone to blame. On Monday, although it was not admitted by the Israel General Staff on that day, the army had been almost as successful as the air force–in Sinai and in Jordan. The little Israeli Navy had also made an audacious but little publicized invasion of Egyptian ports and crippled Russian made submarines and other offensive craft, freeing Israel's sea border and shipping from attack. On the second day the war had continued at an even greater tempo and with more brutality and efficiency both in Sinai and in Jordan. The Israeli Air Force became audacious in its contempt for its Arab opponents. Their planes flew low over each Arab capital in turn. The Arabs were knocked sideways. There was no coordination after the air arm had collapsed. The leaders knew that complete defeat was only a matter of time. The rumor about foreign air intervention was used by Colonel Nasser like the master of propaganda he is. The effects continued to be suffered in the West for months later. The lie became a weapon of psychological warfare which Nasser wielded with all his might. All Arab lands but Jordan believed what he said. Hatred of the West exceeded that wave of hate that spread through the Middle East in 1956. The only foreigners who did not accept Nasser's word were the Russians, for the simple reason that they had covered the British and United States fleet. They had watched the carriers closely all round the clock. They had seen no planes leave any of the ships early on June 5th. Colonel Nasser knew now that he had to be a better diplomat than he was a soldier–words he had used to me and which I quoted at the start. He put into practice every trick, political and psychological, he had ever learned to try to recover diplomatically, with the help of Russia, what he had so far lost militarily.

June 8th was the black letter day for King Hussein as one town after another on the West Bank of the Jordan, Jerusalem included, had fallen into Israeli hands. With his small air force destroyed and his capital exposed to Israel air attacks at any time of the day or night, there was nothing to do but surrender. Hussein's throne had never been in greater danger. Leading subjects on the West Bank told Israeli newspaper men that the King had made a criminal error in flying to Egypt to sign a military pact with Colonel Nasser. The reports were appearing in the press and on the Jordan radio from Old Jerusalem which *Kol Israel* had taken over.

While the Jordan and, later, the Syrian campaigns seemed important when one was in the area, they were, in fact, merely sideshows compared with the terrific campaign in Sinai.

The Russians had wakened to the truth that their Arab allies had failed miserably, that, as Moshe Dayan had said, "they were men of straw." To save their face Russia mounted an offensive in the United Nations. The Soviet Ambassador urgently called on June 7th for an absolute Cease Fire by 8 a.m. GMT. This was a desperate effort to save Nasser. On Thursday, June 8th, Ambassador Goldberg had proposed a new United States resolution when El Kony, the Egyptian Ambassador, handed to U Thant a typewritten note. Egypt had accepted a Cease Fire. There could not have been a greater sensation in that assembly if an Israeli mortar bomb, fired in the Sinai, had fallen on the United Nations building. Russia's Federenko accused Israel of "trampling on the soil of a foreign land in American boots," an odd reference, since it was mainly with French-made planes that Israel had destroyed the cream of the offensive weapons which Russia had sold to Egypt.

A week of war and then a week of mourning. In Israel over 600 families sat in their homes with all the doors on the street open according to the custom of bereaved people, to mourn the loss in battle of a loved one. In one case father and son were among the casualties, the son in the regular army and his father in the reserves. The mourning would continue for a week, just as long as the fighting had lasted.

When the Israeli Army announced that 679 men had been killed and 2,500 wounded * the nation was stunned. The numbers are not large compared with casualties in modern wars, but Israel is a small country with a small population, and disasters of this kind struck very heavily at all communities. Traffic up to the fronts had been mainly one way of carrying soldiers and arms and ammunition, mainly in the night, and now came trucks the other way bringing the belongings of the men who had died for their country. What caused most pain were the letters which arrived from the men who had since been killed. These had been delayed in field sorting offices. It is the custom if at all possible to bury one's dead in the family cemetery, but the Government decided that since the number of dead was so large, they would be interred in military cemeteries close to the scenes of the fighting in which they had been killed. In relation to the extent and duration of the fighting there had been more Israeli casualties in Jordan and Syria than in Sinai. This was explained by the fact that the Sinai battles were mainly between armored formations and mechanized units. Infantry had been used only in skirmishes except on one or two occasions.

The bereaved Israelis showed magnificent courage and fortitude. The women had suffered much in the six days of the fighting. Though they had themselves to work at times long hours to replace men at the front, their minds had been haunted by what might have happened to their husbands or sons. The men had in the first partial mobilization been aroused in the night as they slept and hurried off to their centers. They had had little time to take farewell of their families. They had since been able if they were lucky only to send field postcards or censored letters which said little and made no mention of the role they were to play or the area to which they had been sent. For six days and nights the women waited patiently. Many were the letters received from Jews abroad, and one newspaper spoke of a great wave of sympathy

* The Israeli Defense Ministry amended the number of war dead on July 5th to 730 Israeli soldiers killed. Some 2,800 were wounded, 1,700 of whom were permanently disabled. In the 1956 campaign Israel's losses were 171 dead. A special Israeli fund was set up to help the war widows and their families.

which had spread itself over the country. The Israelis do not exhibit their sorrow, but it was thought that later, when the country had recovered from the heavy blow which the war had made to its economy, a suitable memorial would be erected to the heroic dead.

All Israel, in village as in town, heaved a sigh of relief when the war was over. The lights came on again, and merchants who had lost nothing more than a little trade began to serve small glasses of Israeli wine at the doors of their shops to celebrate victory. Israel could well feel proud. There had been such unity of purpose throughout the land that the new nation made up of such disparate elements felt like a different country, exorcised of all its ethnic inequalities, its political differences and its petty quarrels. The coastal strip from north of Haifa to south of Tel Aviv was no longer exposed to attack. The West Bank of the Jordan was Israeli—for the time being at least. And not far away was Jerusalem, a united city. The economy had been nearly at a standstill for a week. There had been no activity at the Dead Sea, an enormous storehouse of valuable minerals. The potash factory and the bromide plant had only marked time. None of the various chlorides had got far from their source. The salt, phosphate, uranium and gypsum, the sulphur, the bitumen, the copper and manganese lay still where they were a week before, waiting removal. There had been no fishing at Galilee. No oil drilling worth mentioning had taken place. Agriculture had been at a standstill, some crops gathered, some over-ripe in the burning sun. Tractors had been laid aside and the drivers had leapt into tanks and armored cars. Israel's industry, mainly dependent on the agricultural output of the country and the fish of its seas and the raw materials in its soil and waters, had merely been ticking over for six whole days. Men and women had worked twelve and more hours a day. All communities, Orientals and Moslem Arabs as well as Druzes and Bahais, had contributed fully to the war effort. All felt in their hearts the high value of Israel Independence. The Tsahal, as the people lovingly called the army, had called up men and women from every walk of life and from every regional division of Israel to face the foe. Their places in civilian life had been taken by reserves in Chen (Chail

Nashem), the women's units; by Gadna, a contraction of Gedudei No'ar (the youth troops who were a para-military organization which included secondary school age groups), and by numerous students. The mail, for instance, and this was far heavier than usual because of the separation of families, had been efficiently distributed by young people. They also filled numerous vacancies in overworked hospitals.

Israel after nineteen years could at last lift its head and say without any fear of contradiction, "We are a nation."

15

THE ON-OFF RESIGNATION

Israel was already in a deeply thoughtful mood on June 10th before the arrival of the dramatic news that Colonel Nasser had resigned as President of the United Arab Republic. There was, of course, a deep sense of mourning for the brave men they had lost. There was profound gratitude that Israel had won and that the Star of David was flying throughout large Arab areas which earlier had ignored Israel's existence. There was certainly room for rejoicing that the nightmare of a week before had vanished. Israel felt grateful for the way the American and British public had shown sympathy in her hour of trial. Britain, which had its own troubles, had raised 28 million dollars to aid Israel's economy. One man, Sir Isaac Wolfson, had given two and one-half million dollars. A youth had handed over 70 thousand dollars which his father had recently left him in his will. An old woman had given her life's savings. A five-year-old boy had donated the contents of his piggy bank. Such acts warmed their hearts.

The Israelis were genuinely sorry for the refugees. No one was pleased that there were additions to their ranks. Better than any people except the Arabs, the Israelis knew what it meant to be in that position. They were deeply concerned about the Palestinians. For nearly twenty years these displaced people had been obsessed with one single idea—a return to Israel, which they saw as their homeland; but what had happened for the moment, as one man put it, was that Israel had returned to the refugees. Many thousands of people who fled from Palestine in 1948 had become refugees for the second and third time. They had left camps and fled deep into Jordan.

There was also the question of the Russians. The Soviet Union would do all it could do to deprive Israel of the fruits of victory, even of the border security it had won. Russia would try to condemn Israel and demand an immediate and unconditional withdrawal of troops from Arab territory. Russia would condemn Israeli aggression without thinking for a moment how Israel had been subject to Arab aggression for years. Russia would also rearm her Arab allies and make them feel that defeat had been merely a temporary setback.

Israel may have changed, within a week, almost the whole balance of power in the Middle East, but how, the people asked themselves, could that help Israel's economy? Israel was not a rich country by any means. The war had been terribly costly. It had cost 600 million dollars! The struggle ahead would be hard and long. One thing Israel would not tolerate, however, and that was a return to the past. The Israeli people, quite apart from what the Defense Forces or the Government thought, were not prepared to return to the era of sabotage and murder on their exposed borders. No other country in the world would tolerate that for a minute. What they needed was a peace conference and a peace treaty between Israel and the Arabs. The world had other examples of trouble caused because wars had been fought and won and no treaty had been signed. They had to have direct negotiations for a lasting peace with the Arab countries. They did not want a settlement imposed either by Russia or America or by the United Nations.

General Rabin's masterpiece of mechanical war, brilliantly planned and brutally executed, had left in its wake a number of major problems. Israel now had a population not only of 2,800,000 but 1,330,000 conquered Arabs. Her 8,000 square miles by June 10th had become 26,000 square miles. Israel had the problem of caring for 250,000 Palestine refugees in the Gaza Strip which was unrestrainedly anti-Jewish, and some 1,000,000 on the West Bank of the Jordan. There was also the problem of what Israel should do with the territory she had conquered, whether she should annex the Gaza Strip and the West Bank and incorporate Old Jerusalem. Then there were the Gaulan Hills in Syria, which had been a base for attacks on Israel for several years. They certainly must decide what should be done to guarantee border security before withdrawing. There was also the problem of free navigation in the Suez Canal, which had been closed by Egypt when Israel occupied all the Sinai up to the east bank. There was the flash point of the war, Sharm el Sheikh, and the question of how Israel would be able to obtain a guarantee against another possible Egyptian blockade of the Straits of Tiran. There were enough problems to be solved without being faced again by the implacable hatred of the Arabs spurred on by Soviet Russia. So the Israelis were thinking as the lights went on again and preparations were being made to thank God for their victory on the first Sabbath after the war.

Then, suddenly and dramatically, news came that President Nasser had resigned. Israel was accustomed to being the target of propaganda from the Arab world. At first the news was suspect. What they knew of Colonel Nasser told them that the very last thing he would do would be to give up the power he so dearly loved. If he had said he was resigning then it could only be a political maneuver to save his political life. Israel would dearly like to see his resignation, as would America and Britain. He was regarded as the cause of most of the unrest in the Middle East. His fall would make a settlement, and a return to normalcy, far easier, especially if his successor did not make the mistake of accepting Russian advice.

It was not long before Israel knew that the report of Nasser's resignation was true. Their cup of happiness was overflowing. Now it could not be denied that Israel had changed the whole balance of power in the Middle East.

Gamal Abdel Nasser spoke for over twenty minutes over TV and radio from his office at the Republic Palace in Cairo to tell Egypt of his decision to resign. The Egyptians saw him dressed in a dark suit as if in mourning, looking haggard and drawn after a week of sleeplessness. Or they heard his slow hesitant voice, so different from the firm, assured manner in which he had spoken. When he told them of Israel's threats against the Arabs, against Syria, ignoring the threats which he had himself made against Israel and carried out on the borders, there were noises set off to confirm his words. As if the incident had been carefully stage managed by the Property department of Saut el Arab radio network, air raid sirens screamed out. Their banshee wailings mingled with his words. There was no sound of firing or of bombs, and Israel later denied that their planes went over the Egyptian capital at that time. Some Arab countries said otherwise. Nasser's allies could always be relied upon to fill in the gaps. Algeria radio said that Israel attacked the suburbs of Cairo and that bombs were falling five minutes after Colonel Nasser had begun to talk. "The explosions are more violent now," said the Algerian announcer as he repeated Nasser's words.

If there were bombs they did not interrupt Colonel Nasser's address to the Egyptian people.

> Brothers [he told them, according to the *London Times*], we have been accustomed together in times of victory and in times of stress, in the sweet hours and in the bitter hours, to speak with open hearts and to tell each other the facts, confident that through this means alone we can always find our sound direction, however critical the circumstances and however low the light. We cannot hide from ourselves the fact that we have met with a grave setback in the last few days. But I am confident that all of us can in a short time overcome our difficult situation. To do this we shall need much patience, much wisdom and moral courage, and ability for devoted work. Before that we should look at what happened in order to follow developments, and the way they proceeded until they reached this stage. We all know how the crisis began in the first half of last May. There was an enemy plan to invade Syria, and the statements, by his politicians and all his military commanders, declared that frankly. The evidence was ample. The sources of our Syrian brothers and our own reliable information were categorical on this. Even our friends in the Soviet Union told the parliamentary delegation which was visiting Moscow early last month that there was a calculated intention. It was our duty not to accept this in silence. In addition to it being a question of Arab brotherhood it was also a matter of national security. Who starts with Syria will finish with Egypt. So our armed forces moved to our frontiers.

Nasser had already put over the most difficult part of his speech—his justification of the costly venture in mobilizing his army and preparing for war. He now went on to deal with the withdrawal of the United Nations force and the return of Egyptian forces to Sharm el Sheikh, which the Israeli enemy used as one of the results of the tripartite aggression on us in 1956. The passage of the enemy flag in front of our forces was intolerable and so were other matters connected with the most precious aspirations of the Arab nation.

Our estimates of the enemy's strength were precise. They showed us that our armed forces had reached a level of equipment and training at which they were capable of deterring and repelling the enemy. We realized that the possibility of an armed clash existed, and we accepted the risk. There were several factors before us, nationalist, Arab, and international. These included a message from President Lyndon Johnson of the United States which was handed to our ambassador in Washington on May 26th, asking us for restraint and not to be the first to open fire. Otherwise we would face serious consequences. The same night the Soviet Ambassador asked to see me urgently at 3:30 and told me that the Soviet Government strongly requested we should not be the first to open fire.

As Nasser went on to deal with the opening of the war, he repeated that he had been thrown off his balance by the strength of Israel. He had obviously been misinformed by his Intelligence as to their state of preparedness.

On the morning of June 5th, [he went on] the enemy struck. If we say now it was a stronger blow than we had expected we must say at the same time and with assurance, that it was much stronger than his resources allowed. It was clear from the very first there were other forces behind him which came to settle their accounts with the Arab Nationalist movement.

There were significant surprises: The enemy we expected to come from the east and north came from the west. This showed he had facilities beyond his own resources and exceeding the estimate of his strength. The enemy attacked at one go all the military and civil airfields in the United Arab Republic. This meant he was relying on something more than his normal strength to protect his skies from any retaliation from us. The enemy was also fighting on other Arab fronts with other assistance. The evidence of imperialist collusion with the enemy is clear. It sought to benefit from the lesson of the former open collusion of 1956, this time concealing itself cunningly. What is now established is that American and British aircraft were off the enemy's shores, helping his war effort. Also, British aircraft raided in broad daylight positions on the Syrian and Egyptian fronts

> in addition to operations by a number of American aircraft reconnoitring some of our positions. The inevitable result was that our land forces, fighting a most violent and brave battle in the open desert, found their air cover was inadequate in face of decisive superiority.

Colonel Nasser then, in view of the facts that Israel fought unaided, paid a great compliment to the Israeli pilots. "It can be said without fear or exaggeration," he said with emphasis, "that the enemy was operating an air force three times its normal strength."

> This was also faced by the forces of the Jordanian Arab Army which fought a valiant battle under the command of King Hussein who, to be just and honest to him, adopted a fine attitude. I confess that my heart bled as I followed the battles of his gallant army in Jerusalem and other positions on the western coast on a night in which the enemy and the power plotting with him massed at least 400 aircraft to operate over the Jordanian Army. There were magnificent and honorable battles. The Algerian people and their great leader, Houari Boumedienne, gave without reservation to the battle. The Iraq people and their loyal leader, Abdel Rahman Arif, also gave without reservation. The Syrian Army fought heroically, supported by the forces of the great Syrian people and under the leadership of their nationalist government. The peoples and governments of Sudan, Kuwait, Yemen, Lebanon, Tunisia and Morocco adopted honorable attitudes. The peoples of the entire Arab nation, without exception throughout the Arab homeland, struck an attitude of manhood and dignity, an attitude of determination, an attitude of insistence that Arab rights will not be lost nor will they dwindle, and that the war in defense of them continues whatever the sacrifices and setbacks along the road of inevitable and definite victory.
>
> There were great nations outside the Arab world, [he continued] which gave us moral support which cannot be estimated, but the conspiracy was bigger and stronger. The enemy's concentration on the Egyptian front, to which it pushed all its main force of armor and infantry, was backed by an air superiority the dimensions of which I have already described to you.

Then Nasser made a few half-hearted but qualified admissions of the defeat of his army.

The nature of the desert did not permit a full defense, particularly with the enemy's air superiority. I realize that the development of the armed battle may not be favorable to us. I tried with others to use all resources of Arab strength. Arab petroleum played its part. The Suez Canal played its part. And there is still a major role required of Arabs everywhere and I am fully confident they will be able to perform it. Our armed forces in Sinai had to evacuate the first defense line and fought their terrible battles with tanks and aircraft along the second defense line. Then we responded to the cease-fire resolution, following assurances in the recent Soviet draft resolution to the Security Council and following declarations by the French Government that no one could achieve a territorial expansion as a result of the recent aggression, and in view of international public opinion, particularly in Asia and Africa, which watches our position and feels the ugliness of the world-dominant powers which pounced on us.

We now have several urgent tasks before us, [he went on as he approached the purpose of his speech]. The first task is to remove the remnants of this aggression against us and adopt, with the Arab nation, an attitude of firmness and steadfastness. In spite of the setback, the Arab nation, with all its energies and resources, is able to insist on removing the remnants of the aggression.

The second task is for us to learn the lesson of the setback. In this connection there are three vital facts:

(1) The destruction of imperialism in the Arab world leaves Israel with its own strength alone. Whatever the conditions and however long they may last, the abilities of the Arabs are greater and more effective.
(2) The reorientation of Arab interests in the service of Arab rights is a primary safeguard. The U.S. Sixth Fleet was moving with Arab petroleum. There are Arab bases which were forcibly, and despite the will of the peoples, placed at the services of aggression.
(3) What is now needed is a unified voice by the entire Arab nation, that is a safeguard for which there is no substitute in these conditions.

We now reach an important point in this soul-searching by asking ourselves: Does this mean we do not assume responsibility for the consequences of this setback? I tell you truthfully that I am ready to assume the entire responsibility. I have taken a decision with which I want you all to help me.

I have decided to give up completely and finally every official post and every political role and to return to the ranks of the public to do my duty with them like every other citizen. The forces of imperialism imagine that Abdel Nasser is their enemy. I want it to be clear to them that it is the entire Arab nation and not Gamal Abdel Nasser. The forces hostile to the Arab nationalist movement always try to picture it as Abdel Nasser's empire. That is not true, for the hope for Arab unity began before Gamal Abdel Nasser. It will remain after Gamal Abdel Nasser.

I have always told you that it is the nation which survives. Whatever his [Colonel Nasser's] contribution to the cause of his homeland, he is but an expression of a popular will and is not the creator of that will.

In accordance with Article 110 of the provisional constitution, promulgated in March 1964, I have asked my colleague, friend, and brother, Zakaria Mohieddin, to take over the post of President of the Republic and to carry out the constitutional provisions. [The First Vice-President and deputy supreme commander of the armed forces, Marshal Abdel Hakim Amer, along with War Minister Shamseddin Badran, has already resigned.]

Consequently, and after this decision, I place all I have at his disposal in dealing with the critical situation through which our people are passing. I am not liquidating the Revolution. The Revolution is not the monopoly of one generation of revolutionaries. It has brought about the evacuation of British imperialism and the independence of Egypt. It has defined its [Egypt's] Arab character, fought the policy of zones of influence in the Arab world, led the socialist revolution and brought about a profound change in the Arab way of life. It has affirmed the people's control of their resources and the product of their national action. It recovered the Suez Canal and laid down the bases of industrial build-up in Egypt, built the high dam to turn the arid desert green. It has extended generating power networks all over the northern Nile valley and extracted petroleum resources after a long wait. More important than all this, it has placed the workers in the leadership of political action. They are always the source for new leadership, carrying the banner of the patriotic and nationalist struggle phase after phase, building up socialism and winning victories.

Before he had finished speaking, a large crowd suddenly appeared in the center of Cairo crying out, "Nasser, Nasser, only Nasser." Some observers believe that the first group of people came together too quickly for the demonstration to have been spontaneous. They remembered the paid mourners who used to wail at Moslem funerals, and the agitators, paid according to their number and the period of operation, who had occasionally appeared outside some office or house in the past to chant a chorus of discontent. I had witnessed this maneuver myself in the Garden City Suburb during World War Two.

The demonstrators apparently knew exactly where Colonel Nasser went after he had broadcast—to his enlarged bungalow, the standard living quarters for a lieutenant-colonel in the Egyptian Army, in the Moustapha Kamal barracks at Manshiyat el Bakry, where once the Egyptian President entertained me for most of one night. How the crowd got into a barracks, which is well guarded by sentries, I do not know. The gate is some distance from Colonel Nasser's house and a visitor usually has first to go to the Orderly Officer and give full details of his business before being announced, let alone admitted. It seemed that this crowd of civilians was allowed to enter a closely guarded military establishment at a time of war and maximum security, without the normal caution being exercised.

I am told by a friend that the demonstrators travelled by trucks, which were left beneath the high wall of the barracks when they went inside. A TV commentator from Cairo radio also happened to be on hand outside Colonel Nasser's house. He told viewers that the demonstrators were "expressing the will of the Egyptian people" and "that this was likely to be of vital importance in determining events." He added, in an aside to Colonel Nasser: "We stood by you during our victories and we will not abandon you now." The Nasser controlled company which managed TV throughout Egypt continually flashed portraits of Colonel Nasser on the screen. These showed him smiling in one of his characteristic poses, a vivid contrast to his mournful expression earlier. Old newsreels were hastily resurrected which showed multitudes of people cheering Colonel Nasser on the occasion of earlier diplomatic victories. It seemed then that the Egyptian President was, indeed, a better diplomat even than he was a soldier. The crowd did its stint, and then got in the trucks and went home again.

In the interval, people discussed the man Colonel Nasser had proposed to take his place—Zakaria Mohieddin. This 50-year-old former army officer had been one of the Young Officers who had helped in Egypt's 1952 revolution. He was a right-wing socialist. He had, so it is said, at times pleaded with Nasser, when he became extreme, to moderate some of his policies towards the West. He was likely, some of Nasser's opponents said, not to have illusions of grandeur in which the former Egyptian President out-rivalled General de Gaulle. He was more likely to try to build up Egypt economically instead of spending millions on arms and trying to unite the Arabs under his leadership. Even some Egyptians saw that a new leader might the better extricate the nation from the awful position in which it now found itself. It was lucky that Mohieddin was in Cairo at all. He had been prepared to go to Washington to meet President Johnson immediately before the war to discuss the crisis. If he had left early he would have been stranded in Washington. United States planes ceased to fly to the United Arab Republic next day.

It did not take Colonel Nasser long after the visit of the demonstrators to have "second thoughts about his resignation." A second statement by him was read by an announcer over Cairo radio.

> I [the statement ran] will go tomorrow, God willing, to the National Assembly to debate with it and before the people the decision I have stated in my previous announcement. If I request anything of our struggling people at this time it is that they wait until the morning.

Few Middle East observers believe that Nasser intended for one second to resign. The whole thing was a political maneuver, an astute diplomatic gesture. In making known his resignation so dramatically, and before the people had had the time, or the opportunity, to discover the gravity of the disaster into which he had led them, he had compelled them emotionally to plead with him to stay on. Although Nasser has more enemies in Egypt than even he thinks, the masses did not wish to be left at that time with a new leader when they were in a state of acute crisis. Besides, his obsession against the Jews and the Imperialists apart, he was a very capable leader and had a finer record than any other Egyptian leader in history. He was the only man capable of pulling Egypt through the crisis in which she found herself. Colonel Nasser knew also that it was imperative for him to cling to office, and his act had assured him he could do this. He could prevent publication of full casualty lists.* He could conceal the number of planes, tanks and other arms which Egypt had lost in Sinai. He could clamp down on any move to reveal to the public the crippling cost of the war. He could also conceal in the country that which the Pentagon had revealed to the world, the fact that Egypt owed around a billion dollars to Russia for military aid. There were other side costs which had to be concealed. There was the enormous loss sustained by the closure of the Suez Canal, by the absence of a tourist trade and by the interruption in industrial output due to the mobilization of the army in mid-May.

There was another aspect of Nasser's predicament. With the aid of Russia, whom he could persuade to mount a great offensive against Israel in the United Nations, he might even be able to rob Israel of all fruits of victory. He might even emerge as the victor, as he had done after the Sinai campaign in 1956.

A wave of demonstrations followed the reading of the statement. Crowds of Egyptians roamed about the streets. Women shouted in chorus *"Zagrouta,"* a cry which is favored by women at weddings or at the birth of a baby boy. It was stated that one woman burnt herself to death after hearing the news that Nasser had resigned, and an older woman, the mother of two children, took an overdose of sleeping pills. Both women may have committed suicide because of the calamity which had befallen Egypt in the thrashing it had received from Israel. They did not leave behind them letters of explanation. Many women whose husbands were in the

* Early in July UAR authorities stated that "about" 5,000 Egyptians died in the Middle East war, but this is thought to underestimate the position.

army and from whom they had not heard for over a week were terribly distressed. They might have been further depressed by the clear indication of Egypt's defeat seen in Nasser's resignation. There were several reports of suicide from Alexandria about this time, but no one was able to say what was the cause of them. Colonel Nasser said that a referendum would be held later, and this was taken to be in connection with his "resumption" of office. He did not say what question the electorate would be asked to decide. Some observers doubted that the Egyptians would be asked to give Nasser a vote of confidence on his performance in connection with the war. As time passed the Egyptian people would become aware exactly what their leader's adventures had cost them. But Colonel Nasser managed to do two things by his maneuver. He gave himself a new lease on life, and by reacting to the wave of hysteria whipped up on his announced intention to resign, he had dispelled for the time being the black depression that had settled over Egypt.

Colonel Nasser resumed office on Saturday, June 10th, only fifteen hours after his declaration that he was resigning from all posts. So far as can be ascertained he did not take a single step to implement his statement of the previous day, nor did his successor take his own nomination seriously. The President did not even cancel important engagements arranged for the following day.

A message was read on his behalf in the National Assembly by Anwar Salat, the Speaker, to the effect that because of the will of the people he would return to office. This statement, which was broadcast several times by Cairo radio, said in part: "I hoped that the nation would have helped me to carry out my decision to relinquish my post. God knows that in taking this decision I was prompted by no other reason except my reaction to the responsibility in response to my conscience and to what I believed was my duty. I would give this nation, willingly and proudly, all I have, even life, until the last breath. No one can ever be able to understand my feelings in these circumstances towards this astounding reaction of our people and the peoples of the great Arab Nation in their determined rejection of my decision to relinquish my post. Until now I have not known how to express my gratitude. The voice of the people, to me, is an irrevocable order. Therefore, I have made up my mind to remain at my post until the period during which we can all remove the traces of the aggression is over."

After Salat had finished reading the message there was applause in and outside the Assembly building. Prime Minister Mohammed Sidky thanked President Nasser in his absence for "responding to the people's wishes." He called on the crowds who had absented themselves from work to return quietly to their jobs "under the leadership of the man for whom we give our lives."

Colonel Nasser decided that if he was not to resign he had better put the blame on someone and so he took a look round for the guilty man. Field Marshal Abdel Hakim Amer had resigned on Friday night along with Nasser. He was not given the chance Nasser took for himself in retracting his resignation. General Mohammed Fawzy, the former Chief of Staff, was quickly appointed by Nasser to be Commander-in-Chief of the Forces. The resignation was also accepted of the commanders of the army, navy and air force, the commander of the liaison branch and two assistants of Marshal Amer. Four leading generals, including those involved in the Sinai fighting, were pensioned off. More heads fell than after the revolution staged by the Young Officers to oust King Farouk in 1952. Colonel Nasser decided after third thoughts that it might be better if he retained the title of Supreme Commander of the Egyptian Forces. He did not appear to think that his reputation as military leader had suffered as a result of the debacle in the Sinai.

The Russian Ambassador had been kept informed by Colonel Nasser of his various political moves. When the President had concluded his main maneuver and "returned to office," Kosygin sent to him a message of congratulation and promised him that the Soviet Union would stand by the United Arab Republic in the political offensive that was to come.

When the contents of this message was leaked to Israel the Government began to wonder what was now in store for them. Levi Eshkol, the Prime Minister, knew that in the midst of victory they would have to employ all the energy they had to face up to a long political war staged by Kosygin and Nasser. It was not beyond the realms of possibility that there would be attacks on the eastern bank of the Suez Canal as Israel withdrew its main forces along overstretched lines of communication. These fears were realized earlier than was expected. Such outbreaks of fighting, attributed in every case to Israelis, were used to justify the delivery to Egypt by Russia of a large number of the most modern jet fighters. Other arms were not specified, but Soviet ships were reported to have taken tanks and artillery and radar to Egypt.

16

RUSSIAN REACTION

Israel did not have to wait long to know how Russia would express her displeasure. The Soviet Union broke off diplomatic relations, and at the same time warned Israel that it would undertake sanctions if Israeli forces did not stop advancing towards Damascus. The final cease-fire had been imposed earlier and it had survived minor overnight violations and brought the six-day war to an end. There were United Nations observers on both sides of the Syrian-Israeli border. Incidents which took place were stated not to be part of an Israeli advance but local acts of violence. Israeli Ambassador Gideon Rafael, on June 11th, said that no hostile activity was taking place in Syria. He refuted Soviet charges of Israeli violations of the cease-fire which had brought the Security Council back into urgent session overnight for its second meeting within twenty-four hours. Russian Ambassador Fedorenko accused Israel and its representative of lying. Rafael denied the charge. He also said that it was untrue that Israeli aircraft had bombed Damascus. "I deny this," he said and went on to repeat a denial he had made the day before that Israeli aircraft had attacked Cairo while Colonel Nasser was speaking.

The Russian action in breaking off diplomatic relations caused serious disquiet in Israel, the only country which took part in the Israeli-Arab war which had a legal Communist party on its territory. Both Israeli Jews and Israeli Arabs were members. Russia and Israel had enjoyed diplomatic relations ever since Israel was formed in 1948 except for a short period in 1953. On February 11th 1953, Stalin, in the final year of his reign as dictator, broke off relations in the midst of an anti-Jewish campaign in Russia. Diplomatic relations were resumed on July 20th of the same year, just over four months after the death of Stalin. Russia again threatened to sever relations during the 1956 Sinai campaign but thought better of it. In spite of the one-sided attitude of Russia to all things which affected both Arabs and Jews, many Israelis had hoped for an improvement in relations. The breaking off of diplomatic relations came as a great blow. As an indication of the surprising unanimity of opinion by Israeli newspapers, including that of the Communist party, I give extracts from the editorials on the following morning in Israeli newspapers, the Communist organ included:

Kol Ha'am (Communist): The announcement of the Soviet Government to break off diplomatic ties with Israel evoked great regret throughout the Israeli public. On no account can Israel be blamed for aggression in the armed conflict which broke out last week on our borders. . . . We remember quite a few armed conflicts between neighboring countries in various parts of the world, but we do not recollect a single instance where Russia severed ties with one of the parties to the conflict. . . . It seems to us that the use of sanctions, when not based upon an authoritative decision of the United Nations, runs counter to the United Nations Charter and will not further the interests of peace.

Davar (Histadrut): Every Israeli, irrespective of his political viewpoint, will undoubtedly feel regret over Moscow's decision to break off diplomatic ties with Israel. . . . In recent years Israel has made great endeavors to improve relations with Moscow, and if these efforts have remained fruitless, we are not to blame. For some reason the Soviet leaders chose to foster friendly ties with the Arab countries at the expense of Israel. . . . Israel fought for its existence and national security. This was its duty. Let Moscow not pour out its ire upon the defender—even if the defender won, for the defeated party was the attacker.

Ha'aretz (non-party): Egypt and Syria are assured of Russian support, and the Soviet decision to break off diplomatic ties with Israel furnishes demonstrative evidence to this effect. We cannot know how far the Soviets are prepared to go in their support. . . . For the time being the historic fact must be recorded that during the military campaign the Soviets abstained from interference. The impression is that there was some reciprocal understanding between Soviet Russia and the United States that they had better refrain from such interference.

Hayom (Independent): During the last two centuries the Russian people conducted two defensive wars. One against Napoleon and the other against the Nazi invader. . . . In both these wars Russia did not make do with a meticulous observance of the "armistice" after her success on the battle-field. . . . In view of these (and other) events the Jews and the State of Israel were entitled to another attitude from the Russian people, whose rulers promise the entire world a better and more just international future. . . . The Russians knew full well of Nasser's aggressive designs since Radio Cairo revealed the conversations with Egypt in Moscow where they were told that Israel allegedly planned an attack on Syria. A bad smell rises from this news report which Nasser revealed in his latest speech—since it makes the Russian people a partner of Hitler's heir on the banks of the Nile.

Hatzofeh (National Religious Party): Soviet Russia is subject to depressing nervousness. Her protégés have failed her. She has invested a vast fortune in supply and training, both in Egypt and in Syria, with a view to incite the States of the Middle East against each other, in order to exploit their hostilities to penetrate into a key position in the Middle East. . . . Russia apparently induced Nasser to mass his troops in Sinai, to chase out the UNEF, to close the Straits of Tiran and to threaten Israel. Now it transpires that the pro-Soviet Syrians also acted with Russian inspiration.

Al Hamishmar (Mapam): We have received the news of Russia's decision . . . with deep regret. We have received it as an unjust step which does not reflect the state of affairs in the Middle East and is unlikely to serve regional interests. There is nothing left for us but to hope that Soviet Russia will before long reconsider its Middle Eastern calculations and renew relations with Israel—not only on the diplomatic level.

Lamerhav (Achdut Ha'Avoda): Issues of international policy and relations between nations are not always determined according to principles of justice and decency, but Russia's demarche in breaking off diplomatic ties with Israel runs diametrically counter to these principles. Perhaps more than any other global factors, Moscow was able to avoid the aggravation of the Middle Eastern situation to the point of war—but she failed to do so. Instead of checking the flow of arms into Arab countries which never stopped announcing their intention of destroying Israel, she increased that flow.

. . . Soviet Russia now faces the necessity of an agonizing reappraisal of her Middle Eastern policy during the last twelve years. . . . Israel is prepared now, and will be in the future, as she always has been in the past, for an improvement of her relations with Russia.

Omer (Histadrut): These Communist leaders [who severed ties with Israel] turn a blind eye to the threats voiced by the Arab states against Israel during these very days of their defeat—before surrendering to the cease-fire orders and after. They ignore the Syrian Radio appeals to guerilla fighters that "their hour has come," and the continued activity of terrorists on Israeli territory. . . . Russia, no doubt, is angry with Israel. . . . She will do everything to encourage the Arabs—no doubt up to the brink of an entanglement in world war.

Russia followed up its action on June 12th by telling Israel not to delude itself into believing that it would be able to keep the Arab territory it had occupied during the six-day war. Fedorenko, the Soviet ambassador, said at the United Nations Security Council that Israel should pull back her forces to the 1949 Armistice lines.

Legal officials of the United Nations, under the guidance of U Thant, tried to determine if the Soviet ambassador was legally entitled to request an emergency meeting of the 122-nation General Assembly to discuss the question of the withdrawal of Israeli troops. In making the request Fedorenko had called the attention of Ambassador Goldberg to a statement he had made on May 24th that his country was obliged to maintain the territorial integrity of all countries in the Middle East. He asked Goldberg to tell the council if this statement still applied. Fedorenko also demanded that the council should act quickly on the Soviet resolution condemning Israel and ordering her to withdraw her troops.

Israel had little regard for the United Nations. Even lukewarm supporters of the organization had lost faith in it after the action of U Thant in allowing the immediate withdrawal, at the request of Colonel Nasser, of UNEF. Abba Eban made no effort to hide his attitude to some of the organization's actions. Now Major-General Dayan, Defense Minister, told the Israeli cabinet when it met in Jerusalem for the first time after the end of the war, that he saw no one million Russians with or without snow on their boots. Along with others, I stared in bewilderment at the blankets, fingered them and photographed them, though I didn't count them. The mystery was never solved.

Now, with Israel's second Sinai war over, there was a new mystery. An Israeli file was labelled "Abundance Of Tanks And Planes And Other Arms From Russia—Mystery Of." Israeli Intelligence knew that Egypt had approaching 1,000 tanks, most of them Russian. All but about 220 in the Sinai were captured and closely examined by specialists in armaments. It was not so certain how many planes the Arabs had had but about 400 had been shot down or destroyed by Israel. Like the tanks they were mostly Russian. Israeli Intelligence knew that since 1955 Russia had provided the Arabs with 2,000 tanks, of which more than 1,000 went to Egypt. The Soviet Union had supplied the Arabs with 700 modern fighter aircraft and bombers, more recently with ground missiles. Egypt alone had received 540 field guns, 130 medium guns; 200 120-mm. mortars; 229 anti-aircraft guns; 175 rocket launchers; 650 anti-tank guns, 7 destroyers, a number of Luna M and SPKA 2 ground-to-ground missiles, 14 submarines and 46 torpedo boats of various types including missile-carrying boats. That the Egyptian Army had been trained by Soviet experts was admitted by Egyptian officers captured in Israel. Most of the equipment was supplied to the Arabs after the Cairo Summit Conference of Arab leaders in January 1964 had agreed on a specific program for the destruction of Israel. The Arabs hurried to fulfil this plan, accelerating their arms purchases from the Soviet Union whose leaders must have been deaf as well as blind if they did not know what it was all about. The proportion of Soviet assistance was indicated by the fact that in Sinai alone the Egyptians abandoned equipment and offensive weapons of Soviet make to the value of two billion dollars.

Even if the million blankets in the Sinai campaign were not Russian but the foundation of an Egyptian "Bon Marche," what was Soviet Russia up to in 1967? Along with the rest of the world, she knew since 1956 that Nasser and Co. wanted to take revenge on Israel for defeat in the Sinai. So this great peaceful Proletarian Union sold an abundance of

major role for the United Nations in preventing f
breaks of hostilities between Israel and the Ar
United Nations," he said, "keep peace in the Mi
only as long as Colonel Nasser does not want to
again." Later, in an aside, he said he could not re
single important problem that had been solved th
plomacy or the United Nations. The Arab lead
ignore Israel's invitation to negotiate directly. Th
would be a new map, not of the Middle East, but of
they (the Arabs) do not want to sit down with us
shall stay where we are."

Most people in Israel wished to hold direct peace
the Arabs but if there had been any chance of this h
General Dayan had probably ruined it for the time
Colonel Nasser was a better diplomat than he was
General Dayan was certainly a better soldier than
diplomat. He was an exceptionally fine general but
his mind too openly to be a good diplomat. He was
to have said before Syria ceased firing on June 10th
was of the opinion that Israel should retain access
through the Straits of Tiran and the right of passage
the Suez Canal (which had been blockaded illegally
Israel was concerned); should occupy the Old City
salem; the Gaza Strip; and the Western part of Jo
explained that the Gaza Strip would be more a prob
a gift but he didn't think they should "in any way g
the Gaza Strip to Egypt nor the western part to Jord
said that while he would like to see an arrangement
security to Israel while giving the Arabs autonom
western sector, he did not believe they should be a
into Israel, as this would turn the country into an Isr
state.

At the end of the 1956 Sinai campaign there was
every foreign embassy in Tel Aviv labelled: "Blanke
tery Of." One million blankets were found by the
Army near El Arish in north Sinai just about the t
Russians were making threats about what they woul
Israel, Britain and France if they didn't leave little
alone. People said Colonel Nasser was obviously ex

arms without inquiring for a moment what they were wanted for. What had Russia thought Nasser and Co. would do with them?

The Syrian attitude had been ominous because it affected a border that had seen a great deal of infiltration. Syrian war propaganda had been intense. In 1964 the Syrian Defense Minister, General Abdulla Ziada, announced: "The Syrian Army stands as a mountain to crush Israel and demolish her. This army knows how to crush its enemies." Early in 1966 Syria began to carry out what it called a "popular war" against Israel. The Syrian concept of "popular war" meant sending trained groups into Israel territory to blow up water installations and communication centers, to kill or terrorize civilians on farms. The terrorists were trained in Syria and dispatched through Jordan or Lebanon. The terrorist war was formally declared by President Atassi on May 22nd 1966, when he addressed soldiers on the Israeli-Syrian fronts. He said: "We raise the slogan of the people's liberation war. We want total war with no limits, a war that will destroy the Zionist base."

The Israeli case against Russia, as put by Israel's representative in the United Nations, was damning in the extreme. "Your Government's record," he said to the Russian Ambassador, "in the stimulation of the arms race, in the paralysis of the Security Council, in the encouragement throughout the Arab World of unfounded suspicion concerning Israel's intentions, your constant refusal to say a single word of criticism at any time of declarations threatening the violent overthrow of Israel's sovereignty and existence—all this gravely undermines your claims to objectivity. You come here in our eyes not as a judge or as a prosecutor, but rather as a legitimate object of international criticism for the part that you have played in the somber events which have brought our region to a point of explosive tension."

The sight of mainly Russian weapons belonging to Egypt (and French to Israel) in the Sinai was a condemnation of the arms industry of both these countries and of the governments which had granted permits to export arms in such quantities to the Middle East countries which were openly preparing for war. Russia was the biggest offender. She would defend herself, of course, on the grounds that it was and always had been her policy to support wars waged by nationalists who wished to oust colonialists and imperialists who exploited them. Russia supported Egypt and sold to her an abundance of the most sophisticated weapons because she considered that Colonel Nasser was the chief opponent of imperialism in the area. Western countries, learning of Russian arms deals, had corrected the balance by selling arms to the opposing country, in this case, Israel, who was threatened. Both East and West, of course, used military aid to win allies and to influence them. In this way the schism in the world has been deepened and the cold war perpetuated.

Russia had given advice to Egypt from time to time about their policy in the Middle East. When Soviet Foreign Minister Gromyko went to Cairo for a few days on March 30th, sixty-nine days before war broke out, he did not go there for his health. The precise purpose of his visit was never given in a communiqué, but it must have been related to the purpose which had taken his boss, Premier Kosygin, to see Colonel Nasser in May 1966. Kosygin stayed eight days. The two men had displayed mutual interest in creating and maintaining revolutions in the Arab world to oust the imperialists. Kosygin promised Colonel Nasser full support for the revolution in Aden and South Arabia and for Colonel Nasser's opposition to the Muslim Alliance formed by such traditionalists as King Faisal of Saudi Arabia, the Shah of Persia and (more unostentatiously) King Hussein of Jordan. There is little doubt that Kosygin warned Colonel Nasser then to confine himself to revolutions and not to make another venture against Israel. Russia saw in Colonel Nasser a still more useful ally, if he would again cooperate with Syria, with whom in 1958 Egypt proclaimed union under one head of state, a unified army, a common legislature and one flag. He urged Colonel Nasser not to believe that by a demonstration of strength in Sinai he could win advantages for the Palestinians. The Arabs should strengthen their own economies, then their armies. He advised Egypt and Syria to bring into being the Arab Common Market which the two countries (and Iraq and Kuwait) had decided to form in 1964. Premier Kosygin repeated a warning he made to Colonel Nasser about Israel's aggressive intentions towards Syria to the United Arab Republic parliamentary delegation when it visited Moscow in mid-May. He said there was a danger that Israel would not exercise much patience if she felt she was threatened. When Kosygin talked of Russia's great desire for peace he always meant international peace. Internal revolutions were desirable if the imperialists were ousted. It did not matter that when they were ousted he filled the vacuum with his own particular brand of imperialism.

Looking at the sophisticated weapons Russia sold to Syria and Egypt and then at the Syrian and Egyptian prisoners of war in Israeli hands during the war the thought passed through my mind that the Russians had made a grave mistake. They had backed not one but two paper tigers. They had accepted the word of the Egyptian and Syrian Governments that their armies had reached a standard when they could use sophisticated arms. Israeli officers told me that the Arabs were not sufficiently advanced to service such Russian weapons as the latest jet fighters, the fast, complicated tanks, the delicate radar-controlled ground-to-air missiles or the anti-tank recoilless rifles. They were much less able to use them.

Since the Egyptian deal of cotton for Russian arms in February 1958, Nasser had built up his army to be the backbone of the country. He wanted it to be the strongest in the Middle East. Since then Russia had financed all Egyptian armaments. One defense expert believed that the Russians discovered that the sale of arms was the most certain way to influence a country's policy. Arms aid was fairly cheap for the Russians. They had to keep abreast of the United States in arms for a long time. They had a lot of arms that were obsolescent. "If you give countries food," the experts said, "the people eat it and forget you sent it. But if you give arms you have to send hundreds of technicians to teach the soldiers how to use them. You make them dependent on you for supplies. Finally you get them into debt to you, as Nasser is to Russia now." It was estimated in some quarters that Russia had overstocked the Egyptian army with arms. Had these been innocent commercial deals aimed at trade and trade alone, demanded the angry Israelis as they frantically filled sandbags to stack at the entrances to their homes. Russia had obviously tried to bring about a change in the balance of power in the Middle East in her favor but without actual war, by taking advantage of Britain's weakness there and America's involvement in Vietnam to do it. It would have served Russia's purpose excellently if Nasser had united all Arabs under him and driven the last so-called imperialist out of the area. The Russians were identified with Colonel Nasser's theoretical aim of eradicating all forms of imperialism from the Middle East. Russia also supported Arab insistence that Israel should implement United Nations resolutions on Palestine. These provided for repatriation or financial compensation of Palestinians who lost property or homes in the war following the formation of Israel in 1948.

Russia also wanted to build up its power in the Middle East. The United States Sixth Fleet had had its own way too much for too long in the Mediterranean, turning it into an American lake. Russia had had the dream of building up a great fleet and changing its area of operations from the Black Sea to the Mediterranean. Soviet vessels had operated out of a number of Egyptian ports to snoop on the Sixth Fleet and show the flag in the Middle East. Soviet ships in the Mediterranean had increased five-fold in the past three years. They had made their Arab allies navy-conscious. Egypt had fifteen Soviet W-class submarines, ten Soviet destroyers, and a fleet of Lomar motor torpedo boats equipped with guided missiles, which the small Israeli Navy was expecting to attack Tel Aviv. Soviet "show the flag" visits had been used to conceal naval deliveries to both Egypt and Syria.

When Soviet Russia broke off diplomatic relations and made threats about sanctions earlier than was expected she did what she had done before. It showed, however, that she had suffered a terrific setback in the successive defeats of her satellites in the Middle East. With the Arabs in the ascendancy Russia had held political initiative in the Mediterranean, but now she had lost it. The Arab defeat could cause Russia to lose the two satellites and the millions of dollars they owed her. In breaking off relations, Russia showed that there was nothing else she could do to help the Arabs. There was no question of intervention. Soviet policy had always been hostile to Israel, probably because she believed this most stable state was an imperial satellite. Soviet attitude might have meant that there would be political trouble of a higher order. The Israelis feared what Russia might do. She remembered when Russia broke off diplomatic relations in 1953 at the height of Stalin's policy of anti-Semitism. It might mean at the very least that it would be more difficult for the 3,000,000 Jews in Russia to come to Israel. Russia knew that Israel was in great need of new Jewish immigrants to help her economy, which was wavering already before the war. In 1965 there were only 30,750 immigrants compared with an average of twice that number in each of the three previous years. Almost as many people left Israel as arrived last year. Israel and the Russian Jews themselves had made many representations to Moscow that the Jews be allowed to come to Israel where they are so badly needed. Some optimists had hoped Russia would agree. Now, apart from other anti-Jewish measures, Moscow certainly would keep her 3,000,000 Jews. New blood could save Israel from serious economic troubles in the near future.

17

THE REFUGEES

It was apparent at the start of the Arab-Israeli war, just as it was in 1956, that apart from the bereaved relatives of the killed, the people who would suffer most, no matter who won or who lost, were the Palestine refugees in whose name the Arabs claimed to be fighting. Each war waged on their behalf increased their suffering, not only because their camps were often in the line of fire, but because as the victorious army approached they had to flee once again, losing all their possessions. The refugees were promised year by year by leaders such as Colonel Nasser that the hour of their deliverance approached. They were invited, and this time they responded in large numbers, to sacrifice their lives in the cause. They joined commando units, groups of saboteurs, or the Egyptian Army. The refugees in the Gaza Strip, and on the West Bank of the Jordan, were scattered in the first three days of the fighting like so many zombies. They wandered about, tired and listless, muttering Islamic oaths against their enemies. All the world seemed to be against them. They found themselves worse off than before they had moved. They were without food or shelter and found themselves in competition with a new type of refugee who reminded them of what they had once been like when they fled from their settled homes and farmsteads in 1948.

Refugees are like sheep. They follow each other without thinking that they are on their way to create a nightmare for others as well as for themselves. Some of the scenes in Jericho, on the banks of the Jordan, not far from where Jesus is said to have beseeched all children to come unto Him, were so terrible that I defy the hardest onlooker to have kept from weeping. Wretched women, emaciated and worn in child bearing, living for years on low calorie diets, stumbled along glassy eyed, whining for their children, from whom they had become separated when shelling began. I saw women with children who had been seriously hurt, or were sick, who could scarcely walk another step. Their feet were swollen and covered with blisters.

I saw hundreds of children in rags, crying for their parents who lay wounded or dying by the roadside. I saw the disillusionment on the faces of entire families who had left the huts that had been their homes for years to find themselves unwanted wherever they went. They had no means of identity. No nationality. They had even lost their ration cards which stood between them and starvation. When I talked to a woman I found that she had a pitifully one-sided version of the war of which she was again the victim.

UNRWA opened up camps in the areas to which refugee populations had fled. They issued bread and milk to people who had not eaten for days. Many were the stories about Jews driving the refugees out of their villages, firing over their heads to spread them on their way to the other side of the Jordan, or even of transporting them out of the West Bank area into the approaches of Amman. I saw none of these things myself but I was told by people I know and believe. The Israelis, however, had an enormous task to feed all the refugees in the conquered territories. They set about it, after a day or two, in a business-like way. Jordan suffered more than any other Arab country. Some 80,000 new refugees were said to have crossed early from the West Bank of the Jordan with the intention of reaching Amman which already had more refugees than it could deal with. A new camp for about 30,000 refugees was planned for erection near Mafraq. New huts and tents were added to old established camps at Karemeh and Zerqu. The Jordanian Government broadcast helpful information to the newcomers. They told them that all refugees would be granted immediate citizenship so that they could try to secure work or travel on a Jordanian passport.

Soon after all the shooting had stopped, Israel moved civilian officials into the conquered territories to reorganize life that had become shattered. Brigadier Chiam Herzog, a former RAF pilot whose peacetime occupation was managing "Gussies," the big Israeli store owned by Wolfsons' Enterprises, became the Governor of occupied Western Jordan in charge of 80,000 Arabs. The Israelis had concluded their third war with the Arabs. Now they and the Arabs counted the cost. Israeli economists let it be known that while the war had been expensive to prepare for, and wage, it might be even more expensive to maintain the occupied territories. Obviously they would be a great liability. Jordan had been heavily subsidized in the first place by Britain, and later, by both Britain and the United States. Jordan had always been something of an artificial country, and now, truncated, it seemed to have little justification for survival as a sovereign state. Strangely, King Hussein seemed more popular than ever among the majority of the people although it was solely because of his actions, in attacking a nearby country for which Jordan was unprepared to fight, that the disaster had befallen his people. Jordan admitted defeat but said it must have all its lost territory returned before it would join peace talks. This was the modern attitude. One fought to conquer other people's territory, or to cast the inhabitants out of it, and when one lost one asked for the land back, like children who said at the end of some game in which they had failed, that they really were not trying, and that they should start all over again.

Jordan, which had suffered by far the greatest losses, proportionate to its size, demanded the return of both the West Bank of the Jordan and Old Jerusalem. The biggest problem of all was the West Bank, where the population had been about a million and where there had been some 480,000 refugees. The fact that it was cut off from all contact with the East Bank added to the numbers of unemployed. Thousands of West Bankers had been employed in public and other services in Amman. Now they had lost their jobs. Living standards had been low but now the average income was stated to be only 20 dollars a month at the official rate of exchange. The West Bank contained Jordan's best agricultural land as well as major markets for products made on the east bank. Its revenue meant a loss of about 180 million dollars. Jordan's resources were cut by half. The treasury had lost some 44 million dollars or nearly half of the country's income from taxes, duties and services. This situation was aggravated by the fact that the West Bank owed 20 million dollars which some half dozen banking houses had invested in local commerce and industry.

The war had begun at the height of what would have been the tourist season on which Jordan relied for part of its income. Jordan had lost the income that derived from Moslem pilgrims who came in their thousands to visit the Dome of the Rock in Old Jerusalem. There was also the loss of important archeological sites and museums set up with the help of American and British grants. Among losses which could scarcely be described in financial terms were those of the Dead Sea Scrolls which were in Old Jerusalem. Firms had lost valuable buidings, machinery and heavy equipment. Private citizens had lost homes and all their possessions in the heavy bombing. It was perhaps poetic justice that King Hussein, who was given the chance to opt out of the war at a time when it had already been won in the air by Israel, had lost valuables when his Basman palace on the hill in Amman had been bombed. But he had a large comfortable farmhouse and other palaces. The people of Amman had only one home and some 100,000 refugees from the West Bank and the border area had none at all. The Israelis had taken vengeance on the village of Qalqiliya near Nablus in the northern part of the West Bank territory as if to teach it a lesson. Some of their acts there were reprehensible. Qalqiliya had been involved in terrorist raids on Israel in the past. Some 12,000 in the wider area had to live in the open because of the destruction.

Egypt's economy was completely dislocated, though Colonel Nasser made a pretty good job of hiding the fact. He had referred to what had happened as a setback, but even the poorest peasant knew that Egypt had suffered a crushing defeat. The Egyptian President had sacked his generals, who had been merely the instruments of his own policy. Now he floundered on through the wreckage he had caused himself, blaming everyone but himself. The Suez Canal, which had been bringing in nearly as much cash as Egypt's cotton crop, was still closed. The maritime powers had been informed that it would not be reopened until the Israelis left the Eastern Bank. Egypt had suffered more even than Jordan because of the closing down of tourism. Hotels which would otherwise have been full were empty.

The situation in the Gaza Strip was not so clear. This territory of 240 square miles which the Egyptians had held in accordance with the Armistice of February 24th 1949 was a nearly worthless coastal area. It had had a continuous foreign exchange deficit which had been made good by Egypt. The Strip had been valuable to Colonel Nasser because possession had enabled him to exploit the Palestinian refugees, to have them organized into groups which would fight Israel. The total population in the Gaza Strip and nearby area numbered 400,000 persons, of whom 300,000 were refugees. Gaza was without a port worthy of the name. It possessed only a few domestic industries. Its main occupation, growing citrus fruit, was by no means flourishing. The fruit was of low grade and was purchased by the poorer people of Egypt. UNRWA had run schools and health services for the refugees. It had issued low grade rations for the past nineteen years. There was every indication that this arrangement would continue in grim monotony unless there was a political settlement.

On June 28th the Israeli Government passed acts which enabled it to extend its administration over all the former mandated territory of Palestine. This meant that it had annexed the Old City of Jerusalem. The following day Israel opened all barriers in No Man's Land which had divided the city since 1948, and removed by bulldozer unnatural obstacles which the Jordanians had erected. The Jaffa Gate, which was walled up by Jordan nearly twenty years before and had remained walled up ever since, was blown open by dynamite. Israel continued to tighten its grip on the Old City, now joined to the Jewish Quarter. Jordanian residents were informed how to exchange various licenses issued to them by the Hashemite powers for Israeli licenses. Approval was given for the printing of occupation currency in captured Jordan territory, also in Gaza and the Gaulan Hills of Syria. The Government extended the area in which the Israeli dollar was legal tender to the Arab part of Jerusalem. Officials in Jordanian service were told they were to be transferred into

Israeli service. They would be given crash courses in Hebrew. It was rumored that Israel was considering making compensation to the Arabs for lands and property abandoned by them in Jewish Jerusalem in 1948.

The Jordanian authorities had never granted an entrance permit to the Old City of Jerusalem to anyone of Jewish faith since 1948. An application for a permit from a visitor, made through the District Commissioner, was issued in accordance with instructions from the applicant's consul. He had to certify that the applicant was not of the Jewish faith. Further, the Gentile applicant, who probably wanted to visit the shrines associated with the Hebrews, had to carry with him a certificate from a clergyman stating that he was not himself of the Jewish faith.

The Israelis, after the war, reversed this policy. They allowed Arabs from the Old City to visit New Jerusalem and on the same day Jews were allowed to visit the Old City. The two groups of people who had lived sometimes within a few hundred yards of each other for twenty years, and never met, now indulged in the novel experience of crossing the forbidden strip of No Man's Land, fast losing its ugly barbed wire barricades, to visit each other's territory. Both were surprised at what they saw. The Israelis were amazed that the Old City had changed scarcely at all and looked still as it might have looked hundreds of years ago. The Arabs stared in wonder at the modern buildings in New Jerusalem. The Arabs received also another kind of surprise. Some of them were greeted in the streets of New Jerusalem by residents who were Arabs and who had never left Israel, which they call Palestine. These Israeli Arabs told the visitors, as they took them around to see the sights, that they were the largest minority in Israel. They had their own schools where they were taught in the Arabic language. The most promising youths were sent by the Israeli Ministry of Education to the Hebrew University. The visiting Arabs were able to buy *A Yom,* the Arab newspaper, printed in Israel in Arabic script. They were able also to hear local radio programs in their own language. Their Arab hosts explained to them that the Israeli Arabs had their own representation in the Knesset or Israeli Parliament.

The Israeli Government did all they could after a few days

to prevent the Arabs leaving their homes in Old Jerusalem and the West Bank to go to the East Bank of the Jordan just as the Jordanian Government also tried to arrest the movement to over-crowded Amman.

The Israeli Minister of Defense, Major-General Moshe Dayan, was so puzzled by the continuing movement eastward that he tried to discover the reason by personally visiting the Allenby bridge over the Jordan. He spoke to many groups of fleeing Arabs in their own language, for he speaks Arabic fluently. As Arabs mounted the bridge to pass over he asked them why they were leaving their homes. He found they were leaving for a wide variety of reasons and not merely because they did not trust the Jewish administration. They said that their relatives lived on the other side of the river. Some of the men had sent their wives and children over the bridge when the war started. They had stayed to look after cattle. Now they were going to join their families and then decide what to do. Some were frank in saying that they did not want to be ruled by Israel. They were moving pathetic remnants of furniture. Other refugees, mostly women, said that their husbands worked abroad, often in Kuwait. They felt that they would not be able to collect the money their husbands sent weekly unless they were on Jordanian territory. General Dayan told the refugees that they could return as soon as they were so informed by the International Red Cross over the Arab radio service now incorporated in the Israel State radio. Jordanian newspapers described Dayan's offer to let refugees return to the West Bank as "a propaganda gesture."

Meanwhile Levi Eshkol, the Israeli Prime Minister, let it be known that his country would not surrender the territory she had won in battle until the Arabs sat down and negotiated a peace settlement. "We will hold on to the territory as a guarantee that they will come to the conference table," he said.

The refugees would continue to be a problem which no one would solve. The only things that had changed about the refugees in all the time of their existence was their numbers, and that in the wrong direction. Registered refugees had increased from less than 1,000,000 to 1,300,000. Refugees married refugees and produced more refugees to perpetuate the refugee problem. The Arabs maintained camps as a political weapon against Israel, in an effort to compel them to implement the United Nations resolutions on Palestine and provide for repatriation or financial compensation.

Already enough money had been contributed yearly in nineteen years to the UNRWA for rations and accommodation to have provided each family with a lump sum of 3,000 dollars. This would have been enough to have resettled them all. But the problem was worse now than it was when it was created. In Syria three percent of the population were refugees; in Lebanon eight percent; in Jordan thirty-seven percent, and in the Gaza Strip seventy-nine percent. The number registered would continue to increase every year. More than 45,000 refugee babies are born annually, for the refugee men have a vested interest in procreating children. According to a statement I received from UNRWA just before the Israeli-Arab war broke out on June 5th, there were now 1,317,749 refugees, an increase of 36,926 over the total a year before. The most tragic feature of the problem was the high proportion of young refugees. About half of the total number were under the age of eighteen. Some 30,000 refugee boys and girls became adults every year. Many of them by that time were already the father or mother of another new refugee.

The General Assembly of the United Nations had adopted with monotonous regularity worthless resolutions about the refugees year by year since December 11th 1948. It had "noted with deep regret" that repatriation or compensation of the refugees had not been affected. It had "directed attention" time and time again to the continuing critical financial position of the agency, etc., etc. Financial collapse of the organization last year had been averted only by what virtually had been a rescue operation. The time is clearly overdue when the entire organization of UNRWA should be transformed into one which will solve the problem of the existence of the refugees instead of perpetuating it.

The camps should no longer be regarded as breeding centers. Circumstances should not be such that the more babies a refugee woman has, whether in or out of wedlock, below or above the age of consent, the more rations are available for her family. For some girls and women pregnancy was an annual event. The women were well cared for in pregnancy, as were the babies in ante-natal and baby clinics. The mother, for the period of pregnancy, and beyond it, had the feeling of elevated importance. She had helped assure the future welfare of her family and she had another offspring she did not have to provide for. There was not only safety, but better eating in numbers.

All the problems in the camps, like this one of the numbers of refugees themselves, were self-perpetuating. UNRWA existed to provide food, health, shelter and welfare services for the refugees and education and training for their children, including vocational and teacher training and university scholarships so that they could compete in the world with other children. The fact that there were so many young people meant that not nearly enough young people had shown sufficient enterprise to get jobs and start a new life. Being a refugee became a habit as well as a profession. Children absorbed the inertia which the camps created in their parents. They were content to live in idleness, be fed and be looked after by a world which owed them a living. Since the rations cost only a few dollars a month for each person, and provided only two-thirds of the intake in calories of a normal impoverished person in the Middle East, the refugee's health slowly declined. All initiative and self respect left him. It was never envisaged that the refugee problem should go on generation after generation. The United Nations should be ashamed that it has allowed this to happen. A position has been reached now when no one knows what is to be done.

On the half-a-dozen occasions when I have visited the refugees and seen some new faces in the Gaza Strip and on the West Bank of the Jordan immediately after the Israeli-Arab war ended, I have been told parrot-like by responsible leaders that it was their lawful right to return to their former homes in Palestine. The refugees were encouraged to dwell on the past. To let the present and the future take care of themselves. Throughout the years, in all the camps, the defiant attitude has been: "The United Nations has given us assurances regarding repatriation, or compensation, and it is up to the United Nations to keep its word." The foundation stock of refugees, now well advanced in middle age, if they are not long dead, impose on their wives and children and the children they continue to beget even into old age the awful sentence of incarceration in what are little less than concentration camps, until they obtain what they see as justice. And as they wait in vain for someone to do something, their hate of the Israelis, who "occupy their territory," and the West who imposed "a cancer in the heart of Islam" grows in intensity until it has to find expression in sabotage and murder across the border and finally, if they can find a leader, in war. Such a violent upheaval as the recent war, which provided perilous scope for exponents of the cold war to worsen world relationships, should have made responsible members of the United Nations think seriously about marshalling all its resources to tackle the problem at its roots. The United Nations should now bring pressure to bear on Israel and the Arabs alike to contribute ideas, jobs, accommodation and money to facilitate winding up UNRWA's mission, and to distribute the refugees in countries where they can begin to lead normal and useful lives. The oil-rich Arab countries, some of which encouraged the invasion of Israel, should be compelled to donate some of their fabulous wealth to the cause. Anyone with the slightest knowledge of Middle East affairs knows that the refugee problem is a running sore which yields to no symptomatic treatment but demands organic treatment if a cure is to be effected. The refugee problem is traceable in every outrage along the Israeli-Arab borders as it has been clearly traceable in the terrible wars of 1956 and 1967. I have met former Palestine refugees in the Persian Gulf, in the United States of America and even working as responsible officials in UNRWA and UNESCO. They have told me that such is the atmosphere in the camps, although they are excellently run by the Agency, that only a comparatively few refugees have the character, the will power, and the ambition to leave the camps and go abroad to start a new life. The Arabs have a case for repatriation or compensation but the problem cannot be solved easily. Unless they are stupid, the Arabs must see now that the Israelis are as determined as the Arabs to build their own nation in Palestine and, incidentally, are far stronger in their ability to do so.

It is unfair to the babies born into such wretched circumstances. It is unfair to the mothers who are a new kind of slave to maternity. Every possible trick is exploited to obtain more rations as every ruse is adopted in ordinary life by workers to get increased wages. For a long time deaths of refugees were not disclosed, and the deceased refugees were buried in secret and at night in unmarked graves. Newborn babies were borrowed by a succession of sterile women to enable them to obtain more rations. As soon as the officials became wise to one trick, someone thought of another, for the refugees had nothing else to do but plot and plan for their own welfare. The Arab did not think of the welfare of the mothers of the children, but only of the political arguments which the camps provide against Israel at the United Nations in propaganda.

"The conditions under which some one hundred thousand or more newly-displaced persons in East Jordan are living require urgent and effective action," Laurence Michelmore, Commissioner-General of the United Nations Relief and Works Agency for Palestine Refugees in the Near East, announced. He estimated that 74,000 displaced persons from the West Bank were accommodated in Government and UNRWA/UNESCO schools and in other public buildings. A further 30,000 to 50,000 persons were being sheltered by relatives and friends. "The present situation of these displaced persons, particularly those in schools, is a matter of great anxiety to us," said Mr. Michelmore. "There are five or six families—perhaps thirty persons—to each school classroom. Most possess only the clothes they are wearing and a blanket. Overcrowding, the low morale of the refugees and the inadequate sanitary facilities constitute a grave risk to their health." While preventive measures are being taken urgently and UNRWA health teams are treating the sick, whether registered with UNRWA or not, the risk to the health of these persons is ever present until they can be moved to tented camps.

"The recent conflict," said U Thant, Secretary General of the United Nations, "has inevitably brought tragedy and hardship to countless innocent people. Among those whose lives had been most affected by the war were many who had long been refugees in areas which had been occupied by the military forces of Israel. UNRWA was doing its utmost to alleviate the tragic plight of the refugees. UNRWA was, however, already under severe financial stress before the present crisis. The additional emergency tasks and responsibilities which it had to undertake as a result of the fighting would greatly increase this financial strain."

18

PEACE PROSPECT

Wars dating back to the dawn of military conflict have always ended in a peace treaty of some kind. According to whether hostilities have ended with unconditional surrender, or whether they had been concluded before the war had been fought to the bitter end, the peace treaty was either imposed or negotiated.

In 1956, however, when Israel fought Egypt in the Sinai, there was neither an imposed nor a negotiated peace treaty. There was not even an official armistice between Israel and all the Arab nations. The world's two big powers, America with the West and Russia, acting behind the façade of the United Nations, pulled the protagonists apart as if they had been dogs fighting in the street. Because of the Anglo-French Suez campaign, it had been impossible for the Israelis, even if they had wanted to, to carry the fight to the end, which they could otherwise have done in four hours by capturing Cairo and unseating Colonel Nasser.

So the war was merely interrupted, as we can now see, for just over ten years, during which time the big powers who had separated them sponsored one side against the other side, dusted them down, nursed them into a state of fighting fitness, and even gave them modern arms either to replace what they had lost in the 1956 war or to supplement what they already had.

Russia did far more than the U.S. and the West to set up Egypt as the best armed country except America. She also inspired the resuscitation of a military alliance between Egypt and Syria which would assure that Israel, when the next war came, would have to do that which all militarists hate to do—fight on two fronts.

What the two big powers, and the United Nations behind whose pacific façade they operated, were careful not to do was to try to solve the festering problem which was at the very root of the enmity between Israel and the Arabs—the problem of the Palestine refugees.

In the first of three conflicts in under twenty years between Israel and the Arabs, that of 1948, when Egypt, Iraq, Jordan, Lebanon and Syria invaded the day-old state, Israel acquired some of the land belonging to the Arabs, but lost territory west of the river Jordan to Jordan and the Gaza Strip to Egypt. In 1956, when Israel invaded Egypt following provocations similar to those which were the immediate cause of the recent war, the road was paved for the 1967 episode. And in that, among other conquests, Israel won back the West Bank of the river Jordan and the Gaza Strip. Does this all mean that, pursuing the new way of settling wars without a peace treaty, there will in time be a fourth conflict?

Would it not be better in a chronic dispute like this to let the two sides fight it out like a couple of dogs who snarl at each other every time they meet in the street? The Arabs are arming again. The big powers are backing one side against the other. The Arabs are saying that it does not matter if they have to wait for a hundred years they will eventually obliterate Israel from the Middle East. Their hate is implacable. If the two sides fought each other to the bitter end I cannot see the Arabs winning on the form they have displayed in the past three encounters. At the end, therefore, it would mean that the Jews would land up in Cairo, in Amman, in Damascus and in Baghdad. Knowing the Israelis, I do not believe they would misbehave themselves unless they were attacked. They are all too conscious of the need to reach a peaceful settlement with the Arabs. But I can see nothing but good coming from the presence for an occupation period of Israeli soldiers in the Arab capitals. The Israelis would surprise the Arabs, after all the propaganda to which they have been subjected in the past twenty years, by their good behavior.

So far, the only Arabs who have even mentioned the words

"peace conference" have taken up the position that one cannot be held until Israel has returned the territory she has conquered. Egypt says she will not attend a peace conference in any circumstances. On the other hand, Israel says she will not return any of the territory until there is a peace conference.

King Hussein, the man who walked uninvited straight into the war although his army was unprepared to meet such an opponent, went to Cairo for a second time on July 11th to try to push his claim with Colonel Nasser for an early Arab summit meeting. He obviously wanted, as the head of the state which had suffered more than any other state, to try to reach some kind of a conclusion with the Israelis.

So again the position of stalemate has been reached in this most vexed of all the problems which continue to menace the peace of the world.

The Soviet Union, which failed in its efforts in the United Nations General Assembly to help Colonel Nasser win politically what he had been unable to win militarily, has largely replaced the planes which were destroyed on the ground by Israel, and partly replaced the tanks. Russia further encouraged Nasser's defiant policy by sending a force of Soviet warships to Alexandria and Port Said. The type of threat implied was to be seen by the type of ships which made the journey—two guided missile carriers, two submarines, a destroyer, a cruiser and landing craft. Said the force's commander, Rear Admiral Igor Nikolayevitch Moloshov: "We are ready to cooperate with your [Egypt's] armed forces to repel any aggression."

The same ineffective medicine is being doled out again to cure this chronic case in which a surgical operation is badly needed.

As for the United Nations, the organization has never been more confused in its attitude to any issue than it has been to the Six Day War. Under a system in which two-thirds majority of those voting is necessary for the adoption of any resolution, only the resolution declaring invalid Israel's absorption of Jerusalem and a recommendation by the Security Council that UN observers be employed along the Suez Canal were adopted. Resolutions proposed and argued endlessly by the non-aligned nations, the Latin American countries, Albania, and the Soviet Union, all failed. In the case of Russia, the resolution which condemned Israel and demanded immediate unconditional withdrawal to armistice demarcation lines and payment of reparations by Israel, received almost as many votes against as for. The vote finally was in respect of the withdrawal. Other paragraphs received fewer votes.

What had happened up to this point in the UN debate was a temporary victory for Abba Eban and the Israeli Government, but this still did not remove Israel's problems. She had quadrupled her territory in the short way and her problems were now in ratio to its size.

The trouble was that there did not seem to be a man either in the East or the West, or in the United Nations, big enough to lead the way to a settlement of the Palestine refugee problem, without which Israel and the Arabs are unlikely to talk peace.

Let Levi Eshkol, Prime Minister of Israel, have the last word.

> A week ago [he said, speaking in the Knesset (Parliament) on June 12th] the momentous struggle opened. The existence of the State of Israel, the hope of the generations and the vision that has been realized in our days, hung in the balance. Now, only a week after the last session of the Knesset, which took place to the accompaniment of the thunder of the guns, we meet with the tidings of victory ringing in our ears. The aggression of the enemy has been repulsed, the greater part of his power has been broken, his military machine destroyed, the bases for aggression cleared. The threat of war has been lifted from our country. The skies above our heads are safe. The threat to Jerusalem, to the coastal plain, to the villages of the north and the corridor, to the whole of the Negev and Galilee, has been removed. The Israel Defense Forces dominate the Sinai peninsula as far as the Suez Canal, the West Bank of the Jordan and the Gaulan Heights. The passage through the Straits of Tiran to the Gulf of Aqaba is free. Jerusalem has been reunited. For the first time since the establishment of the State, Jews pray at the Western Wall, the relic of our sacred temple and our historic past, and at Rachael's tomb. For the first time in our generation, Jews can pray at the Cave of Machepela in Hebron, the City of the Patriarchs. The prophecy has been fulfilled: "There is a recompense for the work. The sons have returned to their borders."

In the course of the years—confronting, as we did, the constant threats of our enemies—we were compelled to build up the defensive and deterrent power of the Israel Defense Forces, and devoted extensive resources to its training and equipment.

The people stood the test. Hundreds of thousands of young people and new immigrants, in big or little tasks, each according to his age and his abilities, proved that their roots in this country are eternal. It was shown that the spirit of the people flows from the spiritual revival of the state. We saw clearly that this is no mere ingathering of exiles, but a new—yet ancient—nation, a united nation, which has been tempered in the furnace into one Israel, forged out of all our tribes and the remnants of scattered communities—they, their sons and their daughters. A nation has come into being which is ready for any effort or sacrifice in order to achieve its goals.

The state of Israel has stood the test because it knew that it carried the hopes of the entire Jewish people. The unity of our people has been forged anew in these days. All the diaspora communities were keenly conscious of their solidarity with the State of Israel, the heart of the Jewish people. Thousands of our people came forward to help. Hundreds of thousands, millions, are ready to give us all the assistance in their power. Even those who are unable to offer their aid have their hearts with us in our struggle. Just as our own country has attained a higher unity, so has the unity of the Jewish people been reinforced. Jerusalem has been joined together, and in its unit, as our sages said, it has made all Israel brethren.

In the course of the years we found that our neighbors regard agreements as an expedient for gaining time in order to prepare for renewed aggression, with the aim of destroying Israel. The United Nations chose to ignore this attitude on the part of the Arabs. The United Nations Charter obligates member states not to use force or the threat of force, and to solve disputes by peaceful means. Yet the United Nations refrained from condemning Arab hostility towards Israel. Thus, for nineteen years, this unique situation, unparalleled in international relations, persisted. All the nations of the world, their leaders and their representatives heard the incitement of the Arab leaders and the rattling of the swords that were entrusted to them—but they were silent. To the nations of the world I want to say: be under no illusion that the State of Israel is prepared to return to the situation that reigned up to a week ago. The State of Israel arose and continued to exist as a matter of right, and this nation has been compelled to fight and fight again for that right. Alone we fought for existence and our security: we are entitled to determine what are the true and vital interests of our country, and how they shall be secured. The position that existed up till now shall never again return. The land of Israel shall no longer be a No Man's Land, wide open to acts of sabotage and murder. We have already explained to the nations of the world that we look, not backward, but forward—to peace.

A new situation has been created, which can serve as a starting point in direct negotiations for a peace settlement with the Arab countries. The historic contribution which the people of the world, headed by the great powers, can make towards the establishment of peace in our area is clear and unmistakable. They must address their demands, not to Israel, which has sought peace since she came into being, but to the Arab States, which have turned the Middle East into a focus of tension and a hot-bed of ceaseless hatred during the past two decades. Justice, logic and morality demand that, after those twenty years of impotence, the powers should have the courage to tell the Arab states that the United Nations Charter obligates them, just as it obligates every other member-state, to solve disputes by peaceful means.

Today our area is at the cross roads; in one direction lies peace and true cooperation, resting upon the sincere desires of the peoples in the area and their true interests. In the other direction lies the danger of continued hostility and hatred because of the absence of stable peace. The international community is faced not only with a moral test, but also with a test of its political sagacity. The sooner the arms race in the area is ended, the sooner steps are taken to bring peace nearer in the Middle East, the greater, perhaps, will be the contribution to the relaxation of general international tension.

To the Arab peoples I want to say: We did not take up arms in any joyful spirit. We acted because we had no alternative if we wanted to defend our lives and our rights. Just as you have a right to your countries, so we have a right to ours. The roots of the Jewish people in this country go back to primeval days. Throughout the generations, Israel in dispersion maintained its spiritual and material links with this country; it was never severed from it even when it went into exile. Similarly, this land has kept faith with us, it has not given itself to any stranger. This historic and spiritual right of ours has been confirmed by international law and forged on the anvil of reality; today the entire world realizes that no force can uproot us from this land. There is no parallel in the annals of the nations to this unique bond between our people and its land. Perhaps the fact that we have successfully survived the three wars that have been forced upon us will finally convince those who refuse to recognize this fundamental truth that our ties with this land are deeper than the sea, because without it our people cannot live. In these days, when false hopes for the destruction of Israel have been shattered, perhaps the Arab leaders will think again, perhaps they will consider the extensive suffering and losses which they have caused to their peoples—and which we, too, regret, perhaps they will realize the valuable resources that have been squandered on weapons of war instead of being utilized for economic and social progress, perhaps they will ponder on the blessings that can flow to all the peoples of the area from sincere cooperation between them. Only through such cooperation will the Middle East take its rightful place in the total picture of world culture and human progress.

I am confident that, in national unity, we shall meet the tests that lie in store for us, ready for the political struggle and always seeking peace. May the coming days deepen still further that wonderful feeling of devotion, unity and spiritual exaltation, the bond between future generations and the unity of the entire House of Israel. Israel has emerged stronger than before from the test of fire and blood. Faithful to herself and looking with confidence to the future, with the aid of the Rock and Redeemer of Israel, this nation shall yet dwell in safety.

APPENDIX

Egyptian Air Attack Preparations

Translation of a Top Secret Document taken by Israeli forces at El Arish after its capture, indicating a plan to attack Israel:

TOP SECRET
UNITED ARAB REPUBLIC HEADQUARTERS,
EASTERN AIR REGIONS STAFF HEADQUARTERS

No. 10/67/3/35
Date 27.5.1967
BATTLE ORDER No. 67/7

Further to Appendix No. 1 to Battle Order 67/2 of 21.5.67, orders will be amended as follows:

1. *Target for Group 2*

A. Air Squadron 18, in a formation of 12 airplanes concentrated at air-base 258, shall bomb the airfield of Ekron (Aqir) and its radar installations, on condition that it shall be above the target at H hour.

Armament: Rockets and cannon.

B. Squadron 25, consisting of 12 aircraft located at air-base 260, shall have as its No. 1 target the bombing of three Hawk bases at co-ordinates 123147/140158/142166.

Time over the target area: H hour.

Armament: Rockets and cannon.

2. *Target for Air Group 12*

A. Squadron 24, consisting of 12 aircraft located at air-base 248, shall have as its No. 1 target the bombing of three radar installations at co-ordinates 121073/124130/145973.

Time over the target area: H hour.

Armament: Rockets and cannon.

The air-group shall also study the bombing of Halsa airfield as its target No. 2, as an alternative to a previous target area.

B. Squadron 31 shall consist of the Sukhoi course and of the battle-training and MIC 17 PRFS courses entitled to use air-bases 228 and 206 and of the mechanics attached to the Sukhoi and battle training courses. This squadron shall serve as a reserve group.

3. *Target for Air Group 1*

A. 6 aircraft from Squadron 55, located at air-base 260, shall bomb the command center and American-type long-range radar station situated at Mount Aricha.

Time over the target area: H hour.

Armament for all planes: 2 bombs, an empty tank and 2 rocket carriers.

B. 10 aircraft of Squadron 55 shall be located at air-bases 233 as a reserve group.

4. *Target for Air Group 61*

A. A formation of 9 planes shall bomb the airfield of Hatzerim at H plus 2 hours, and shall coordinate its action-time with Squadron 24, so that the special unit bombing the Hatzerim radar shall provide direct support to the air group engaged in this action.

B. 6 planes shall be charged with the bombing of Beer Menucha airfield as target No. 1 at H hour. They shall also study the bombing plan of the Matsada airfield as their target No. 2, as an alternative to the Beer Menucha objective.

C. 6 planes shall be charged with the bombing of the Akeda airfield, target No. 1 at H hour. They shall also study the bombing plan of Timna airfield as their alternative target No. 2, and of Eilat airfield as their alternative No. 3.

5. *Target for Air Group 65*

A. A formation of 3 planes shall bomb the Petach Tikva airfield at H hour plus 3.

B. A formation of 3 planes shall bomb Lod airfield at H hour plus 3 and shall study the bombing-plan of Petach Tikva airfield as their alternative target No. 2.

C. A formation of 6 planes shall bomb Hatzor airfield at H hour. The Air Group shall study the plan of Ramat David airfield at Haifa as a possible alternative objective.

General

All Air Squadrons shall study the enemy targets in accordance with the report of the Intelligence Branch and of low-altitude tactical-range observations from their present position.

Determination of bombing targets shall be effected before take-off.

The Air Defense Branch shall issue orders in connection with air defense and protection during concentrated bombing.

Coordination among units taking part in this concentrated bombing shall be effected as circumstances develop.

Signed: L/A Jelal Ibrahim Ziz,
Chief of Staff, Eastern Air Command

INDEX